BIOGRAPHY AND CRITICISM

General Editors
A. NORMAN JEFFARES
R. L. C. LORIMER

2
SEAN O'CASEY
The Man Behind the Plays

SAROS COWASJEE

SEAN O'CASEY
The Man Behind the Plays

OLIVER & BOYD
EDINBURGH AND LONDON
1963

OLIVER & BOYD LTD
Tweeddale Court
Edinburgh 1

39A Welbeck Street
London W1

First published 1963

PRINTED IN GREAT BRITAIN
AT THE PRESS OF THE PUBLISHERS

Foreword

Mrs O'Casey's Letters to the Author

Torquay, Devon.
July 8, 1961.

My dear Saros,

    I enclose a letter giving some idea of Sean's life today and if you will use it in the preface as a letter. I have no time to correct or think out for a preface as such. Sean is really well, he gets easily tired but is his same old fighting self. He went to London twice recently for his eyes and the specialist seemed to help the pain of them a great deal, he will go up now and again.

    Shivaun is coming home soon, and Breon and his girl, so with all I shall be busy.

All the best.
Signed: Eileen O'Casey.

P.S. Please correct spelling?[1] I am very bad!

July 61.

My dear Mr Saros Cowasjee,

    I have so little time to write the preface you asked me to do, instead I am writing you this letter, and tell you briefly about Sean's everyday life at 81 years of age.

    The pattern of his writing life has not changed much. His life over the years of our life together, has of course changed.

    The children took up a great deal of his time when they were young, he loved to be with them, and spent many, many hours, playing and laughing with them, sketching for them, and reading to them. I remember him reading *Moby Dick* with great action and gusto to Breon the eldest. At all times his

---

[1] [It has scarcely been necessary.—*Ed.*]

mind seemed to be taking notes of any odd thing a person would say, or a comic situation which might happen.

Now his day starts at 9 a.m. after breakfast, we read the letters and settle what to reply to them. He always has Irish newspapers in his mail; he has an order for them in Dublin, these he reads during the morning, he generally relaxes and may go for a walk, or sit on the balcony in the sun, if warm enough; but mostly the morning is an easy time. Unless he has practically finished a work, then he will type at any time in the day. When he is completing a play he will sing and hum, this I feel sure he does unconsciously.

Sean loves to get a song into any recorded interview he does, the family know this and we look at each other in good natured humour, he will manage to get the song in somewhere, somehow. It's a sure thing.

To go on with his day after lunch he rests, mostly to give his eyes a rest; this is a regular habit now, over many years, then tea and around 5 p.m. he starts to get into action on his typewriter and write; and he writes on and off all evening; has his evening meal, and goes on again of course some days with more gusto, and naturally there are days when he thinks or relaxes—looks at odd T.V. pictures mostly sport, or zoo series, listens to music he likes Mozart, Mendelssohn and Haydn and others and traditional airs of most countries. All must depend on how far he is in the creating of his work, it is a slow process, he will write into a copy book in small minute writing, cover pages, I am sure none could untangle this but himself, then he writes on to the typewriter, it is a very old typewriter he has had for years, ever since he came over from Ireland, then he makes a second copy on the typewriter, altering the work as he goes on. He will leave it on the typewriter and sit in his armchair for some time and rewrite what he wants to alter, writing it down in longhand over and over, then back to the typewriter to finish. So the whole writing may take 6 months a year or whatever time it will to complete a work. This means a great deal of work for him, no one can help him, as he doesn't like to dictate, but weaves his own pattern in his own way; this must get slower as he gets older and also battling with poor eyesight.

He always writes even when he is ill in bed, he will have a

notebook and pen beside him to write down his thoughts and comments, he cannot rest from this. In the last 2 years he has written 3 new plays and is writing a book of "Comments" to be called *Under a coloured Cap*,[1] you know he usually wears a coloured cap; this book he writes chapters for when he feels like it, and has no other work on hand.

Crowds were always a great joy to Sean, he would like to be on the edge unnoticed and listen and watch all, he would catch the humour or tragedy. Hyde Park on a Sunday evening, the speakers near the gates, his play "Within the Gates" was written from this park, a play about the life within a park during one day, from opening to the shutting of the gates.

The market place in Totnes was another place he loved and the wonderful character of Brennan in "Red Roses for Me" came from Totnes market place.

The beaches, when the children were young. Now he cannot mix, or stay at the edge of crowds, he misses this very much I am sure.

Sean's great love for Ireland is very true and real. It is clear to read in all his works, as in G. B. Shaw's and James Joyce's. Not a sentimental love, but a hope that the great intelligence, energy and humour of the Irish people will be used to the best, education to thrive, and ignorance and superstition to pass away. His love for his mother, his admiration for her courage her humour and steadfast fight to make the best of her poverty; such a fine person. He knows there are many such fine women even now struggling for existence, and his fight is that life must be better for them, in fact that they really live.

He does not believe in a pessimistic outlook, he always sees the way of a better living, and better life for all human beings. All Sean's plays have a note of hope and going on further with life, they all end in this way.

He went to America in 1936 for the production of his play "Within the Gates." When there he made many friends, and has a love for New York. Each summer these Americans and others telephone to see him, and he used to see a great many visitors; but he cannot see many now, and tries to see only people connected with his work, or productions; or a few

---

[1] London (Macmillan) 1963.

friends. He always hates to refuse to see young people, students who ask for help with a thesis, or any problem when studying his plays. He will try and answer and has in past written so many letters to young students; he cannot do this as much now, and this is another thing I know he wants to do and misses doing. His outlook is very young and I have not time to tell you of his intense interest in all new sciences.

I must mention his admiration for Gael Linn, in Ireland, the Gaelic movement, they run a pool and with the money do various things, such as getting new motor boats for the Irish fisherman and more up-to-date equipment, and other useful things to help. Also the cultural side has a fine collection of songs and poems, they have recently made a very fine film of Irish life. The traditional music is very fine, and Sean, who speaks Gaelic is in close touch with them.

Well now the O'Casey day ends the same way whether we be one two or more. Around midnight Sean gets up from his armchair and goes to the kitchen to see how much milk we need, he asks me each night, "How much shall I ask for?" and I say 1 or 2 or more pints. Sean makes a piece of paper in a dart and puts this in an empty milk bottle, with the words one or two pints written on it. That is the last O'Casey writing on most days. He may go back and listen to more music, or write, but often he just sits and thinks—having written his request for the morning milk.

I hope somehow you get a picture of Sean O'Casey as he is now.

Eileen O'Casey.

To My Mother

Preface

IN this study of O'Casey I have tried to relate his plays to his life. In other words mine is a biographical approach: to show the author's life, purpose and convictions in relation to his work as a dramatist. I had first thought of doing a purely critical study of O'Casey's plays, but soon discovered that such an attempt, however valuable, would be incomplete. The problem is not where O'Casey succeeds or fails, but why. To answer this we must inevitably turn to the man: one whose life is to an extraordinary degree interwoven with his writings. What Professor Jeffares said of Yeats, "His life throws light on his works and his works reflect that life,"[1] is even more true of O'Casey, for Yeats's primary concern was art, O'Casey's concern is man.

Since no study of O'Casey's plays can be complete without some knowledge of the man, I have devoted my first and third chapters to tracing his life: from his early childhood to the time he left Ireland in 1926. For two reasons, I have concentrated on the first forty-six years of his life. First, to keep my study from becoming unwieldy, thus preventing me from getting down to a critical evaluation of his plays. Second, and perhaps more to the point, it is the first forty-six years of his life that are eventful, and that have made him into the dramatist that he is today.[2] Though O'Casey takes us to the fifties in his last two autobiographies, he himself once thought of ending his life story with his departure from Ireland. This can be seen from a letter he wrote to Mr Jack Daly, in which he said:

> I am working at the "last" volume of biography. It ends at the time when I leave Ireland for England, "The Last Glimpses of Eirean" [*Inishfallen Fare Thee Well*].[3]

---

[1] A. N. Jeffares, *W. B. Yeats : Man and Poet*, p. vii.
[2] For similar reasons, I have not discussed O'Casey's latest volume of plays, published in 1961. It is impossible to provide an up-to-date discussion of O'Casey's works so long as he himself is still writing.
[3] Letter dated 26 Nov. 1946. In Mr Daly's possession.

Every effort has been made to get information about the man from sources outside his own writings. I am especially grateful to Mrs O'Casey for her account of her husband as he is today. Mr O'Casey supplied the dates which are missing in his autobiographies, and many of his friends gave me valuable and interesting information that I have used freely. I have also quoted at length from several letters that O'Casey wrote to his friends and to me. Use has also been made of Joseph Holloway's diary, *Impressions of a Dublin Playgoer*, housed in the National Library in Dublin. Holloway visited the Abbey Theatre regularly from 1895 to 1944, recording vividly his impressions of the plays and the people he met there. According to what he told O'Casey in April 1924, he wrote some two thousand pages per year.[4] One may argue that there is more weight in the paper used than in the thoughts expressed, yet even this allows him a measure of credit when one takes into consideration that his works are bound in 221 volumes, each volume consisting of roughly 350 pages. A very interesting, and perhaps revolutionary, story of the Abbey Theatre could be written from Holloway's diary alone: but the possibility seems remote, on account of the bulk of the material and the illegibility of the script.

In conclusion I wish to acknowledge my debt to those who have made this work possible: to the J. N. Tata Endowment and the late Sir Cowasjee Jehangir for a scholarship to study in Leeds; to Professor G. Wilson Knight for his guidance and for enlightening me with his knowledge of O'Casey's plays; to Professor A. N. Jeffares for helping me to acquire the necessary background of Irish history, and for ungrudgingly seeing me through many difficulties, any of which could have prevented this work from being completed; to Mr O'Casey for his several informative letters in which he most frankly answered some very embarrassing questions; to Mrs W. B. Yeats and Mr Cyril Cusack for allowing me to read O'Casey's correspondence in their possession; to Mr Ernest Blythe and Mrs Woods for permitting me to consult the Abbey Theatre Library, and for arranging interviews in Dublin with people who knew O'Casey; to Miss J. A. Anderson and Miss A. Orde for their painstaking

[4] Joseph Holloway, *Impressions of a Dublin Playgoer*, MS. 1885, Apr.-Jun. 1924, p. 732.

editing of the manuscript, and to Mr David MacIver for his valuable assistance in reading proofs.

Among others to whom I feel special gratitude are the late Dr Lennox Robinson, Miss May Craig, Miss Ria Mooney, Mr Jimmy Boyle, Mr James Boyle, Mr P. MacDonnell, Mr K. Eason, Mrs Schweppe, Mr Frank Robbins, Mr Gabriel Fallon, Mr Tom Sutton, Mrs Susan Elliott, Mr John Beary, Mr Tony Quinn, Mr Wedge, Mr Ron Ayling, Mr S. O'Tallamhain, Mr B. Macnamara, Mr D. Spillane, Mr D. W. Jefferson, Dr M. H. Millgate and Miss A. C. Stead.

I also wish to extend my thanks to the staff of the following libraries for their assistance: in Dublin to the National Library of Ireland, Trinity College Library, National University College Library, Catholic Library, Rathmines Library, the library of *The Irish Times* and the *Irish Independent*. In England I am indebted to the Brotherton Library, Leeds, Leeds Central Lending Library, Leeds Library, the British Museum and the Bodleian Library.

SAROS COWASJEE

Bombay 1963

Acknowledgments

For permission to quote from the works of Sean O'Casey acknowledgments are due to Macmillan & Co. Ltd and The Macmillan Company.

Acknowledgments are also due to the following: *Irish Independent; Irish Times;* Alfred A. Knopf, Inc. (George Jean Nathan: *Art of the Night*); National Library, Dublin; *New York Times*; The Macmillan Company (Allan Wade (ed.): *The Letters of W. B. Yeats*).

Contents

I

The Making of a Dramatist 1880-1923

What to such as they, anyhow, such a poet as I? Therefore
  leave my works,
And go lull yourself with what you can understand, and
  with piano tunes,
For I lull nobody, and you will never understand me.
  O'Casey, "A Stand on *The Silver Tassie*," unpublished.

SEAN O'CASEY was born at 85 Lower Dorset Street, Dublin,
on 31 Mar. 1880, dropped, as he says,

into a world that was filled up with the needs, ambitions, desires,
and ignorances of others, to be shoved aside, pressed back,
beaten down by privileges carrying godwarrants of superiority
because they had dropped down into the world a couple of
hours earlier.[1]

He was named John, much against the wishes of his mother
for she had already buried two Johnnys and thought that
calling this child John would be a challenge to God. But he
soon outlived his mother's superstitions to attack them in later
life with the same doggedness with which his father had
named him John.

A delicate and imaginative child, he grew up under the
direct care of his mother. His father, Michael O'Casey,[2] died
at the age of forty-six from a spinal injury while Johnny was
still a child. Michael, though born of a Catholic father, had
been brought up as a Protestant and knew the Bible well,
"most of it in the letter and all of it in the spirit." Being a
learned, upright and a fearless man, he was always expressing
his opinions, arguing that Popery was repugnant to the
plain words of the Scripture and that between man and God
there need be no middleman. These traits Johnny inherited

---

[1] *I Knock at the Door*, p. 3.
[2] O'Casey in his autobiographies writes of his childhood and boyhood days
under the name Casside, the reason being, according to the dramatist, "to
become a little more detached from my conscious self." Letter to me from
O'Casey dated 27 Jun. 1963.

B   1

rather than learnt from his father, for the two seldom came in contact: his father feared that Johnny would grow up into a dunce because of his poor eyesight, and this prospect was hateful to him.

With the death of his father, the first shadow of misery fell across the O'Casey doorway. Before long, Johnny's two elder brothers, Michael and Tom, were impressed by what Bugler Benson—their sister Ella's lover—had to say about the army, and both threw up their respective jobs of telegraph clerk and sorter in the Dublin General Post Office to take the "Queen's shillin." Ella got married to Nicholas Benson much against the wishes of her mother, and moved out to start a new home. Johnny, his mother and his third brother, Archie, moved into a tenement house in a slum district in the north of Dublin. A good summing up of the Dublin slums of 1913 is given by Arnold Wright, an English spokesman of the Federated Employers of Dublin:

> The Dublin slum is a thing apart in the inferno of social degradation. Nowhere can there be found concentrated so many of the evils which are associated with the underworld of our modern civilization. To say that men and women live like beasts of the field is the merest truth. In buildings— old, rotten and permeated with both physical and moral corruption—they crowd in incredible numbers. At the Government Inquiry into Dublin housing conditions, held in November 1913, some astonishing facts were brought into prominence. . . . Altogether there appear to be in the city 5,322 tenement houses accommodating, if such a word can be used, 25,822 families, or a total population of 87,305. No fewer than 20,108 families occupy one room each, 4,402 of the remainder have only two rooms each.[3]

Johnny's eyes had begun to trouble him when he was about five. Little pearly specks appeared on his eyeballs and the least light would throw him into agonies of pain. The treatment for this varied from plunging his head into a bucket of cold water and swearing at him to open his eyes, to taking him to attend St Mark's Opthalmic Hospital. As time passed, his eyes grew better and he could play about in the sun. One day when Johnny was playing marbles, the rector of the parish,

[3] Arnold Wright, *Disturbed Dublin*, p. 29.

the Reverend Mr Hunter, intervened, disapproved of Johnny wasting his time, and took him straight to school. He was not long at school before the pains in his eyes were at him again. Once more the visits to the hospital became a regular feature, and Johnny very gladly stopped attending school on the strict instructions of the doctor. Soon Mr Hunter was at the door to press Mrs O'Casey to send Johnny to school, and she, fearing her son would grow up into a dunce, consented. At school he was bullied by boys older and stronger than himself, but in Georgie Middleton—the strongest boy in the school—he at last found a friend who offered him protection.

His short stay in school was drawing to a close. Once, while he was keeping an eye out for the school-teacher, "oul Slogan," as Georgie Middleton and a few others gambled, Slogan caught them all. Leaving the bigger boys to be punished according to their consciences (Slogan had heard them say that they would break his skull if he ever attempted to cane them), he picked out Johnny, mercilessly caned him and made him stand on a chair facing the class. But when Slogan's head was bent in prayer, Johnny slipped down, picked up the heavy ebony ruler and brought it down with all his force on the bald head of the teacher, and fled. Johnny's mother firmly turned down Mr Hunter's proposition that Johnny should present himself the following morning at school for a sound thrashing. With that Johnny's schooling came to an end; in all it had lasted for about three years.[4]

This incident is of particular significance, not simply because it deprived him of an opportunity of primary education, but because it was the first of the many instances of injustice he was to face in life. And his answer to every injustice that befell him later had some semblance to the blow he had dealt at Slogan's head. He had seen through the hypocrisy of the Church and its ministers, and was to voice his thanksgiving some forty years later.

Poverty had been knocking at the door even while his father was alive. But now with his death, and the departure of Michael and Tom to join the army, the door opened. His third brother Archie was bringing in fifteen shillings a week

[4] See O'Casey's autobiographical sketch in *Twentieth Century Authors*, edd. Kunitz and Haycraft, p. 1039.

for a fourteen-hour-a-day job in the publishing house of the *Daily Express*. But this was not sufficient for the three of them, and a good many meals consisted of nothing but dry bread and tea; an occasional herring was a treat. Johnny's clothes had become threadbare; the soles of his boots had long ago worn out and were reinforced with cardboard soles which soaked up the water. He slept between the few old coats and the puff felts that Archie had managed to pilfer from the office of the *Daily Express*.

But life, however hard, was not without its joys. A sensitive child, he found pleasure in watching the baker's horse trotting along the road or the milkman's cart jingling in the street. There were games like "Duck on the Grawnshee," or "Ball in the Decker," which he played with other children when his eyes were free from pain; and this was fun with no school to attend, no whining out numbers and words, no "maps that made the living world a thing of shreds an' patches."[5]

He would dream and build a world of colour and joy around himself where cherry-faced women walked about "to lash out with the canes at any kid who missed for a single second the joy that was to be got out of the things the place provided, and so made it sure that no kid could forget for a moment that he was a member of Christ, a child of God, and an inheritor of the Kingdom of Heaven."[6]

And so Johnny grew up into boyhood in a world of dreams which was now and again shaken by the strong breeze of reality: the pain in his eyes, hunger, Ella's insistence on teaching him geography and grammar, his mother's warning that she would deprive him of the weekly *Boys of London and New York* if he did not study, and his first little sweetheart Jennie Clitheroe's cry that she would tell her mother that he had printed two hard kisses on her mouth.

Johnny obtained his first job at the age of fourteen, earning three shillings and sixpence per week for a ten-hour working day at Hymdim, Leadem and Co., a firm of wholesale chandlers. Soon he was promoted to the position of dispatch clerk at six shillings a week, which he skilfully supplemented by petty

[5] *I Knock at the Door*, p. 112.
[6] "The Dream School," *Op. cit.*, p. 138. This was first published in the *Yale Review*, Summer 1937.

pilfering. He gave his mother four and six every week out of his wages, telling her that he earned only five shillings; "fair and square," for Johnny needed books now. But the job was short-lived. When he was about sixteen, and earning seven and six a week, he was fined two shillings for impertinence— and that at a time when he had set his heart on buying the works of Milton—at which he protested so forcibly that he got the two shillings back and his dismissal with it. And the Milton "for nix," for he had already filched it from the bookshop.[7]

Apart from earning a living, Johnny at the age of fourteen had also determined to read and write. *The Boys of London and New York, Deadwood Dick,* or *Frank Reade Junr.* no longer sufficed for him, and he was soon struggling through Merle d'Aubigné's *History of the Reformation,* Sullivan's *Geography Generalised* and an American encyclopaedia, *The Comprehensive Summary.* Soon he came to know a great number of people: Cyrus, Zeus, Semiramis and Ninus, Aurelius, Hector, Ulysses, Xerxes, Leonidas, Alexander, Hannibal, Caesar, Datis, Agricola and a horde of others. By the time he took leave of Messrs Hymdim, Leadem and Co., he could say:

> He hadn't done badly so far—he had three of Dickens' and four of Scott's; two of Balzac's and one of Hugo's; Ruskin's *Seven Lamps of Architecture, Sesame and Lilies, Ethics of the Dust, The Crown of Wild Olives,* and *Unto This Last;* Darwin's *Origin of Species and Descent of Man* to be read when he knew more about things in general; two by Fenimore Cooper and three by Dumas; Tacitus' *Germania* and the *Life of Agricola* with *Plutarch's Lives* to keep them company; Reade's *Cloister and the Hearth;* Carlyle's *French Revolution* and Mignet's, too; Bunyan's *Pilgrim's Progress* and *Sheridan's Plays;* Taylor's translation of *The Aeneid* and a *Classical Geography;* Ball's *Story of the Heavens;* and, in poetry, the works of Byron, Shelley, Keats, Goldsmith, Crabbe, Tennyson, Eliza Cook—a terrible waste of sixpence—Gray, and the Golden Treasury, with the glorious Globe Edition of Shakespeare falling to bits; all backed up with Chambers's Dictionary, a stiff purchase, costing three shillings, bought after an old one, left behind by his father, had faded away in fragments. All these, with the old religious controversial works of his father, looked grand,

---

[7] The shop as O'Casey has described it in *Pictures in the Hallway* is to-day known as "Dublin Book Shop," at 32 Bachelor's Walk, Dublin.

and already made a fine show, above the delft, on the top shelf of the old dresser.[8]

Of the books he read at this period of his life, Shakespeare made the strongest impression on his mind and he felt that he was on the threshold of a new life. He had learnt a good bit by heart, and when his brother Archie and his friend Tommie Talton got possession of some unused stables and formed the "Townshend Dramatic Society," Johnny found a vocation which, if not paying, was at least interesting. Here were played scenes from Shakespeare, Boucicault and other playwrights to be found in Dick's *Standard Plays*. Johnny played the part of Henry VI, of Cassius and Brutus, of McClusky in *The Octoroon* and so on. Archie had become a friend of Talton's brother-in-law, Charlie Sullivan, and plays began to be staged on a larger scale; Johnny saw on a free pass Irish plays mixed with *The Corsican Brothers, Saved from the Sea, The Shaughraun* and others. He himself played Father Dolan in *The Shaughraun* at the Mechanics Theatre[9] when the regular actor Cleggett fell ill, and he played it so well that Sullivan exclaimed that only once had he seen a better Father Dolan—the time when he played it himself.

When Johnny was sixteen or seventeen, Archie went with a theatre company to tour the west and south of Ireland. His two brothers, Michael and Tom, had had what may be termed their day in the army. Tom, who loved a soldier's life but could not play a "spying bully," returned home to get a porter's job at fifteen shillings a week; while Michael, who hated the army, found rest in a military cell for thrashing a company sergeant-major who had called him a good-for-nothing Irish bastard. The O'Caseys folded their tents and moved into another two-roomed flat at 18 Abercorn Road, in the same district. Their temporary comforts were cut short by Tom's illness, and then by a strike in which he got involved. Johnny, on the recommendation of the new rector, the Reverend Harry Fletcher, got the job of van boy at Eason & Son (O'Casey refers to them as "Jason and Son" in his *Pictures in*

---

[8] *Pictures in the Hallway*, pp. 172-3.

[9] The theatre was later bought by Miss Horniman and converted into the Abbey Theatre under the supervision of the architect Joseph Holloway, who became a regular patron.

the Hallway) for nine shillings a week. Apart from the dreadful task of pushing a van full of newspapers to Amiens Street Station, his work also included "parcelling papers and magazines; pasting labels; tying string endlessly; in the midst of floating dust, dim light, the passing to and fro of heavy, tired, dragging footsteps, and the murmur of voices saying nothing."[10] By the end of the week Johnny had decided to throw up the job, and he did so with a defiant gesture, refusing to take off his cap while receiving his pay.[11]

Loss of his job brought the inevitable poverty, but his time was not wasted. He read Goldsmith, Ruskin and Marlowe and devoted his time to learning Irish from O'Growney's *Simple Lessons in Irish*. The study of the language not only brought him into the Gaelic League, which Padraic Pearse, the leader of the 1916 rebellion, called "the most revolutionary influence that has ever come into Ireland,"[12] but it also developed in him a nationalistic fervour, and a keen desire to see Ireland freed from the British yoke.

Tom, who had secured temporary employment as a postman, was recalled to the army to fight against the Boer Republic; while Archie, who had thrown up the stage as a "mad and bad job," found better luck as the confidential clerk of Messrs Harmsworth's Agency for a pound a week, and married a clergyman's grand-daughter. He got Johnny a temporary job with this firm for five shillings a week.

At this period of his life Johnny was won over by the charm and gentleness of the Reverend Harry Fletcher. Under his guidance he passed through the rite of Confirmation, renewed

---

[10] *Pictures in the Hallway*, p. 249.

[11] As the story narrated by O'Casey in *Pictures in the Hallway* seemed rather highly coloured, I contacted Mr Keath Eason, a retired Director of Eason's, and this is what he wrote to me in his letter dated 26 May 1958 :

"When *Pictures in the Hallway* was first published about 1946 [*sic*] it was clear to me reading the three chapters about his week's employment at the wholesale newsagent that, however coloured it might be in the retrospect, it was the story by an eye-witness with a keen vision.

"There is evidence that boys were used by us to trundle a truck with parcels of newspapers, in the early morning, from Abbey Street to the G.N. Ry. at Amiens Street well into the 20th century." In a private conversation Mr Eason told me that after Johnny's dismissal an inquiry was held into the matter, and an attempt was made to stop this inhuman practice of making boys trundle vans by bringing in the use of horse vehicles. This would be O'Casey's first service to his people.

[12] Quoted in Dorothy Macardle's *The Irish Republic*, p. 61.

his baptismal vows openly and helped in the singing of *Veni Creator Spiritus*. Harry Fletcher's influence was cut short by the extreme Orange element in the parish who objected to the ceremonies he had introduced as Popery. Johnny's sympathies were wholly with the rector. This may partly be because he was always drawn towards ceremonies and processions of all kinds; and partly because he had a High Church outlook. Ernest Blythe in his autobiography *Trasna na Bóinne* (Crossing the Boyne) tells us that O'Casey had an inclination to copy Catholic services, that he objected to the name Protestant and called himself Catholic, as distinct from " Roman Catholic."[13]

Johnny at this stage could do little to win public support for the rector, who subsequently had to leave the parish and whose place was taken up by the Reverend E. M. Griffin. Later when Mr Griffin faced similar opposition from the Orangemen, Johnny, who was very fond of this minister too, played an active part in organising the rector's supporters. The difficulty was solved by the defeat of the opponents at the election to the Select Vestry.

The influence of the Church on Johnny was strong but short-lived. He was too much of a rationalist to bask for long in the warmth of faith. The grim realities of life that he saw everywhere around him, his own hard struggle for existence, the death of Ella's husband and the misery that Ella and her children suffered, the death of Tom who had returned from the Boer War and had married a stupid Catholic girl; all this, and the startling things that he read in Darwin's *Descent of Man*, weakened his belief in religion. However, he continued to read the Bible for its sheer "beauty of language," so that by the time he began to write plays he knew much of it by heart.[14]

When Johnny was nineteen or so he secured a job with a big gang of navvies who were working on a railway siding. The work was hard and taxing for a boy of his physique, and his attempt to use pick and shovel gave amusement to his workmates. At night he suffered torments from aching muscles. But he struggled on with determination, so that in course of time he became a lusty fellow of twelve stone ten pounds who could perform his task as well as anybody in the gang. From

[13] Eárnan de Blaghd, *Trasna na Bóinne*, p. 105.
[14] Mícheál Ó Maoláin, *Feasta*, VIII, May 1955.

now on till the Larkin strike of 1913 he had a more or less regular job as a labourer and was able to afford a square meal for himself and his mother. But they were far from being comfortably off, for the wages were meagre and there were additional expenses such as the purchase of books and subscriptions to the Gaelic League and the Irish Republican Brotherhood. Often they were faced with hunger and poverty, and he tells us that at the time when his sister died he had only twopence-halfpenny in his pocket.

Though he had been taking an interest in the Gaelic League and the Irish Republican Brotherhood since his later teens, it was not till about 1903 and 1905 that he became a member of these two movements.[15] How wrong they are who think that he was a man in whose mind there was room for only one idea at a time may be judged from the various bodies and influences that attracted his interest. We have already touched upon his thirst for knowledge. Another passion that was to draw him with equal enthusiasm was his love for Ireland and the Irish people, and the next fifteen years of his life were to be devoted to the service of his country. His interest in the Gaelic League, the Irish Republican Brotherhood, the Labour Movement and the Irish Citizen Army were all manifestations of his love for Ireland in different shapes: an all-round attempt to find a means to serve his country and his people.

The Gaelic League was founded on 31 Jul. 1893 by Dr Douglas Hyde. Though primarily a movement to stimulate knowledge of the Irish language it soon achieved a political status, and had much to do with the shaping of those men who guided Ireland's destiny during the stormier days of her struggle for Independence. The Gaelic League was the first organisation that O'Casey admits having joined, though Joseph Holloway narrates a story which is worth glancing at before we brush it aside:

> He [O'C.] was once an Orangeman himself and a member of the Purple Lodge, and was getting on well till his love for processions and bands got him into disfavour with the members of his Lodge, and he left the body and joined a Gaelic League class. . . . It was in this way it happened. He always liked

---

[15] Letter to me from O'Casey, postmarked 23 Oct. 1958.

to go out to see the annual Parnell procession to Glasnevin
and usually went up near the cemetry to see it without being
seen by his sort. He had a Protestant friend in the Foresters
and one year he was looking on at the procession passing
when his friend marched along with a green sack across his
shoulder, and he [O'C.] being in the front row of sightseers,
his friend pulled him into the space behind him . . . and
walked along till they came to the Brian Boru pub, and the
Forester being a thirsty soul, said he was off for a drink and
as O'C. was a teetotaller at the time, the other said, "here's
the sack" and he took it off and threw it across O'Casey's
shoulder. . . . O'Casey marched on to the cemetery with
the procession and when it was over he took off the green sack
and concealed it under his coat. The Lodge called him to
account for his marching in a rebel procession to a papist
Churchyard and summoned him before them, and he being
always of a pugnacious disposition real [*sic*] up about Parnell,
and defended him and his own action instead of apologising,
and he got three years expulsion from the Lodge and was
stripped of all his masonic trappings. In leaving the hall
after sentence he told them all they might go to hell and went
and joined the Gaelic League, learned Irish and became a
Nationalist there and then.[16]

The account touches on so many of O'Casey's idiosyncrasies
with which we are familiar from his autobiographies that there
is little doubt that this story must have been related to Holloway
by O'Casey himself. However, when I wrote to O'Casey and
asked him if he had ever been an Orangeman or a member of
the Purple Lodge, he replied:

> No. I knew all the Dublin Brethren well, from Grand
> Secretary, Frank Donaldson, to the members of rank and
> file. I worked for several weeks with the Northerners who
> played the part of James II: the Second in the sham Battle
> of Scarva.[17]

The truth probably is that O'Casey was never an Orangeman
but that he told Holloway—in fun—that he had been one in
the past. J. L. Hodson's observation that O'Casey "says a

---

[16] Joseph Holloway, *Impressions of a Dublin Playgoer*, MS. 1877, Apr.-Jun. 1923,
pp. 742-3. Hereafter cited as J. Holloway, MS.
[17] Letter to me from O'Casey, postmarked 23 Oct. 1958.

good many things for devilment"[18] is perhaps true, and this story a fine instance of it.

The Gaelic League, however, exercised a potent influence on him and, more even than Shakespeare had been, was the source of a new life. He soon adopted the Gaelic form Sean for Johnny, though his mother continued to call him by his former name. He began attending regular classes in Irish at the League branch in Talbot Street and began to speak the language fluently, though not with grammatical perfection.[19] In 1906-07 he became the secretary of the Lamh Dearg branch of the Gaelic League in Drumcondra. So enthusiastic was he for the cause that every night he would go to the branch office, sweep the floor, light the fire, and teach the language to the pupils.[20] It was at this time that *The Playboy of the Western World* was first performed. Sean was nearly turned out of the Gaelic League for declaring that he liked the play,[21] though from his third autobiography, *Drums Under the Window*, it would appear that he could not afford a shilling to see it.

A man of his fiery temperament had to endure many a snub from the League. He was hampered in his attempt to get the Protestants interested in it because some members foolishly feared that it would bring sectarianism into the movement. He was criticised for attending the meetings untidily dressed, and was once asked to wait outside as he was not suitably clad to appear before the Dean of St Patrick's. Still he worked zealously for the League, doing his best to rouse public interest in the movement. He wrote vigorously —and often under the most trying conditions, as when his widowed sister's children slept on the floor of his room—for the *Gaelic Manuscript Journals* (*c.* 1907) which normally consisted of articles of topical and political interest. These articles were read once a month at the Branch office and then thrown open to discussion. He also wrote short stories which were published in these journals. The stories were about an imaginary brother of his called Adolphus, who was continually trying to push his way into polite society. Sean's stories were

[18] J. L. Hodson, *No Phantoms Here*, p. 153.
[19] My interview with Mr Ernest Blythe in Dublin on 22 Apr. 1958.
[20] My interview with Mr P. MacDonnell in Dublin on 2 Jun. 1958.
[21] J. Holloway, MS. 1881, Sep.-Dec. 1923, p. 596.

so popular that people flocked to the Branch and so increased the League's membership.[22]

The Gaelic League led him to join the O'Toole Pipers' Band and the Ard-Chraobh or Central Hurling Club of the Gaelic Athletic Association.   Sean was the first secretary of the Pipers' Band, which was a national band under the presidentship of Tom Clarke.[23]   Holloway writes:

> I had a chat with Lame Maguire. . . . Speaking of Sean O'Casey, he remembered him as being one of the first to join the People's Band [*sic*] and wear the kilt, and an ungainly figure he cut in it.[24]

It was perhaps his love for music, colour and processions that led him into the band.   His autobiographies are flooded with long, enchanting descriptions of processions and meetings; and his plays are soaked in music and song and dance.

His interest in hurley may seem a little curious, for Dublin working men generally preferred Association football to hurley: but "everything in this proletarian was abnormal, or unusual."[25]   He was good at the game but not good enough to get into the team.[26]   Perhaps his weak sight prevented him from excelling at hurley, and it is said that once in a match "he killed a sparrow—thinking he was striking at a ball."[27] What he most developed here was a feeling of fellowship, so that later on he was able to induce about ninety per cent of his comrades in the Pipers' Band and the Athletic Club to join the Irish Republican Brotherhood.   Mr Ernest Blythe, the present Director of the Abbey Theatre, was one of them.[28]

Among his associates in the Gaelic League were members of the I.R.B., the lineal descendant of the Fenian Organisation, and they persuaded him to join the Republican movement. Soon he was as enthusiastic over the I.R.B. as he was over the Gaelic cause, and even more violently nationalistic.   This is

[22] My interview with Mr Ernest Blythe on 22 Apr. 1958.
[23] My interview with Mr P. MacDonnell on 2 Jun. 1958.
[24] J. Holloway, MS. 1884, Jan.-Mar. 1924, p. 496.
[25] M. J. Lennon, *The Catholic World*, cxxx, Dec. 1929.
[26] My interview with Mr Ernest Blythe on 22 Apr. 1958.
[27] J. Holloway, MS. 1884, Jan.-Mar. 1924, p. 496.
[28] Mr Ernest Blythe has related the story of how he came under O'Casey's influence in his autobiography, *Trasna na Bóinne*.

how Desmond Ryan describes Sean attending a Sinn Fein meeting:

> Sean O'Casey sits in silence at the back of the hall during the lecture, a dour and fiery figure swathed in labourer's garb, for he works on the railways just then. His neck and throat are bound in the coils of a thick white muffler, and he looks a Jacobin of Jacobins as his small, sharp and red-rimmed eyes stab all the beauty and sorrow of the world. He speaks first, and very fluently and eloquently in Irish, then launches out into a violent Republican oration in English, stark and forceful, Biblical in diction with gorgeous tints of rhetorics and bursts of anti-English Nationalism of the most uncompromising style.[29]

The I.R.B., for all it professed, did not live up to his expectations. He felt that the leaders, though brave and sincere, were not alive to the problems of the common man, and that they paid little heed to the rough energy and splendour of the working class. He tried hard to convince the Republican leaders that if they wished to succeed, they must bring Labour into the movement. He also criticised them vigorously for the weaknesses in their policy. Sean's criticisms were resented by the Republicans and he was asked to stop them, but he would not give up the freedom to speak his mind. He says:

> Who has done more for the I.R.B. in relation to his condition and chances than I? he asked. Isn't it because the criticisms are justified that they want them stopped? he asked again. Quite a few have got jobs through its influence: have I? Bar ill health, pain, and poverty, I have got nothing. Nor do I want anything; but I am determined to hold on to what is mine own; my way of thinking, and freedom to give it utterance.[30]

Freedom to give utterance! The freedom that he had cherished from the day he was sacked from his first job was his, and he left the I.R.B. Mr P. MacDonnell told me that the immediate cause for his leaving was his failure to get Jim Larkin accepted by the Republicans.[31] This may be so, for Larkin championed the cause of the Labour Movement and Sean had an unbounded admiration for him.

[29] Desmond Ryan, *Remembering Sion*, p. 82.
[30] *Drums Under the Window*, p. 273.
[31] My interview with Mr P. MacDonnell on 2 Jun. 1958.

Even in the midst of this hurly-burly he had maintained his interest in reading. He had bought Emerson's *Essays*, Zola's *La Débâcle*, Whitman's *Leaves of Grass* and a cheap edition of Eithne Carbery's *Four Winds of Eireann*. He had read Prescott's *Conquest of Peru*, Frazer's *Golden Bough* and works of Darwin, France and others. But it was not till his friend Kevin O'Loughlin introduced him to Shaw's *John Bull's Other Island* that he was passionately moved. He devoured all the available works of Shaw, finding in him a man after his own heart who could view things objectively without drawing a romantic veil over reality. His affection for Shaw has been one of the most dominating passions of his life, and he has paid splendid tributes to his literary hero in his autobiographies and critical writings.[32]

Sean's admiration for Larkin, and his deep-seated love and desire to serve Ireland and the cause of Labour, brought him into Larkin's camp. Before long he had refused to sign the document handed to him by his employers asking him to promise that he would not join Larkin's Union, and he was thrown out of the job that had been the mainstay of his mother and himself. During these days "O'Casey played the part of a ranker, but of the ranker who is near the staff."[33] He helped the Workers' Union to carry on work without the support of the employers, but it fizzled out. He took active part in the socials held at Liberty Hall to provide entertainment for the locked-out workers.

> Liberty Hall was the nerve centre of the Union and, when the lock-out had lasted some weeks, it was decided to hold entertainments and social evenings there to keep the men from brooding over their sufferings. Sean O'Casey, the foremost post-war Irish dramatist, tried his prentice hand at play-making. An enthusiastic Larkinite, he tramped to the hall each day in boots reinforced with cardboard soles, cutting out new soles before beginning the homeward journey.[34]

During the period of the lockout his mother's pension kept them alive on dry bread and tea. To add to his troubles

[32] For a letter from O'Casey to a friend pointing out what was common between him and G. B. Shaw, see Appendix B, p. 253.

[33] M. J. Lennon, *The Catholic World*, cxxx, Dec. 1929.

[34] R. M. Fox, *Green Banners*, p. 125.

Sean developed paralysis of the legs which the doctors wrongly diagnosed as a congenital spinal disease. It took him nearly two years to get over this, and after that he suffered a tubercular swelling on the neck and was admitted to St Vincent's Hospital. He was on his way to recovery when a certain Sister Paul made some unpleasant remark about Jim Larkin, and he "forthwith rose from his bed and cleared out of the place."[35]

While suffering from paralysis he lay in his bed reading, and writing articles for *The Irish Worker* and *Irish Freedom*. They had little literary merit, and were packed with quotations and commonplace ideas: but still they revealed the force of his personality, his extreme nationalism, and the part that he felt Labour must play in the Irish struggle. All this may be seen in the passage quoted below, from an article of his:

> Allow me to blow a blast on a little trumpet of my own that I may add melody to the discord of these "beaters of drum and twanglers of the wire." The Separatist movement is, from the lowest root to the uppermost bough, a Democratic movement, living, moving, and having its being in the fibres of the Irish people. Our work will not have been accomplished when we stand over the grave of the "last of the English." Ireland's star of destiny will not be at its full brilliancy when England's grip is loosened; it will indeed be radiant, but the work of recreation will daily make it glitter with an ever increasing glow. Our work is not alone to drive far from us our connection with England, but to enter into our inheritance; not to repeal the Union, but to overthrow the conquest; not alone to end our subjection to England, but to labour that we may have life and have it more abundantly. . . .
>
> But surely, there would be union between the Separatist and the railway labourer, the factory hand, and the transport worker. Surely Democracy follows hard on the heels of Republicanism. "Reparee" advises wrongly when he urges that National ideals should weave a bandage round the toilers' eyes. The men who are linked to Wolfe Tone's soul are mainly toilers, and their condition must be bettered in a Republican Ireland. We do not demand all the good things of this life, but we do want bread that we may live.[36]

---

[35] Gerald Griffin, *The Wild Geese*, p. 217.
[36] S. O'Cathasaigh, *Irish Freedom*, Mar. 1913.

It was this attempt to persuade the Irish Republican Brotherhood to side with the Labour Movement that brought him
prominently before the eyes of the Labour leaders. He was
appointed secretary of a committee formed to provide clothes
and boots for women and children of locked-out workers. Far
from well, he would hobble to Liberty Hall to do his bit for
the workers. Later, when the Irish Citizen Army was formed,
he was elected secretary of this organisation. Both from *Drums
Under the Window* and from *The Story of the Irish Citizen Army*
it is clear that he was unable to advance its policies and found
it extremely difficult to come to an understanding with Captain
J. R. White, the president of the I.C.A., and Countess
Markievicz, the treasurer. This, as usual, was the result of
his habit of criticism and a certain incapacity to see another's
point of view. He was continually expressing his opinions,
and was often referred to as "one of the step committee
members"[37] because of his habit of standing on the steps of
Liberty Hall and criticising the organisation's policies. He
himself admits that he "had always had a bent for criticism,"[38]
and some of those who came to know him remarked on this
quality in him. Joseph Holloway records a certain Maguire
having told him that O'Casey "agreed with nobody and believed
in nothing."[39] He also quotes a remark by a Mrs Fay on
O'Casey:

> He has one peculiarity—he is always in opposition to other's
> opinions at first, and contradicts flatly what one said—after-
> wards he expresses agreement with what he had previously
> disagreed.[40]

Apart from the many minor differences in outlook between
him and the I.C.A., there was his suspicion of the Irish
Volunteers, an organisation which was sprinkled with employers
who had opposed the Larkin Union. Captain J. R. White and
Countess Markievicz were keen to bring about better understanding between these two movements that had the common
aim of freeing Ireland, but Sean remained a bitter critic of this

---

[37] My interview with Mr Frank Robbins in Dublin on 3 Jul. 1958.
[38] *Drums Under the Window*, p. 191.
[39] J. Holloway, MS. 1884, Jan.-Mar. 1924, p. 496.
[40] *Op. cit.*, MS. 1900, Jan.-Mar. 1926, p. 520.

union. Diarmuid Lynch records the following in his book, *The I.R.B. and the 1916 Rising*:

> Tom Clarke [one of the chief signatories of the Provisional Government of the Irish Republic, 1916] in a letter to John Devoy dated 14th May 1914, wrote: "Larkin's people for some time past have been making war on the Irish Volunteers. I think this is largely inspired by a disgruntled fellow named O'Casey." How right Tom Clarke was in this is borne out by O'Casey's story of the I.C.A.[41]

Matters came to a head when Sean proposed a resolution to the committee of the I.C.A. calling upon the Countess to sever her connexions with either the Citizen Army or the Volunteers. O'Casey's motion was opposed and a vote of confidence was passed in the Countess's favour by seven votes to six. Sean was then asked to apologise to the Countess, and Larkin asked him to withdraw anything he had said, but Sean refused and resigned.

Frank Robbins told me that when O'Casey brought the resolution against Countess Markievicz for her sympathies with the Irish Volunteers, Jim Larkin was not against it. But O'Casey made one mistake in stating from the platform: "that he feared no man, morally or physically, not even Jim Larkin."[42] This turned Larkin against him. The man who took an active part in seeing that O'Casey resigned was Thomas Foran, one of the Vice-Chairmen of the Army Council and the General President of the Irish Transport and General Workers Union.[43] There may be some truth in this account, for the Volunteers were not favourably disposed towards Larkin,[44] and Larkin may have himself thought it best for Countess Markievicz to devote all her loyalties to the I.C.A.

When the Easter Rising of 1916 took place, of which Dermot O'Byrne has sung:

> And such a broth of love and hate
> Was stirred ere Monday morn was late
> As Dublin town had never seen—[45]

---

[41] D. Lynch, *The I.R.B. and the 1916 Rising*, p. 88.
[42] My interview with Mr Frank Robbins on 3 Jul. 1958.
[43] *Ibid.*
[44] See R. M. Fox's *History of the Irish Citizen Army* and *Jim Larkin*.
[45] D. O'Byrne, "A Dublin Ballad-1916," *The Oxford Book of Irish Verse*, edd. D. MacDonagh and L. Robinson, p. 205.

C

Sean, having disassociated himself from the I.C.A., was left to wander far from the scene that he had dreamed of and struggled for during so many years. He was imprisoned for a night in St Barnabas' Church and later removed with the other men of the neighbourhood to be detained in a granary. This must have been a bitter blow for one whose life had been a preparation for this day, though he comforts himself by saying that he didn't approve of this sort of rising, and that as "he grew in grace and wisdom, he was growing less and less of a hero."[46] His autobiographies and early plays bear this out.

When he was released, his old companions taunted him with "Where were you in Easter Week?" He gave his answer some ten years later when the Abbey curtains went up on *The Plough and the Stars*. He told them in unmistakable words not only where he had been, but also where they had been: they who had brought death, destruction, suffering on innocent women and children; and all in the sacred name of patriotism. He showed them the incongruity between their heroic words and their unheroic actions, between their extrinsic courage and their ingrained cowardice: they who were "afraid to say they're afraid!"[47]

After the Rising he discovered that he was no longer welcomed by his associates. Save for odd days of employment he had no work and so lived with his mother on her old age pension of ten shillings a week. He suffered from extreme hunger, and once told his friend MacDonnell that "he did not remember the taste of meat."[48] Holloway records a Mrs Corrigan [*sic*] telling him after she had met O'Casey:

> Often he was hungry almost to starvation and he recalled how once when he was possessed of only trousers and coat he saw a man discard a portion of a bit of bread, and he not having had anything to eat for days pounced upon it and instead of eating it at once, placed it between his coat and bare breast, and in the joy of its possession walked on elated. Hunger at one time almost drove him to madness. He felt its pangs so keenly that he almost felt that he could kill a person to secure food.[49]

---

46 *Drums Under the Window*, p. 329.
47 *The Plough and the Stars*, Act III, p. 221.
48 My interview with Mr P. MacDonnell on 2 Jun. 1958.
49 J. Holloway, MS. 1885, Apr.-Jun. 1924, p. 782.

It was not simply that jobs were not available, but also that he would not stick to one when he got it. Hannen Swaffer wrote of him:

> He is irritable, and he is lazy. He boasts of it. "Work is meant for—slaves", he shouts, sometimes.[50]

To keep himself occupied, he joined the tiny Socialist Party of Ireland and went about campaigning for meals for hungry school children. He helped in the forming of a dramatic club which performed plays in both English and Irish. The plays were rehearsed at Oriel Hall but staged at 41 Parnell Square and at the Olympia Theatre. In a play called *Naboclish* (Never Mind It), Sean played the part of an Englishman who was terrified by what was happening in Ireland.[51] His acting capacity was limited and he never looked his part,[52] but he had a sweet voice and he wrote songs which he sang at the "Sgohuid-heachta" (the social evenings at the Oriel Hall). Presumably these were the songs that were later published as *Songs of the Wren* by Fergus O'Connor, Dublin. When exactly he took to writing these songs is difficult to say; the earliest that I could trace was "The Bonnie Bunch of Roses, O!" published in *The Irish Worker* of 11 Jan. 1913.

Unemployment meant hunger and pain, but there were compensations for what the body suffered. Sean found time and leisure to read and write. He wrote two laments[53] and a small prose tract on the patriot Thomas Ashe. The laments possess the tone of Romantic poetry without its force; they are spoilt by an excess of imaginary grief and a conscious effort on the poet's part to give the tragedy a cosmic importance. His prose piece, *The Sacrifice of Thomas Ashe*, like his earlier newspaper writings, is packed with quotations, and in addition suffers from most of the faults of his poetry. The straining after effect, the purple passages, the repetition of words, the "excess": all go to show that he is not certain of himself and the medium in which he frames his thoughts.

There is not much to be said of his songs published under

---

[50] H. Swaffer, *Who's Who*, p. 17.
[51] My interview with Mr P. MacDonnell on 2 Jun. 1958.
[52] *Ibid.*
[53] One of these is included in his *The Sacrifice of Thomas Ashe*, and a copy of the other is in the possession of Hodges Figgis & Co. Ltd., Dublin.

the title *Songs of the Wren* and *More Wren Songs*, and priced at
a penny and twopence respectively. Though they were not
written for money, he was paid £5 for the full copyright by
the publishers.[54] The influence of the Romantics, specially of
Burns and Byron, is strong. And whenever the influence is
strong, the poem is tolerably good. His "Mary is Faithful to
Me" has the ring of Byron's "Stanzas to Augusta," as can be
seen from the last two stanzas:

> Tho' the future's broad sky that is o'er me
> Is dark, with a darkness drear;
> And in Life's winding pathway before me
> No symbol of Hope is near;
> Yet bright as the sun's beaming splendour
> Soft as gentle star-shine on the sea—
> Is the gleam of thy love, true and tender,
> That lightens Life's roadway for me.
>
> I know, dearest love, that thou carest
> For me in my woe and pain,
> And for this fearless love, that's the rarest,
> I'd bear all my sorrows again.
> Let troubles and cares come thronging,
> For now they are nothing to me—
> Losing all that's to Pleasure belonging,
> I find a joy deeper in thee.[55]

Of greater interest to us are some of the themes that he used
for the songs. Songs such as "The Man from the *Daily Mail*,"
"The Demi-Semi Home Rule Bill," "The Divil's Recruitin'
Campaign," and others distinctly show how alive he was to
the political unrest of his days. He was using his talents,
however limited they may have been at the time, to express
his thoughts on some of the burning problems Ireland was
facing between the years 1913 and 1918.

His first book written for money, which brought him
fifteen pounds from the publisher, was *The Story of the Irish
Citizen Army*.[56] Though he had been a secretary of the I.C.A.,
and had followed the Rising with profound insight, the historical

---

[54] Letter to me from O'Casey, postmarked 23 Oct. 1958.
[55] *Songs of the Wren*, New Series, No. 1, p. 3.
[56] All his writings up to the publication of his plays were generally under his
Gaelic name O'Cathasaigh.

validity of the book is open to question. Diarmuid Lynch tells us that the flag hoisted on the occasion was not the Irish Tricolour as O'Casey states.[57]   Frank Robbins told me that it is still on record that at a meeting at Dún Laoghaire O'Casey himself supported the motion that uniforms should be distributed to the I.C.A.,[58] though from *The Story of the Irish Citizen Army* it would appear that O'Casey was against the distribution of uniforms. O'Casey also judges James Connolly rather harshly, blaming him for sacrificing his love for Labour and for international humanity to Irish Nationalism. Captain J. R. White, comparing O'Casey's contribution with that of Connolly, writes:

> I judged O'Cathasaigh once because he took a literary prize [Hawthornden Prize] from the hands of Asquith, Prime Minister of the Government that shot Conolly, his old chief—for it may not be generally known that O'Cathasaigh was secretary of the Citizen Army Committee under Conolly and for a time under me; but men have their function at their time and place and according to their lights; O'Cathasaigh to write in ink, Conolly in blood.[59]

The book was not well received and members of the Citizen Army went round persuading the public not to buy it. It is possible that either O'Casey or his publisher realised the limitations of the book and so called it the "Story," rather than the "History" of the Citizen Army. The hero of the story is Jim Larkin,[60] and it is written in a style that combines an objective and straightforward narrative with rhetorical flights such as:

> The disappearing Artist Sun had boldly brushed the skies with bold hues of orange and crimson, and delicate shades of yellow and green, bordered with dusky shadows of darkening blue, which seemed to symbolise the glow of determination, the delicate hues of hope, and the bordering shades of restless

---

[57] D. Lynch, *The I.R.B. and the 1916 Rising*, p. 74.
[58] My interview with Mr Frank Robbins on 3 Jul. 1958.
[59] J. R. White, *Misfit*, pp. 249-50.
[60] Larkin was at this time locked up in an American prison. A splendid tribute is paid to him by O'Casey in the song "A Son of Granuaile."   The poem does not bear the author's name, but from the manner and method of its composition I am certain it is O'Casey's. See Appendix C, p. 255.

anxiety that coloured the hearts and thoughts of the waiting, watching masses of men that stood silently beneath the oriental-coloured panoply of the sky.[61]

But now and again there are lines of exquisite beauty which we miss in his earlier writing, and which distinctly portend the birth of a poet, even though a poet only in prose.

Here, with one's head in the bosom of Nature, to what a small compass shrinks even the Constitution of the Irish Citizen Army! How horrible is a glistening, oily rifle to one of the tiny daisies, that cowers in a rosy sleep at my very feet, happy in itself, and giving to the world to which it has been born the fullest beauty and fragrance that its simple nature has to give.[62]

O'Casey next wrote *Three Shouts on a Hill*. It was a vigorous attack on the three movements for which he had sacrificed so much. The Republican Movement was too self-centred to entertain a broader vision which might lead to something more than political emancipation; Labour, too engrossed in its own petty struggles to spare a glance towards life and literature, scoffed at the idea of taking a fuller share in the birth of a new nation; the Gaelic League had dried into a skeleton, and was shirking its responsibility towards the workers.[63] The book was never published, for after completing it O'Casey sent the manuscript to George Bernard Shaw who returned it with his comments. O'Casey destroyed it.[64]

His mother died in 1919, worn out by poverty and hunger. This was a bitter blow, for she alone had cared for and protected him. His three brothers and his sister Ella had shown scant love or consideration for him. It may be for this reason that we find no strong family ties in his plays, except occasionally the love of a mother for her child.[65]

With his mother's death O'Casey found it difficult to get on with his brother Michael, who had long since left the army

[61] *The Story of the Irish Citizen Army*, p. 2.

[62] *Op. cit.*, p. 39.

[63] See, "The Gaelic Movement Today," by O'Cathasaigh, *Irish Opinion*, 23 Mar. 1918.

[64] Letter to me from O'Casey, postmarked 23 Oct. 1958.

[65] Walter Macken in his plays, *Home is the Hero* and *Mungo's Mansion*, shows the same bitter parent-child relationship as O'Casey does. His plays deal with the slums of Galway, just as O'Casey's deal with the slums of Dublin.

and now revelled in drunken and half-imagined escapades. Archie had left for Liverpool, where he was sweeping the floor of a Dunlop Rubber factory. It was probably in December 1920 that Sean, after a violent row with Michael, left his home at 18 Abercorn Road to stay with his friend Mícheál Ó Maoláin at 35 Mountjoy Square. He went for a night[66] but stayed on for nearly five months.[67] It was the time of the Anglo-Irish wars when the Black and Tans were having their Satanic reign in Ireland:

> They [the Black and Tans] roamed through the country by night in their armoured cars bellowing with drunken fury in search of vengeance for some successful ambush or captured barrack: set fire to defenceless villages or blew them up with bombs; flogged, tortured and murdered without ceremony the men whenever they could find them, under conditions too loathsome to be particularized; whenever the men were missing they extorted their last penny from the terror of the women, outraged them with drunken obscenities more hateful than their flourished revolvers, and left with a whole generation of Irish children memories of their midnight devilries more horrible than any Dante could imagine for his *Inferno*.[68]

The house in which O'Casey stayed was under suspicion for Republican activities and was visited by the police, Black and Tans, soldiers and Auxiliaries some eighteen times.[69] During 1917, 1918 and 1919, 12,589 raids were carried out in private houses.[70] It was one of these raids that O'Casey witnessed and immortalised in *The Shadow of a Gunman*.

Soon after the raid O'Casey moved to 422 North Circular Road, where he stayed till he finally left for England in March 1926. While he was at Mountjoy Square he had got employment with Jim Larkin's sister, Delia Larkin. She had taken a hall at Langrishe Place where she ran the "House Game," and O'Casey was employed for thirty shillings a week to come in the mornings and tidy up the place for the nightly

---

[66] My interview with Mrs Schweppe at 35 Mountjoy Square, Dublin. She was a next-door neighbour and figures as Bessie Ballynoy in *Inishfallen Fare Thee Well*.

[67] Mícheál Ó Maoláin, *Feasta*, VIII, May 1955.

[68] William O'Brien, *Irish Revolution*, p. 426.

[69] Mícheál Ó Maoláin, *Feasta*, VIII, May 1955.

[70] R. M. Fox, *Green Banners*, p. 311.

session.[71]   For the first time for years he was able to feed himself regularly, though he devoted the greater part of his earnings to buying a complete set of Balzac, a new set of Shakespeare's works, and a volume of Goya's paintings, as well as giving ten shillings a week for a typewriter which was to be handed to him as soon as he had made the full payment of twenty guineas.

O'Casey worked at Langrishe Place for about six months, making some extra money by writing newspaper articles.   His personal needs were few and he could live on less than ten shillings a week.[72]   When this job was over he took work as a labourer, but there were intermittent periods of unemployment. It was not till the success of *Juno and the Paycock* that he threw up his manual work and decided "that one job is enough for any man."[73]

Though O'Casey wrote his first play for the Drama Club, attached to the National Movement, about 1911,[74] it was after 1916 that he became passionately involved in playwriting. *The Frost in the Flower* was perhaps the first play he sent to the Abbey Theatre, some time in 1919.   The play was about a young man (a friend of his, Frank Cahill),[75] who, though full of confidence on great issues that did not concern him, was timid on simple questions that touched him closely.   The Abbey returned the play to him saying, "that they thought well of it, but that the central character stood out too dominantly, dwarfing the others.[76]"   It was amended on the lines suggested by the Abbey, but the play was returned again

---

[71] About his work at Langrishe Place, O'Casey wrote to me in his letter postmarked 23 Oct. 1958:

> By the way I worked in Langrishe Place mainly to see how best funds could be gathered for Jim Larkin, when he returned from the American jail. We knew the opposition Jim would meet, when he came back, from the self-centred, conventional, horo-frightened [sic] leaders of the Labor Movement, that took over power when Larkin left for America, and Jim [James] Connolly was executed.
>
> I was then Secretary of the Dublin Committee working for the release of Jim Larkin. A busy time, with no help from official Labor, only bitter and malicious opposition.

[72] Letter to me from O'Casey, postmarked 23 Oct. 1958.

[73] J. L. Hodson, *No Phantoms Here*, p. 151.

[74] Letter to me from O'Casey, postmarked 23 Oct. 1958.

[75] My interview with Mr P. MacDonnell on 2 Jun. 1958.

[76] Letter to me from O'Casey dated 20 Apr. 1958.

—now with the comment that the stature of the character had been reduced too much.[77]

The second play O'Casey sent to the Abbey was *The Harvest Festival*, which was returned with a note saying that it was finely conceived but badly executed. In view of his past experience O'Casey abandoned the play[78] and sent in a third one called *The Crimson in the Tri-Colour*, which dealt with the tussle between Labour and Sinn Fein. This they liked, especially Lady Gregory, who told him: "I believe there is something in you and your strong point is characterisation."[79] How right Lady Gregory was, and how much O'Casey is indebted to her, may be seen from the history of his first three major plays. Lady Gregory was anxious to give the play a performance but Lennox Robinson mislaid the manuscript, and after a year when it was found Yeats refused it.[80] One of the characters of this play was later elaborated and became The Covey in *The Plough and the Stars*.[81]

There are two one-act plays which should be mentioned here, as very little is known about them. *The Robe of Rosheen*, a fantasy, was O'Casey's first play to be printed, in a Republican weekly called *The Plain People*.[82] Several searches have been made for it, but so far it has not been found.[83] O'Casey in his letter to me says that he "cannot recall the manner and mind of it" except that it "was written in a vain effort to persuade against the Irish Civil War—the rending of Rosheen's Robe."[84]

---

[77] MacDonnell told me that O'Casey wrote a sequel to his first play called *Nipped in the Bud* which also dealt with Frank Cahill, and that when he asked him to send it to the Abbey O'Casey replied: "Nobody will ever prostitute my brains." The play MacDonnell refers to may possibly have been the revised version of *The Frost in the Flower*.

[78] Letter to me from O'Casey dated 20 Apr. 1958.

[79] Lady Gregory's *Journals*, ed. L. Robinson, p. 73.

[80] Dr Robinson told me in an interview in Dublin on 13 Sept. 1958, that he still had the play but could not find it. When I met Mrs Robinson in July 1959 she said that she had gone through the papers of her late husband but could not trace the play. This is what O'Casey has to say about it in his letter to me dated 20 Apr. 1958: "Mr Robinson still has the original MS—he told Mrs O'Casey so when she was in Dublin on the occasion of *The Bishop's Bonfire* production; and, afterwards the Librarian of Trinity College when he was organising a Book Exhibition, and asked me for an MS. It seems that Mr Robinson can't lay his hands on it; it seems to have a magical power of disappearing. It has been lost, found, and lost again for the past 35 years."

[81] Letter to me from O'Casey dated 20 Apr. 1958.

[82] *Ibid.*   [83] *Ibid.*   [84] *Ibid.*

The other was *The Cooing of Doves*, which was sent to the Abbey Theatre with another one-act skit on Irish politics of the day, *Cathleen Listens In*. Much to O'Casey's surprise the former (which he thought to be a better play) was rejected while the latter was acepted.[85] *The Cooing of Doves* afterwards became the second act of *The Plough and the Stars*.[86]

Unfortunately, we know very little about these early plays. Perhaps they no longer exist though Holloway writes of O'Casey having told him:

> Fay wanted his earlier plays that were refused by the Abbey but he [O'Casey] wouldn't give them to him or anyone. He said he destroyed them but he didn't. He hopes to use some of the dialogue later on.[87]

This is possible. We know that O'Casey incorporated a character from *The Crimson in the Tri-Colour*, and the whole of *The Cooing of Doves* into his masterpiece *The Plough and the Stars*.

The little we do know of these plays is from what O'Casey wrote about them in *Inishfallen Fare Thee Well*, and from what Lady Gregory jotted down in her journals. Lady Gregory writes of O'Casey having told her, on the first night of *Juno and the Paycock* at the Abbey, that they were right in rejecting *The Crimson in the Tri-Colour*, and that he could not read it himself now.[88] Holloway records something very similar:

> I had a chat with Sean O'Casey in Vestibule. He told me that when he started to write plays he thought he was a second Shaw sent to express his views thro' his characters and was conceited enough to think that his opinions were the only ones that mattered. It was Lady Gregory who advised him to cut out all expression of self and develop his peculiar ability for character drawing. At first he didn't take kindly to the advice but afterwards, on consideration felt she was right.[89]

But O'Casey nowhere says that he thought of his rejected plays as poor stuff. On the contrary he writes that years after he had left Ireland he began to realise that the plays which the

[85] Letter to me from O'Casey dated 20 Apr. 1958.
[86] *Ibid.*
[87] J. Holloway, MS. 1886, Apr.-Jun. 1924, p. 1041.
[88] Lady Gregory's *Journals*, ed. L. Robinson, p. 74.
[89] J. Holloway, MS. 1884, Jan.-Mar. 1924, p. 475.

Abbey had refused were a lot better than most plays that they had welcomed at the time, and that this filled him with bitterness and scorn.[90]

The fault in O'Casey's earlier attempts, according to Yeats, was that he wrote about the vices of the rich about which he knew nothing.[91]   Lennox Robinson told me that they dealt chiefly with wicked landlords and "girls who were led into the most compromising situations."[92]   This time it was Yeats and not Lady Gregory who advised him rightly.   Yeats "implored him to write of life as he knew it—it chanced to be the life of the Dublin slums."[93]   That O'Casey took Yeats's advice to heart is obvious from the realism of his Abbey plays, and his gratitude is clear from the words that he inscribed in the copy of *Juno and the Paycock* which he gave him: "The man who by the criticism of a bad play of mine made me write a good one."[94]   That he later felt bitterness towards Yeats and the Abbey Theatre was partly due to his temperament, but chiefly because of the shabby manner in which the Abbey treated him.   To this we shall turn after we have discussed his Abbey plays.

[90] *Inishfallen Fare Thee Well*, pp. 121-2.
[91] Lady Gregory's *Journals*, ed. L. Robinson, p. 75.
[92] My interview with Dr Lennox Robinson on 13 Sep. 1958.
[93] L. Robinson, *Curtain Up*, p. 138.
[94] *Op. cit.*, p. 139.

II

The Abbey Plays

THE immediate outcome of Yeats's advice to O'Casey was *The Shadow of a Gunman*. It is perhaps the most autobiographical of his plays; and this shows how he took Yeats's advice to heart, and how he remains indebted to Yeats in the eyes of all who consider his three Abbey plays to be his best. From *Inishfallen Fare Thee Well* it would appear that this was the fourth play he had sent to the Abbey, though Andrew E. Malone writes that it is said that as many as eight of his plays were rejected before *The Shadow of a Gunman* was accepted.[1] This is possible, for O'Casey might not have felt the necessity to record in his autobiographies all his rejected plays. The actor, Tony Quinn, who is a friend of O'Casey, told me that O'Casey showed him a play written before *The Shadow of a Gunman* which he is certain was *Red Roses for Me*,[2] while the correspondent of the *Daily Graphic* writes of O'Casey having told him of a play called *The Corners*, which the Abbey rejected.[3] It is a pity that we know so little about his earlier attempts at playwriting, for whatever their worth they are bound to throw interesting light on the man. Few dramatists have dramatised themselves and their convictions as O'Casey has done.

There is some mystery surrounding the early history of *The Shadow of a Gunman*. The story that Yeats came to O'Casey to ask him to change the title of his play *On the Run* as another play of that name existed, and that O'Casey fell into a sleep, and dreamt he saw a "gunman in a mirror" which reminded him of another name for his play,[4] remains a story. It is true that the play was initially called *On the Run* and that the name was changed to *The Shadow of a Gunman*, but that is all we know

[1] Andrew E. Malone, *The Irish Drama*, p. 211.
[2] My interview with Mr Tony Quinn in London on 26 Aug. 1958.
[3] *Daily Graphic*, 6 Mar. 1926.
[4] H. N. Kirwan, *Crystal*, Feb. 1926.

for certain. The other story, that Lady Gregory declared that they were "putting on the play for three nights only just in order to let the poor fellow see how bad it was,"[5] is fantastic. Lennox Robinson tells us that the play was immediately accepted, possibly with no revisions;[6] and Tony Quinn, who played the part of "An Auxiliary" in its first production, told me that Lady Gregory's comments were: "We think we have discovered a new author."

The reasons for these stories that got about regarding O'Casey and his plays are obvious. The Abbey was facing bad days: "Synge had ceased to excite people, and Yeats thinned the stalls down to a few ecstatic readers of poetry, most of whom came in on their cards."[7] The theatre was near bankruptcy, the plays performed at the time were sterile and commonplace and no new dramatist was in sight on the Abbey horizon. And then all of a sudden—sudden to all but himself —O'Casey turned up with a play that packed the theatre to its capacity and made his reputation in a single night. His success was so sudden and unexpected that there were "some who were convinced that Sean O'Casey was a myth and that some well-known Abbey author had adopted the name as a pseudonym."[8] His shy and reticent nature, his abhorrence of interviews in the fear of being misrepresented, and perhaps the back-stage gossip "that the author was a strange fellow, a labourer—wears a cap, no less and hob-nailed boots,"[9] may have given support to the stories that went round.

The play was first performed at the Abbey Theatre on 12 Apr. 1923. The reaction of the Irish Press may be judged from what the correspondent of the *Evening Herald* had to say:

> It was indeed a welcome and wholesome sign to sit last night in the Abbey Theatre and listen to an audience squirming with laughter and revelling boisterously in the satire which Mr. Sean O'Casey has put into his two-act play. Not for a very long time has such a good play come our way. It was

---

[5] Gabriel Fallon, *The Irish Digest*, Nov. 1946.
[6] L. Robinson, *Curtain Up*, p. 139.
[7] Micheál MacLiammóir, *All for Hecuba*, p. 53.
[8] Quoted by Holloway from an article by I. I. Hayes published in *The Boston Transcript* of 13 Feb. 1926. See MS. 1900, Jan.-Mar. 1926, p. 384.
[9] Gabriel Fallon, *The Irish Digest*, Nov. 1946.

brilliant, truthful, decisive. . . . His characters were as perfect and his photography, for one really felt his men and women were but photographs, was nothing less than the work of a genius.[10]

And Lady Gregory recorded in her journal on 15 Apr. that the play was an "immense success, beautifully acted, all the political points taken up with delight by a big audience."[11] But when it was performed at the Court Theatre, London, on 27 May 1927, and later at the Goodman Memorial Theatre, New York, the reception, though good, was not as warm. This was because the English and American audiences were unfamiliar with O'Casey's setting, and could not therefore appreciate some of the "political points" that Lady Gregory refers to. Dorothy Macardle's description of the Dublin of 1920 is very much a description of the Dublin of O'Casey's play:

> Dublin during the summer [of 1920] was a scene of intense military activity. The streets were full of British Regulars in khaki and steel helmets who carried rifles with bayonets fixed, of Auxiliary Cadets in black and the oddly attired Black and Tans, as well as the Dublin Metropolitan Police, while at every point of vantage lingered men in plain clothes, more or less recognisable as detectives of the G. Division employed in political espionage. Military cordons drawn around sections of the city with barbed wire, military lorries and tanks in attendance were a familiar sight. At night searchlights played on the house fronts, while the rumble of lorries shook the streets. The stopping of a lorry outside a house was the signal for the occupants hastily to throw on garments and rush to open the door, in the hope of being in time to prevent its being broken in. Then followed the rush of armed men upstairs and into every room, attic and cellar, swinging revolvers and shouting threats, the bursting open of cupboards, tearing up of floor boards and ripping of mattresses. If, as frequently happened, the raiders were drunk, or in a savage temper as the result of a recent ambush, shots would be fired through the walls and ceilings and breakables smashed. Any man found on the premises was in danger of being shot out of hand. Those taken away in lorries were sometimes shot

---

10 *Evening Herald* (Dublin), 13 Apr. 1923.
11 Lady Gregory's *Journals*, ed. L. Robinson, p. 71.

dead and reported as "shot while attempting to escape."
Articles looted from the raided houses were carried openly
through the streets.[12]

It is on this background that O'Casey has woven his plot,
and should this prove weak, as indeed it does, it nevertheless
does justice to the intricate period of Irish history in which the
play is set. What the critic Milton Waldman said for *The
Plough and the Stars* may as rightly be said for this play:

> Apparently he [O'Casey] sees the sequence of revolutionary
> episodes as one vast drama, and from it selects for his own
> purposes dramatic episodes which he places against a shrewdly
> observed background of Irish proletarian life. This would
> seem to explain the very real lack of structure. . . . He
> himself sees so clearly a beginning, an end, and a middle in
> recent Irish history, that he conceives it unnecessary to stress
> these dramatic props in the segment of that history which he
> chooses to dramatise.[13]

The plot of the play revolves round a tenement poet,
Donal Davoren, who is being continually hampered in his
attempt to compose verses by the other residents of the tenement. First there is a loud knock at the door by a neighbour
to arouse Seumas Shields, his pedlar friend. Once Seumas is
up all sorts of discussions take place between the two: the
subjects range from Shelley's poetry to braces which Seumas
professes would hold Cuchullain's trousers, but to the delight
of the audience do not hold his own. There is a visit from
Seumas's friend, Maguire, who leaves a bag behind; and from
the landlord, Mulligan, who comes to collect his rent and
exchanges hot words with Seumas. When Seumas at last
goes out to sell his wares it appears there will now be a spell
of peace for the poet, but in comes Minnie Powell to ask for a
drop of milk. She is a pretty girl, and in love with Davoren
because he is supposedly a "gunman" and a poet. A tender
but humorous love scene follows which is abruptly cut short
by the entry of the bragging Tommy Owens, who indulges in
a fit of maudlin patriotism. He is followed by Mrs Henderson,
and Mr Gallogher who brings a letter addressed to the Irish

---

[12] Dorothy Macardle, *The Irish Republic*, p. 355.
[13] M. Waldman, *The London Mercury*, XIV, Jul. 1926.

Republican Army. The act ends with the frustrated and
tired poet exchanging a quick kiss with Minnie Powell.

When the second act opens it is night and there is hope
that Davoren will find some peace. But this hope is soon
shattered by a visit from Mrs Grigson who comes in to complain
that her husband has yet not returned from the snugs. This is
followed by the drunken entry of her boastful husband,
Adolphus Grigson, and finally by a raid by the Auxiliaries.
Donal Davoren and Seumas are frightened, and more so when
they find that the bag left by Maguire—who in the meantime
had been shot dead—contains bombs. Minnie Powell arrives
on the scene and takes the bombs to her room. They are
found in her possession and she is shot while trying to escape.
Davoren, when he hears of Minnie's death, gives a cry more
poetic (in its echo of Ecclesiastes XII.6) than anything he has
composed so far: "Oh, Donal Davoren, shame is your portion
now till the silver cord is loosened and the golden bowl be
broken. Oh, Davoren, Donal Davoren, poet and poltroon,
poltroon and poet!"[14]

The story lacks a conventional plot and consists of a string
of incidents, which are often not well connected. And yet the
play succeeds. Is it because of strong characterisation? P. S.
O'Hegarty writes that the "characters are puppets—the only
character that one really remembers afterwards is the realistic
Black-and-Tan, who is on the stage only about ten minutes."[15]
But a play's success does not merely depend on plot and
characterisation. Yeats in a letter to Brinsley Macnamara,
dated 29 June 1919, wrote: "After all a play is merely a bundle
of acting parts."[16] Even if we do not wholly agree with Yeats,
it is undoubtedly true that much of the success of *The Shadow
of a Gunman* rests on its "acting parts." And O'Casey has
given each character an interesting part, whether Davoren
who is on-stage throughout, or the Auxiliary who comes in for
a few minutes.

I have already said that *The Shadow of a Gunman* is perhaps
the most autobiographical of his plays. O'Casey got his
material from an actual raid that took place while he was

[14] *The Shadow of a Gunman*, Act II, pp. 156-7.
[15] P. S. O'Hegarty, *The North American Review*, Jun. 1927.
[16] *The Letters of W. B. Yeats*, ed. Allan Wade, p. 658.

staying with his friend Mícheál Ó Maoláin at 35 Mountjoy Square in 1920. O'Casey's description of the room in the play with its two windows, a stretcher bed, etc., tallies with that given by Ó Maoláin in his article on Sean O'Casey.[17] Bombs were kept in the workshop in the back-yard of the house, but the story of Maguire leaving a bag full of them in Davoren's room is fictitious. Tony Quinn told me that O'Casey had mentioned to him that there were two revolvers in the room which he hid on a high wall-shelf, while Ó Maoláin writes that during the time of the raid O'Casey had with him the reports of the Irish Citizen Army.

Davoren is more or less a picture of O'Casey himself, or rather "that part of his own character which every great writer chooses to castigate."[18] This is clear from his autobiographies and from Ó Maoláin's article in *Feasta*. It is interesting to note, for it is something that Ó Maoláin has avoided mentioning, that he himself was introduced into the play in the character of Seumas Shields.[19] O'Casey, though he does not spare himself in the role of Donal Davoren, still plays the part of a poet; while Ó Maoláin—who in actual life was a school-teacher—figures as a comic, cowardly but literary pedlar. But Ó Maoláin had his say thirty-one years later. He tells us that O'Casey used to get up early in the mornings and sing songs from Burns while he stayed in bed listening, that they discussed various literary and political questions but seldom religion (note the discussions between Davoren and Seumas), that at the time of the raid O'Casey was so frightened that not a sound came out of him, and his toes were parted in fear. But the most valuable information he gives us is that the neighbours suspected O'Casey of being a "gunman," and so were kind to him and willing to help him.[20]

The other characters in the play are also modelled on real people. Lennox Robinson says in his autobiography:

> He [O'Casey] disturbed me by saying at rehearsal that all
> the characters were taken literally from life, that so-and-so

---

[17] Mícheál Ó Maoláin, *Feasta*, VIII, May 1955.
[18] Frank O'Connor, *Holiday*, XIX, Jan. 1956.
[19] See *Life* (international edn.), 23 Aug. 1954.
[20] Mícheál Ó Maoláin, *Feasta*, VIII, May 1955.

D

was Jackie — and another character Jim —. Would they, I wondered, come to the back pit, recognize themselves and wreck the theatre? He reassured me. They never visited a theatre, he named the pubs in which they would inevitably be found.[21]

Joseph Holloway records in his diary that a Mr Kavanagh told him that "The Orangeman [Adolphus Grigson] in O'Casey's play *The Shadow of a Gunman* lived in rooms in the same house, as well as others of the characters introduced."[22] Tony Quinn told me that O'Casey once pointed out Mr Grigson to him. Grigson was then working as a printer's compositor, and used to hang around Abbey Street.

Minnie Powell perhaps has a realistic basis in many of her type who were encouraged "to forget their sex and play at gunmen."[23] Perhaps she may have her seed in Linda Kearns, who was arrested for carrying ammunition and sentenced by court martial to ten years' imprisonment.[24] Many women who fought for Ireland's freedom belonged to the upper class: Maud Gonne Macbride, Countess Markievicz, Eva Gore-Booth, Grace Plunkett and others. Minnie belongs to a different class altogether, but a class whose sacrifice was equally great. Maguire is modelled on a pedlar, Seumas McGowin, who was once in the Citizen Army but later went about selling laces, pins, etc.[25] The landlord, Mr Mulligan, is a caricature of the owner of 35 Mountjoy Square, Mr Keegan, who knew that bombs were kept in the back-yard.[26]

Though O'Casey permits his characters to develop in the roles allotted to them, at times he sacrifices their development in the interest of conveying his own views. This is partly because he is anxious to express his ideas (an influence of Shaw), but mainly because he himself figures as a character in the person of Donal Davoren. This reduces the stature of Seumas Shields, "a scamp on the grand scale, a Fluther Good in the making."[27] He is made to say things that are inconsistent

21 L. Robinson, *Curtain Up*, pp. 139-40.
22 J. Holloway, MS. 1877, Apr.-Jun. 1923, p. 743.
23 P. S. O'Hegarty, *The Victory of Sinn Fein*, p. 125.
24 R. M. Fox, *Green Banners*, p. 299.
25 My interview with Mr James Boyle in Dublin on 24 Apr. 1958.
26 My interview with Mrs Schweppe on 25 Apr. 1958.
27 Ivor Brown, *The Saturday Review*, CXLIII, 18 Jun. 1927.

with his comic development so as to provide Davoren a chance
to speak his philosophy:

> SEUMAS [*sitting up in bed*]: . . . I don't profess to know much
> about poetry—about poetry—I don't know much about the
> pearly glint of the morning dew, or the damask sweetness of
> the rare wild rose, or the subtle greenness of the serpent's
> eye—but I think a poet's claim to greatness depends upon
> his power to put passion in the common people.
> DAVOREN: Ay, passion to howl for his destruction. The
> People! Damn the people! They live in the abyss, the
> poet lives on the mountain-top; to the people there is no
> mystery of colour: it is simply the scarlet coat of the soldier;
> the purple vestments of a priest; the green banner of a
> party; the brown or blue overalls of industry. To them
> the might of design is a three-roomed house or a capacious
> bed. To them beauty is for sale in a butcher's shop. . . .[28]

In the discussion that takes place between Seumas and Davoren,
O'Casey speaks through both characters. Seumas expresses
the horrible state to which Ireland has been reduced by the
Anglo-Irish wars, while Davoren conveys the reaction of a
vain and sensitive poet to the grim conditions. Though
Davoren turns to poetry as an escape from the present realities,
he still remains a tenement dweller; the call of the Muse is
not strong enough to lift him up from the world around. Take
the conversation between the two:

> SEUMAS: . . . How peaceful the heavens look now with the
> moon in the middle; you'd never think there were men
> prowlin' about tryin' to shoot each other. I don't know
> how a man who has shot any one can sleep in peace at night.
> DAVOREN: There's plenty of men can't sleep in peace at
> night now unless they know that they have shot somebody.
> SEUMAS: I wish to God it was all over. The country is gone
> mad. Instead of counting their beads now they're countin'
> bullets; their Hail Marys and paternosters are burstin'
> bombs—burstin' bombs, an' the rattle of machine-guns;
> petrol is their holy water; their Mass is a burnin' buildin';
> their De Profundis is "The Soldier's Song", an' their creed
> is, I believe in the gun almighty, maker of heaven an' earth
> —an' it's all for "the glory o' God an' the honour o' Ireland."

---

[28] *The Shadow of a Gunman*, Act II, p. 127.

DAVOREN: I remember the time when you yourself believed in nothing but the gun.

SEUMAS: Ay, when there wasn't a gun in the country; I've a different opinion now when there's nothin' but guns in the country. . . .[29]

The words of Seumas sum up O'Casey's own development from a revolutionary who believed in guns to one now seeking for peace. O'Casey himself believed in guns as long as there were few of them in the country. But the 1916 Rising, followed by the brutalities of the Anglo-Irish War and the Civil War, turned him towards pacifism. This was not simply because he himself knew fear—of that he makes no bones in his autobiographies—but because he felt that it was always the innocent poor who had to suffer most. Tony Quinn told me that O'Casey once said to him during a rehearsal of *The Shadow of a Gunman*, that "whatever the idealist may think it is only the poor who get it in the neck." This is well borne out in all his Abbey plays. Donal Davoren who, if not a "gunman," was at least the shadow of a gunman, escapes; while Minnie Powell dies, not so much for the Republic as for her love for Davoren.

O'Casey further goes to show that among the poor it is the women who bear the brunt of the tragedy, and in most cases heroically. The heroines are the heroes of his plays: it is they who see rightly and act bravely. Professor Wilson Knight justly observes:

> O'Casey's women see, with the author, all masculine quarrels, politics and war as absurd and trivial, his plays being rooted in the feminine. . . .[30]

O'Casey's plays are indeed rooted in the feminine: in the brave but rash Minnie Powell in *The Shadow of a Gunman*, in the nagging but heroic Juno in *Juno and the Paycock*, in the weak but affectionate Nora Clitheroe in *The Plough and the Stars*. Just as there is the shadow of a gunman in the character of O'Casey himself, there is more than a shadow of his mother in his three great heroines. He has ridiculed himself in the figure of Donal Davoren, he has ridiculed all the things he

---

[29] *The Shadow of a Gunman*, Act II, p. 131.
[30] G. Wilson Knight, *Christ and Nietzsche*, p. 122.

loved for the sake of something he loved more: "the gay laugh of [his] mother at the gate of the grave."[31]

Minnie Powell is only on the stage for a short while in the first act and makes only one brief entrance in the second, yet she still remains the chief character in the play. She towers above the others because she at least lives up to her illusions and gives her life for them. O'Casey does not give her fine words to speak or great thoughts to voice, but he endows her with something finer still—courage. It is the wastrels and good-for-nothings that are fine phrase-makers; and the incongruity between their words and deeds is a source of continual laughter.

Mrs Grigson is a real creature of the slums, epitomising in her appearance and conversation all the characteristics of slum dwellers. Here is O'Casey's description of her:

> She is a woman about forty, but looks much older. She is one of the cave-dwellers of Dublin, living as she does in a tenement kitchen, to which only an occasional sickly beam of sunlight filters through a grating in the yard; the consequent general dimness of her abode has given her a habit of peering through half-closed eyes. She is slovenly dressed in an old skirt and bodice; her face is grimy. . . . Her hair is constantly falling over her face, which she is as frequently removing by rapid movements of her right hand.[32]

Her tragedy is the tragedy of the Dublin slums: a drunken boastful husband out in the snugs after the curfew hour and fear and poverty knocking at the door. What is she to do? What if anything should happen to him? "Not that I'd be any the worse if anything did happen to him,"[33] she admits; and then, "Do the insurance companies pay if a man is shot after curfew?"[34] In two sentences O'Casey has summed up the tragedy of the very poor, who fear nothing more than the poverty they have been facing all their lives.

Adolphus Grigson comes close to Captain Boyle in comic grandeur, while Tommy Owens is another Grigson in the making. They are not just permanent features of slum life but the very pillars on which the slums rest. As one hears their

---

[31] O'Casey dedicated *The Plough and the Stars* to his mother with these words.
[32] *The Shadow of a Gunman*, Act II, p. 135.
[33] *Op. cit.*, p. 136.   [34] *Op. cit.*, p. 137.

drunken tales and cheap boastings, one feels that the Dublin slums will endure for ever. Drunk on whiskey or stout, they are able to lift themselves out of their sordid existence and indulge freely in flights of imaginative heroics, while their wives and children live on, fighting a losing battle against poverty and death. It may be for this reason that *The Times* critic commented:

> For the tragic message of the play is that splendid deeds are as fugitive as splendid words and that, though one may die for it, life goes on unchanged and human nature remains unaltered, after its first shocked tribute to death, and everything will always be the same, neither better nor worse.[35]

A word is necessary about the Black and Tans. They were a force of 5,800 armed men recruited in England to take the place of the Royal Irish Constabulary, which was not wholly reliable. They began arriving in Ireland on 25 Mar. 1920, and were dressed in khaki coats with black trousers and caps. This costume, it is said, promptly gave rise to the nickname "Black and Tans,"[36] though another version is that they were called after a famous local pack of hounds when the first company was sent to Limerick.[37] Whatever its origin, the name stuck to these recruits and was often applied generically not only to the Black and Tans proper, but also to another force, the Auxiliaries, which consisted of ex-army officers. The raid that takes place in the play is by the Auxiliaries, but since there was so much in common between these two forces critics often refer to the raiders as Black and Tans.

O'Casey's handling of the raid in the play is masterly. The Auxiliary remains on stage from seven to ten minutes, but in this short time reveals all the characteristics for which his army earned a name in Irish history. As soon as he hears from Mrs Grigson that a bottle of whiskey has been found he rushes out of the room for a drink. Davoren's fear that "They're bad enough sober, what'll they be like when they're drunk,"[38] is soon answered by Minnie's death.

There is one serious flaw that comes near to spoiling the

---

[35] *The Times* (London), 26 Jan. 1953.
[36] Dorothy Macardle, *The Irish Republic*, p. 340.
[37] Frank Pakenham, *Peace by Ordeal*, p. 41.
[38] *The Shadow of a Gunman*, Act. II, p. 150.

play. The scene in which Mrs Henderson and Mr Gallogher bring a letter addressed to the Republican Army is unnecessary, and much too long. The humour falls flat in spite of all the malapropisms of Mrs Henderson, a slum lexicographer, taking pride in the letter of her friend Mr Gallogher, which she says is as good as any that "was decomposed by a scholar."[39]

There seem to be three reasons why O'Casey introduces this scene. Firstly he wishes to stress again, quite unnecessarily, that the neighbours respect Davoren because they think him to be a "gunman." Secondly he wants to show that in a tenement house there is hardly any privacy. Finally, perhaps, the need to introduce these two characters arose because he had still some way to go before he could conclude the act. He could not extend the love scene between Davoren and Minnie, for it was based on an emotional attachment which would flag if lengthened. Tommy Owens had emptied himself out in the first ten minutes. There was no option for O'Casey but to introduce new characters even if they contributed very little to the development of the play. Therein lies the chief danger of a play that lacks a conventional plot. O'Casey solves this difficulty better in his next two major plays by his rich characterisation and brilliance of words, and by an extremely successful juxtaposition of tragedy and comedy. A good example of this last is in the scene where Adolphus Grigson's boast of his heroic conduct during the raid is followed by the news of Minnie's death.

It is this mixing of tragedy and comedy in rapid succession that finally results in confusing the mind of the audience so that they are unable to carry a definite impression of the plays. In *The Shadow of a Gunman* this juxtaposition is not very prominent, except in the later part of the second act, yet one feeling or the other is evoked throughout. This causes an undiscerning critic to fail to grasp the "general philosophy" of the play, which, in the author's own words, is "the bewilderment and horror at one section of the community trying to murder and kill the other."[40]

In spite of its success *The Shadow of a Gunman* brought O'Casey less than £4. This was not even enough to pay his

---

[39] *The Shadow of a Gunman*, Act I, p. 116.
[40] *New York Herald Tribune*, 16 Nov. 1958.

debts, so he immediately sat down to write his next play, *Cathleen Listens In*,[41] a one-act fantasy. The play was given its first performance at the Abbey Theatre on 1 Oct. 1923. It ran for seven nights and was very coldly received. Later, Lady Gregory and O'Casey sat down together for an hour and revised the play.[42] The revised version was given six performances at the Abbey from 3 Mar. 1925. Since then it has not been revived.

The play was a failure. Joseph Holloway, who was at this time sympathetic towards O'Casey, writes: "Somehow or other despite *Cathleen Listens In* being a good shot, it missed the mark I think and fizzled out somewhat," and, "The audience was eager to laugh with him but couldn't; only by fits and starts."[43] Gabriel Fallon, who played the part of the Man in the Kilts, wrote that the curtains were lowered on a "frigid silence."[44] O'Casey himself has written that the play was received in dead silence, and that there was not so much as a timid handclap; a fate that no Abbey playwright had ever suffered.

The play was not condemned by the Irish Press as one might expect, but gently brushed aside. The critic of *The Irish Statesman* wrote:

> The new play at the Abbey Theatre, *Cathleen Listens In*, calls itself a Phantasy, and is not, we imagine, taking itself very seriously as a play; but it invites some serious consideration as an allegory, or perhaps we might say a rough-and-tumble morality play.[45]

And the *Evening Telegraph* commented:

> All expectations as to the wittiness of the play and its aptness and interest were more than fulfilled; but it was a play to slightly puzzle a first night audience. To begin with, utter

---

[41] The play has not been published and most students of O'Casey know little about it. The Abbey typescript copy was destroyed in the fire on the night of 17 Jul. 1951. But I was fortunate enough to find, through the very generous help of the Abbey Theatre secretary, Mrs Woods, a half-burnt copy of the parts of the various characters in the revised version of the play. With the help of a friend, Robert Caswell, I typed out the parts and have attempted to put the play in order. It is difficult to say how far we were success ul.

[42] J. Holloway, MS. 1892, Jan.-Mar. 1925, p. 373.

[43] *Op. cit.*, MS. 1881, Sep.-Dec. 1923, pp. 676-8.

[44] G. Fallon, *Theatre Arts*, Jan. 1950.

[45] *The Irish Statesman*, 6 Oct. 1923.

phantasy, however direct of meaning, is not gathered in completely at first to the mind of any audience unless they have been extraordinarily well prepared for it.[46]

There are two reasons for this apologetic approach of the Irish critics. Firstly, the play followed fast on the heels of *The Shadow of a Gunman*, which had brought unstinting praise from some of these very critics. Secondly, and perhaps more to the point, the critics themselves failed to get to the bottom of the fantasy. If the audience was not "extraordinarily well prepared for it" neither were the critics, and this is best shown by their criticisms.

O'Casey told Holloway that "nobody but himself rightly understands his phantasy."[47] Quite possible, for nobody except O'Casey thus aligned himself with one political body after another, and nobody was ever left so disillusioned as he was. In this play the tragedy of Ireland, as O'Casey sees it, lies not in the rivalry between the political parties alone, but in Ireland herself—brought into the play in the person of Cathleen—who is given to ephemeral pleasures and is not conscious of her destiny.

The play bears a close resemblance to George Shiel's *First Aid* which also had a poor reception at the Abbey when performed on 26 Dec. 1923. In Shiel's play, Nora, an old woman representing Ireland, falls into a well and the neighbours, who symbolise the various political parties, gather round to pull her out: but in their anxiety to help Nora they betray their hatred and suspicion of one another. In O'Casey's play,[48] Ireland is signified by the young and flippant Cathleen, whose suitors, among them a Free-Stater, a Republican, a Business-man, a Farmer and a Labourer represent the different bodies and political parties that are out to win her. The feeble old Man in the Kilts stands for the timid Gaelic League fanatics who thought that Ireland's destiny was bound up with the compulsory teaching of Irish. O'Casey, though a strong Gaelic Leaguer himself, was against the ramming of Irish into the children of the workers,[49] and in this play he

[46] *Evening Telegraph* (Dublin), 2 Oct. 1923.

[47] J. Holloway, MS. 1881, Sep.-Dec. 1923, p. 696.

[48] The theme is based on a short story he wrote called "The Seamless Coat of Kathleen" published in *Poblacht Na h-Eireann* in March 1922.

[49] See *The Irish Statesman* of 29 Nov. 1924, and 10 Jan. 1925.

satirises the extreme element of the Gaelic League in the person of the Man in the Kilts.

Apart from showing a chaotic picture of Irish political parties and the sad state to which Ireland has fallen, there is little in the play. There is nothing of a plot, the characters are all insipid and static. This is the only play in which O'Casey holds forth no vision, no hope. In almost all his other plays there is at least a ray of light, a dream that things could have been different, may one day turn out to be different. But here he sees nothing. The reason may be that he cannot see objectively where Ireland's destiny is concerned. He had been a participant too long in the country's struggle for freedom, and for bettering the lot of the workers; he had spared neither himself nor the little he had, and had at last emerged from the fight disillusioned and disgusted. The theme of the play touched him so closely that he failed to exercise the dispassionate gaze of the artist. This is seen in the timid manner in which he approaches the central theme. The plot turns on the wooing of Cathleen by the representatives of the various political parties, but they are not introduced till we are nearly two-thirds of the way through the play.

Similarly, O'Casey's personal involvement is responsible for the lack of genuine humour. The tragedy of his own life looms in the background: the failure of the Irish struggle is analogous with his own failure. Thus every attempt to laugh is stifled by a cry from the heart. In *The Shadow of a Gunman*, *Juno and the Paycock* and *The Plough and the Stars* he freely evokes laughter, for he himself is laughing. Though he is one with the characters in these plays and feels for their misery, their tragedy is, strictly speaking, not his tragedy. But in *Cathleen Listens In* the theme touches the author too closely, and the subjectivity of it smothers the attempt to laugh wholeheartedly.

Though O'Casey liked fantasies he soon realised that this was not the time nor the place for them, and that, if he was to make a living and earn a name for himself, he must return to Yeats's advice and write of the life that he knew intimately. His fame and future depended on the Abbey playgoers, and they wanted him to portray the tragi-comedy of their existence.

There was little choice for him, and on 3 Mar. 1924 the Abbey curtains went up on *Juno and the Paycock*.

The play, which remains to this day his most popular work in England,[50] was an instantaneous success in Dublin. The critics praised it unstintingly, though a few pointed out its structural weakness. The message was no longer cloaked as in *Cathleen Listens In*. \The author's cry of anguish that man should exist in such degradation moves through scenes of uproarious farce, cutting its way through the easy laughter and the foolish boastings./ The critic of the *Freeman's Journal* wrote:

> No one who saw the *Shadow of a Gunman* will ever forget its strong ironic bite. Here we have that same irony, centrifugal and indiscriminating as to character, but with a finer point. If the point is finer, however, the thrust is deeper. In the last act, touching the vitals, it becomes unbearable.[51]

And later on Dawson Byrne wrote:

> It is no wonder this play instantly brought Dublin to the feet of a new and unknown dramatist. It is more than a mirror held up to nature. It is nature itself—human nature, so living and quick that Dublin must have forgotten proscenium and footlights as it watched. . . .[52]

O'Casey's understanding of human nature, coupled with his keen observation and a sound knowledge of his characters was the immediate cause of the play's success. He had known Jack Boyle and Joxer Daly intimately, and in the case of Boyle he had not even changed the name. Holloway records in his *Impressions* that Joxer Daly was always shrugging his shoulders and falling in and out with his pal Jack Boyle, just as we see him in the play.

I did not fully comprehend how directly these two characters were drawn from life till I met Jimmy Boyle, son of Jack Boyle, and James Boyle, brother of Jack Boyle, in April 1958. Joxer and Captain Boyle have not passed from "literature into

[50] *The Times* (London), 18 Aug. 1956. See also Norman Veitch, *The People's*, pp. 177-8.
[51] *Freeman's Journal*, 4 Mar. 1924.
[52] D. Byrne, *The Story of Ireland's National Theatre*, p. 128.

reality"[53] as Walter Starkie says, but from reality to immortality. James Boyle told me that O'Casey was once a great friend of theirs, and used to visit their two-room apartment in Gloucester Street, Dublin. It was here that he came across Jack Daly, the inseparable snug-mate of Jack Boyle. Jack Daly, who did not have as much as a sixpence to call his own, visited the Boyles' daily for a "cup o' tay." The two friends would sit and gossip for hours. O'Casey, if he happened to be there, would sit near the fire listening to their talk, or writing something on bits of paper. Neither Boyle nor Daly suspected that O'Casey was fast jotting down their conversation to give it to the world at a later date. This was O'Casey's technique of success, and this is what Holloway quotes in his diary from the *Daily Express*:

> The remarkable realism of his work is due to the fact that he used to jot down on the back of envelopes all sorts of remarks made by his friends. These he incorporated in his plays. As it was the practice of many of these friends to use forceful language, it is not surprising that his plays in parts are a little lurid.[54]

James Boyle also said that Jack Daly was a self-educated man and spoke good English—by Boyle's standards, of course. He had a fine memory and could quote widely. He also had a quick temper and this is brought out in the play, and in what Holloway writes about him:

> On reflection—Daly is another slum character down Bally-bough way. A lady gave him a suit and boots so that he could go respectfully to church, and when next he met her he was profuse in his thanks and praised the boots highly and added that he now could kick any who annoyed him into a [blooming] pulp.[55]

It was not altogether easy for me to question the Boyles about the accuracy of Captain Jack Boyle's portrayal. They told me, however, that Jack Boyle was not in life the character that O'Casey had depicted in the play; and that the confusion arose because of the truth in the character of Jack Daly, and

---

[53] W. Starkie, *The Irish Theatre*, ed. L. Robinson, pp. 156-7.
[54] J. Holloway, MS. 1900, Jan.-Mar. 1926, pp. 339-40.
[55] *Op. cit.*, opposite p. 458.

also because O'Casey gave the name Jack Boyle to the "Captain." On the other hand Holloway records that Captain Boyle had "even more twists and turns than [O'Casey] gave him in the play."[56]

Where exactly the truth lies is hard to fathom, all the more because O'Casey told me that the real Jack Boyle did not live in Gloucester Street but in Malahide, a district in the north of Dublin. However, it cannot be disputed that O'Casey drew the character of the "Captain" from someone he knew intimately. Of course, it is only too likely that while portraying the man he might have exaggerated some peculiarities and invented others.

Jimmy Boyle also told me that his father wrote verse, and this is brought out in the second act of the play. When Mrs Madigan presses Boyle for a song, he, on Joxer's suggestion, recites a poem:

> Shawn an' I were friends, sir, to me he was all in all.
> His work was very heavy and his wages were very small.
> None betther on th' beach as Docker, I'll go bail,
> 'Tis now I'm feelin' lonely, for to-day he lies in jail.
> He was not what some call pious—seldom at church or
>   prayer;
> For the greatest scoundrels I know, sir, goes every Sunday
>   there.
> Fond of his pint—well, rather, but hated the Boss by creed
> But never refused a copper to comfort a pal in need.[57]

Could this be one of Jack Boyle's poems, that O'Casey, with slight changes, has incorporated into the play? Very likely, for O'Casey told me that this poem was written by a friend of his and published in a local Dublin paper. Shawn in this poem obviously appears to be O'Casey himself. We have already seen that his wages were very small and work heavy, and that he was employed for a time as a docker. The phrase "he lies in jail," may refer to his internment during the Easter Rising. It is also true that O'Casey seldom went to church, that he hated his boss by creed, and was always willing to share the little he had with others.

It was interesting to learn from James Boyle that his

---

[56] *Op. cit.*, MS. 1884, Jan.-Mar. 1924, p. 476.
[57] *Juno and the Paycock*, Act II, p. 57.

brother and Jack Daly went with a lawyer, a Mr O'Hudaigh, to see the performance of the play with a view to suing O'Casey for defamation. Jack Boyle at the end of the show decided to drop the matter for he felt that the cap did not fit him, but Jack Daly kept protesting that it did. James Boyle also told me that at one time Jack Boyle was working in a printer's shop whence he often brought paper for O'Casey who was then so poor that he could not afford to buy his own.[58] If this is true, and if it is also true that O'Casey used to take down the conversation that went on between his friends, it is only too likely that the first rough draft of Captain Boyle's character was sketched on the paper that Boyle himself supplied.

Juno Boyle seems to be modelled on O'Casey's own mother, Susan O'Casey, whose courage and forbearance she shares. She also has much in common with Mrs Rainey, a character in St John Ervine's *Mixed Marriage*. Like Mrs Rainey she keeps the family together and sees things in their right perspective. Compare Mrs Rainey's words on strikes with Juno Boyle's:

> Mrs Rainey: There ought to be some other way o' settlin' these things nor stracks. It's wicked, that's what it is, an' it's the weemen that has to bear the worst o' it. Awe, yes, indeed it is. You men don't have to face the rent agent an' the grocer wi' no money.[59]

This is what Juno tells Mary when the latter goes on strike for a principle:

> Mrs Boyle: Yis; an' when I go into oul' Murphy's tomorrow, an' he gets to know that, instead o' payin' all, I'm goin' to borry more, what'll he say when I tell him a principle's a principle? What'll we do if he refuses to give us any more on tick?[60]

The other characters are all definite types that O'Casey may have come across at one time or another. Jerry Devine is the typical Labour man, "knowing enough to make the mass of

---

[58] Joseph Holloway records O'Casey telling him that he was so poor that he could not buy writing paper, and that a friend of his working in a printer's shop used to filch some for him. See MS. 1884, Jan.-Mar. 1924, p. 475.

[59] St John Ervine, *Mixed Marriage*, Act I, p. 6.

[60] *Juno and the Paycock*, Act I, pp. 6-7.

his associates, who know less, a power."[61] Mary Boyle
in her vanity, her learning, and her unsympathetic attitude
towards her brother Johnny, has something in common with
O'Casey's sister Ella. Charles Bentham, the school-teacher,
may be compared as a character with Ella's fiancé, Bugler
Benson, but the woes that he brings on Mary are far more
horrible than those Ella suffered through marrying Benson.
Johnny Boyle, Mrs Madigan, Mrs Tancred and others are all
slum types, moving in a groove in which chance, circumstances
and heredity have placed them.

We can now turn to the plot. The play has for its background the heart-rending Civil War between the Free-Staters
and the Republicans, which followed on the signing of the
treaty between England and Southern Ireland in 1922. War
often bears hardest on those who have least to do with it, and
in this play the victim is Juno Boyle, the only prop of the
Boyle family. She works and supports the family while her
drunken husband, Captain Jack Boyle, struts about like a
"paycock" with his "butty" Joxer Daly. Her daughter Mary
stays at home on strike, and her son Johnny—an invalid—
haunts their two-room dwelling like a ghost. Then, all of a
sudden, into Juno's dismal world comes the news of an unexpected legacy, brought by the school-teacher Bentham on
whom Mary has pinned her love after throwing up the Labour
leader, Jerry Devine. On the strength of this legacy the two
dingy rooms are decorated with cheap paper festoons and
glaring, vulgar furniture. Neighbours are entertained and
Captain Boyle, saturated in stout and voluptuously stretched
on the sofa, spins yarns about his adventures at sea. But the
joy does not last for long: two months, and "the sails of
comedy swell no more in the wind of his invention and we
beat up against the cold wave of disaster."[62] Tragedy breaks
in with the news of Mary's pregnancy and Bentham's flight to
England. Captain Boyle reveals that the Will has fizzled out
due to being vaguely worded. Johnny Boyle, who alone had
taken no part in the Paycock's illusory prosperity, is taken
out and shot by the Republicans for betraying a comrade to
the Free-Staters. Juno and Mary leave the house for ever,

---

[61] *Juno and the Paycock*, Act I, p. 8.
[62] Ivor Brown, *Saturday Review*, CXL, 21 Nov. 1925.

and the curtains descend on the drunken entry of the Captain, who, unmindful of his loss, raises his "drunken downfall to the universal plane and endows his fate with cosmic significance: 'The whole worl's in a tur-rible state of chassis' [*sic*]."[63]

Though the plot of *Juno and the Paycock* is more closely knit than those of O'Casey's other Abbey plays, it has not escaped scathing criticism. Ivor Brown feels that it does not make a shapely play,[64] and Camillo Pellizzi says that "There is no trace of a theme, or rather there are a thousand themes and yet none at all. . . ."[65] Milton Waldman, after calling it a bad stage play, goes on to say:

> There are thus three lines of plot, the Boyles' elusive inheritance, Mary's unfortunate love affair, and Johnny's treachery. Neither of the former two has any relation to the last, and their connection with each other is, to say the least, slender.[66]

Theatrical success has shown that *Juno and the Paycock* is not a bad stage play. As for the three lines of the plot, this is true; and it is also true that the former two have no relation to the third. But then, is a connexion necessary? Are all events in the life of one person connected with the events in the life of another, even if the two are father and son? O'Casey is giving us a realistic picture of tenement life, and he often sees in each life a rounded plot in itself. Even if Mr Waldman's objection to this is just, he fails to see that the three lines of plot are connected with each other—where they should be connected —in the person of Juno Boyle, the heroine and the most ennobling character in the play. It is her tragedy that the "Paycock," living on an imaginary nautical prestige, should drink himself into debt, that Mary should be seduced and then deserted by a worthless liar, that Johnny should be led to his doom for betraying a friend. The play is brought to a focal point in the character of Juno Boyle.

The late George Jean Nathan, the American critic for whom O'Casey had an unbounded admiration, and who later

[63] E. V. R. Wyatt, *The Catholic World*, CL, Mar. 1940.
[64] Ivor Brown, *Saturday Review*, CXL, 21 Nov. 1925.
[65] C. Pellizzi, *English Drama*, p. 237.
[66] M. Waldman, *The London Mercury*, XIII, Feb. 1926.

described the play as "one of the richest tragi-comedies,"[67] had earlier said of the third act:

> His second act is almost entirely in the low comedy vein and his third act, cut off from the other as with a meat axe, piles tragedy upon tragedy so exaggeratedly that it would take a professional pallbearer to profess any show of sympathy over his characters' plight. The impression is of a man stopping suddenly short in the midst of a comic story to tell the plot of *Œdipus Rex*.[68]

Nathan's criticism is not off the mark, but still we cannot blame O'Casey for piling up the tragedy. Johnny's fate was inevitable and explicit from the start; his death was a matter of time, and for dramatic reasons it could not be carried out in the second act. Every other mishap that overtook the Boyles was in one way or another the result of the failure of the legacy. As a realist of the most uncompromising kind, O'Casey spares his audience nothing. Once the fallacy of the expected legacy has been unmasked, it is reasonable to expect that every creditor will try to recover whatever he was owed. There is a piling of tragedy on the stage because there is a piling of tragedy in tenement life. But on the whole O'Casey does not forget that the tragedy of the Dublin slum-dweller is not without its comic side. Captain Boyle remains so irresistibly comic that we often forget to pity Juno and Mary. Tragedy and comedy are so well juxtaposed that our emotions remain in a continuous state of flux for the greater part of the play. The final impression that emerges is of "an extraordinary blend of ugliness and beauty, squalor and splendour, tenderness and brutality."[69]

Though *Juno and the Paycock* is a much better play than *The Shadow of a Gunman*, the purpose and the message remain the same. The background now is the Civil War instead of the Anglo-Irish War, the tragedy again is the tragedy of the very poor, and the only signs of courage and common sense are shown by women: in this play they are shown by Juno Boyle, "the greatest mother in drama, even though her influence be limited to two rooms in a Dublin slum."[70] Unlike Minnie

[67] G. J. Nathan, *Newsweek*, 29 Jan. 1940.
[68] G. J. Nathan, *Art of the Night*, p. 187.
[69] R. M. Fox, *The Irish Statesman*, x, 23 Jun. 1928.
[70] Andrew E. Malone, *The Irish Drama*, p. 213.

E

Powell she is rooted in the present, her feet firmly planted on the earth. She is the ideal O'Casey heroine, possessing those qualities that he values in women. In *Rose and Crown* O'Casey has written:

> Women were nearer to the earth than men; they had their feet in the soil. Men went lightly over the ground; women trod firmly. They are closer to common things, and so have a more ready and lasting knowledge of life. Men shout dogmatically, they gesture, and run here, run there; women stay more still, speak more quietly, and say more in their silence.[71]

And, speaking to the reporter of the *New York Herald Tribune* in a transatlantic telephone conversation, he said:

> They're much more near to the earth than men are. Men are more idealistic, stupidly idealistic. They're not as realistic as the women. The woman has to be nearer the earth than the man.[72]

Juno's courage and common sense are felt from the beginning almost to the end of the play. As each misfortune overtakes her, she rises above it and finally, when another character would have doubled up under the weight of her misery, she goes out to begin her life struggle anew. Her grasp of reality is not only brought out in every scene of the play, but is made to contrast with the stupid idealism and imaginative flights of the other members of her household. Captain Boyle solves his problems through bottles of stout, Mary through books, and Johnny by cutting himself off from the others into a living death. Juno alone faces the facts of life. See the wisdom in her retort when Johnny boasts that he is prepared to go through the mill again for Ireland's sake:

> JOHNNY [*boastfully*]: I'd do it agen, ma, I'd do it agen; for a principle's a principle.
> MRS BOYLE: Ah, you lost your best principle, me boy, when you lost your arm; them's the only sort o' principles that's any good to a workin' man.[73]

A shattered hip and an amputated arm have taught Johnny

[71] *Rose and Crown*, pp. 292-3.
[72] *New York Herald Tribune*, 16 Nov. 1958.
[73] *Juno and the Paycock*, Act I, p. 31.

nothing. He is one with the O'Casey heroes in for ever re-
maining stupidly idealistic. But the best instance that sums
up her being is brought out at the end of the play when she
and Mary hear the news of Johnny's death:

MARY: Oh, it's thrue, it's thrue what Jerry Devine says—
there isn't a God, there isn't a God; if there was He wouldn't
let these things happen!

MRS BOYLE: Mary, Mary, you mustn't say them things.
We'll want all the help we can get from God an' His Blessed
Mother now! These things have nothin' to do with the
Will o' God. Ah, what can God do agen the stupidity o'
men![74]

The climax comes when she leaves Mary behind—fearing that
the sight of her dead brother would be painful to her—and
goes out to receive the body of Johnny alone. As she goes out
she repeats the beautiful prayer of Mrs Tancred, said when the
latter's son was shot by the Free-Staters:

. . . Mother o' God, Mother o' God, have pity on us all!
Blessed Virgin, where were you when me darlin' son was
riddled with bullets, when me darlin' son was riddled with
bullets? Sacred Heart o' Jesus, take away our hearts o' stone,
and give us hearts o' flesh! Take away this murderin' hate
an' give us Thine own eternal love![75]

Much has been said about the pathetic beauty of these lines
which are reminiscent of the first three lines in the second
stanza of Shelley's *Adonais*:

Where wert thou, mighty Mother, when he lay
When thy Son lay, pierced by the shaft which flies
In darkness?

and of Ezekiel XI.19, which reads:

And I will give them one heart, and I will put a new spirit
within you; and I will take the stony heart out of their flesh,
and will give them an heart of flesh.

Lady Gregory after hearing Juno's prayer told Yeats, "This is
one of the evenings at the Abbey that makes me glad to have

[74] *Juno and the Paycock*, Act III, p. 86.   [75] *Op. cit.*, p. 87.

been born."[76]   But all critics have not shared her enthusiasm. The critic of the *Freeman's Journal* wrote that Juno's outburst "savoured just the slightest of what we now know by the odious name of propaganda";[77] and Milton Waldman has referred to it as "little short of bathos."[78] My own feeling is that these lines are most touching and very much in harmony with Juno's religious nature.

Mrs Tancred is another Juno Boyle in embryo.   She is on the stage for not more than seven minutes, but in this short space she displays those qualities for which O'Casey's women are known.   When she is going out to receive the dead body of her son, a neighbour tries to comfort her.

> NEIGHBOUR: Still an' all, he died a noble death, an' we'll bury him like a king.
> Mrs TANCRED: An' I'll go on livin' like a pauper.   Ah, what's the pains I suffered bringin' him into the world to carry him to his cradle, to the pains I'm sufferin' now, carryin' him out o' the world to bring him to his grave![79]

These touching lines are, I am sure, modelled on what Mrs O'Kelly said on the death of her son Conn the Shaughraun in Boucicault's *The Shaughraun*:

> Mrs O'KELLY: . . . There'll be eating and drinking, and six of the O'Kelly's to carry him out as grand as a mimber of parliament—och hone! my darlin' boy, it will be a grand day for you, but your poor ould mother will be left alone in her cabin buried alive while yourself is going to glory—och —o—hone![80]

Mrs Madigan is a typical slum type who has somehow escaped the crushing misery of tenement existence.   She is ignorant, vulgar and forward, but her heart is generous.   She does not express O'Casey's views, but she has in abundance what most of his heroines have—sympathy.   She can sip Captain Boyle's whiskey at one moment and walk off with his gramophone at another, for he deserves no pity.   But no sooner is anyone in

[76] Lady Gregory's *Journals*, ed. L. Robinson, p. 75.
[77] H. L. M., *Freeman's Journal*, 4 Mar. 1924.
[78] M. Waldman, *The London Mercury*, XIII, Feb. 1926.
[79] *Juno and the Paycock*, Act. II, p. 54.
[80] Boucicault, *The Shaughraun*, Act III, Sc. 1, p. 49.

genuine trouble, as in the case of Mrs Tancred or Juno, then the good in her character reveals itself. George Russell shrewdly observed that "The women in his plays alone keep some incorruptible spiritual atom of pity or love in their hearts, the men are all lost souls blighted by weakness of will, or infected by God knows what spiritual disease through environment or heredity."[81]

O'Casey's approach towards Mary is more cynical than unsympathetic. Such attitudes have led a few critics to feel that he has no conscious reforming purpose in his plays. We know that O'Casey has throughout advocated that the working class should shed their ignorance and take a fuller share in life and literature. Yet in this play it is the very attempt to grasp "life and literature" that he ridicules in the person of Mary. And he does it so violently that for a moment we even tend to agree with the "Paycock's" contention: "What did th' likes of her, born in a tenement house, want with readin'? Her readin's afther bringin' her to a nice pass—oh, it's madnin', madnin', madnin'!"[82]

Though women alone command his love and pity, some of his strongest convictions and views are expressed through his male characters. In *Juno and the Paycock* this may not be very noticeable, for the chief male characters are drunkards and so possess the liberty to say what they like.

George Jean Nathan has said that "The hero of a popular play is always seen by the audience through the heroine's eye."[83] The truth of this statement is so evident with regard to this play that it requires no illustration: we hold on to what Juno thinks of her husband and Joxer to the very end of the play. We get the first glimpse of these two wastrels through her eyes, and when we see them on the stage we cannot restrain our laughter. We share Juno's views but Juno does not, partake in our mirth; it is her tragedy and she sees nothing uproarious in it.

Audrey Williamson refers to Captain Boyle and Joxer as "three-dimensional figures."[84] Of the two, Boyle is the more

---

[81] A. E., *The Irish Statesman*, III, 7 Mar. 1925.
[82] *Juno and the Paycock*, Act III, p. 75.
[83] G. J. Nathan, *The World in Falseface*, p. 23.
[84] A. Williamson, *Theatre of Two Decades*, p. 186.

arresting character. Dawson Byrne gives a lovable description
of him:

> A vast pagan figure of a man, lying about his adventures at
> sea; falling victim to pains in his legs whenever a job threatens;
> scorning the Church and deriding the clergy one day and
> defending them the next; swaggering in gaudy, vulgar
> exuberance when he thinks he is coming into an inheritance;
> and at last finding forgetfulness of the dishonour of his daughter,
> the murder of his son, and the martyrdom of his wife in a
> drunken stupor on the bare floor of the room from which the
> instalment-house men have removed the last stick of furniture.[85]

And another critic sums him up equally well:

> There have been Captain Jack Boyles in every literature—the
> clowning rascal who conceals the tears he causes with a
> laugh; whose unshaken belief in himself and his lucky planets
> inevitably attracts a satellite and who can cover even his
> downfall with an epigram.[86]

This is not the place to discuss Boyle as a comic character:
here we may see only how O'Casey uses him to express his
views—mainly on the Roman Catholic clergy. *Juno and the
Paycock* is as anti-clerical as some of his later plays, but the
undiscerning Irish audience failed to see this for two reasons.
Firstly, they did not know, as they now know from O'Casey's
plays and autobiographies, that through Captain Boyle O'Casey
was expressing his own firmly held views. Secondly, and this
reason holds good even today, Boyle is shown as a drunkard
and a wastrel and therefore his decrying the clergy is lightly
brushed aside. But we have only to weigh Boyle's denunciation
of the clergy with what we know to be O'Casey's own views
on the subject and the truth is clear. Here is the work-
shy Boyle denouncing the clergy to Joxer when Father Farrell
offers him a job:

> BOYLE: If they do anything for you, they'd want you to be
> livin' in the Chapel. . . . I'm goin' to tell you somethin',
> Joxer, that I wouldn't tell to anybody else—the clergy
> always had too much power over the people in this un-
> fortunate country.

---

[85] D. Byrne, *The Story of Ireland's National Theatre*, p. 129.
[86] E. V. R. Wyatt, *The Catholic World*, CL, Mar. 1940.

JOXER: You could sing that if you had an air to it!

BOYLE [*becoming enthusiastic*]: Didn't they prevent the people in " '47" from seizin' the corn, an' they starvin'; didn't they down Parnell; didn't they say that hell wasn't hot enough nor eternity long enough to punish the Fenians? We don't forget, we don't forget them things, Joxer. If they've taken everything else from us, Joxer, they've left us our memory.[87]

Of course the very next minute he is upholding the clergy, but his defence is so weak and foolish[88] that without any doubt we can see where the author's opinion lies. Further, O'Casey's autobiographies show that he strongly condemned the attitude of the clergy towards both Parnell and the famine of 1847. Again the following words on religion: "Isn't all religions curious?—if they weren't, you wouldn't get any one to believe them. But religions is passin' away—they've had their day like everything else. . . ."[89] are not in keeping with Boyle's character; hence all the more reason for us to believe that O'Casey is putting his own opinions into Boyle's mouth.

The drunken frolicking of Boyle and Joxer which ends the play is controversial. James Agate called it the "work of a master,"[90] and so have others, but there have been a few critics who have disapproved of it. One critic called it a "disaster,"[91] and another suggested that the piece "should be speeded up to half it's length."[92] As it is the scene is brief, and reducing it would make it unintelligible. The point to be considered is whether it could profitably be removed as was attempted in the Columbia recording of the play.[93] To cut

[87] *Juno and the Paycock*, Act I, pp. 24-5.

[88] *Op. cit.*, Act II, p. 38.

[89] *Op. cit.*, p. 44.

[90] James Agate, *Red Letter Nights*, p. 232.

[91] See *Green Crow*, p. 24.

[92] H. L. M., *Freeman's Journal*, 4 Mar. 1924.

[93] When the long-playing gramophone record was made of the play, the concluding scene between Boyle and Joxer was cut—unknown to the author and to the leading actor, Cyril Cusack. To a correspondent who enquired the reason for the cut, Cyril Cusack replied in a letter dated 23 Nov. 1956:

First may I tell you in reply that this 'cut' was not authorized by me. It was made without my consent and without my knowledge, and I'm afraid I do not agree with it, either from the point of view of emphasizing 'Juno' or even as a matter of taste, or for any other reason. To my mind it lends— with loss of interest—an almost sentimental conclusion to the play. It

this scene would mean that the play must end on the sentimental prayer of Juno. This would not only be against the dramatist's intention of showing how men live in a world of fantasy and escape their miseries by means of drink or vagaries, but it would mean denying O'Casey the credit for a splendid juxtaposition of tragedy and comedy. Slum life, however drab or tragic, is not without its comic side and O'Casey does not fail to see this. Here, in this play, it is only too fitting that the curtains should descend on a drunken "Paycock," who, unmindful of his loss, prophesies that he will serve his country after having failed to support his own family.

Joxer, the "daarlin' man," is no less a creation than Boyle. Spare and loosely built with a face like a bundle of crinkled paper, he is ever ready with apt proverbs for all occasions. A "masterly bit of life," he has a plenary insight into Boyle's character: he alternately flatters and insults him as he gulps down his friend's stout and tea. Without him the "Captain" could not have ventured to sail the high seas of fancy. Though O'Casey uses him to bring out the fustian genius of Boyle, still he has bestowed on him many risible qualities. While Joxer inwardly giggles at the Captain, we remain under the spell of an uncontrollable laugh at them both.

O'Casey does not normally use Joxer as a mouthpiece to express his own views, though now and again he makes him say things in which we may see a little of the dramatist himself.

---

rejects the intention of the playwright and that of myself and my company; and it also interferes with the intention of the prospective purchasing public. . . .

I am of the opinion that the 'cut' was a concession to what is considered to be a commercial exploitation, it probably being thought that the present ending to this play would have greater current appeal to the American public.

He also quoted O'Casey's views on the cut:

Here then is O'Casey in a letter dated 7 May 1956: ". . . By the way, Columbia sent me neither Brochure nor record. Forgot I dare say. . . ."; then on the 25 May: ". . . Now I know why I got no record of *Juno*. They didn't wish me to realize that the epilogue had been cut out. I was not informed of the cut, and it never crossed my mind that such a god-damned stupid thing could be done to spoil a play. God damn these bastards who think that they know more about a play than he who wrote it; or, even if they do, they have no right to make amends [sic] without the knowledge and consent of the author. . . . The cut from *Juno* is in my opinion the comic highlight (and tragic highlight too) of the play."

For instance when Boyle asks him to see who is knocking at
the door, Joxer shewdly replies: "An' mebbe get a bullet in
the kisser? Ah, none o' them thricks for Joxer! It's betther to
be a coward than a corpse!"[94] We have already seen how
O'Casey described himself as growing less and less of a hero as
he grew in grace and wisdom.

Charles Bentham and Jerry Devine, though minor characters, have in common with other of O'Casey's heroes the
endemic quality of professing great and doing small. The
school-teacher Bentham, on a little query from Juno Boyle,
expounds his Theosophical creed like a schoolboy who has
learnt his lessons by heart, speaking of the existence of an
all-pervading spirit or "Universal Life-Breath." Having
impressed the Boyles and seduced Mary, he silently slips away
to England. The half-intoxicated Boyle rightly spouts: "The
scoundrel, I might ha' known what he was, with his yogees
an' his prawna!"[95]

Jerry Devine appears like the Reddleman of *The Return of
the Native* gone wrong at the last minute. Like most of
O'Casey's male characters, he professes what he cannot live
up to. In his portrayal O'Casey wishes to show the incongruity
between great words and poor deeds: the "odd combination
of romantic illusion and sordid meanness,"[96] which paves the
road to tragedy. If Davoren could have lived up to his pre-
tensions of being a "gunman," Minnie would not have been
sacrificed; if Boyle could have sailed from "the Gulf o' Mexico
to the Antanartic Ocean,"[97] Juno would not have had to slog
from morning till evening; if Fluther Good and his like could
have given some practical shape to their maudlin patriotism,
the 1916 Rising would not have been a failure. In the same
way if Jerry Devine could have acted up to what he once said
to Mary, "No matther what happens, you'll always be the
same to me,"[98] Mary and Juno would at least have had a roof
over their heads. But the Labour leader forgets his mighty
promises and shrinks back in fear when he hears that Mary is
carrying a child. Mary, with a sigh, sums him up in a single

[94] *Juno and the Paycock*, Act I, p. 22.
[95] *Op. cit.*, Act III, p. 74.
[96] Cyril O'Connor, *Unitas*, xxvii, Jul.-Sep., 1954.
[97] *Juno and the Paycock*, Act I, p. 26.
[98] *Op. cit.*, p. 19.

sentence; "it's only as I expected—your humanity is just as narrow as the humanity of the others."[99]

Johnny Boyle has been introduced into the play with masterly effect. He provides the link between the Boyle tragedy and the Civil War, without which the action could have been placed in any period of Irish history. Haunted by his fears and shadowed by his grief, he takes no part in the "Paycock's" imaginary prosperity. The news of the inheritance brings just one utterance of hope which we know too well to be false: "We'll be able to get out o' this place now, an' go somewhere we're not known."[1] Tragedy looms in his person, and his presence on the stage, or even in the wings, is a constant reminder that the joys of the forthcoming legacy cannot last. He is the one discordant note in the "boozy low melody" of the play, the one figure that keeps reminding us that tears must follow mirth. The cause of his wretched fear is skilfully revealed bit by bit, and though a quick eye may guess the reason when he bursts into a neurotic cry on seeing Robbie Tancred's ghost, it is not till the end of the second act that we are certain that he has betrayed a comrade to the enemy. Had O'Casey exposed the secret of Johnny's disloyalty to a comrade in the first act, we would have lost our sympathy and curiosity; and the tragic end would have become so definite from the start that we would have failed to participate in the joy of Captain Boyle's elusive inheritance.

Johnny differs from O'Casey's other male characters in that he partly fulfils the principles he stands for. This should have ennobled him in our sight, but the cynic in O'Casey breaks through and asks: What are such principles worth? What are such sacrifices worth? Nothing—"Sacrifices are made for, and in the name of, the Motherland, but the mother of flesh and blood is spurned, derided, sacrificed, or ignored! Ireland, the Motherland, is loved as an abstraction; Juno is compelled to live in a slum, to see her children sacrificed, but she is ignored because she is merely a reality. Even her own son will fight for the abstraction instead of working for his mother!"[2]

But O'Casey does not use Johnny alone to foreshadow the

[99] *Op. cit.*, Act III, p. 81.　　　[1] *Op. cit.*, Act I, p. 33.
[2] A. E. Malone, *The Irish Drama*, pp. 215-6.

tragic end; he often conveys it ironically through the words he places in the mouths of his other characters. For instance, when Juno hears of Robbie Tancred's death, she says, "— thanks be to God that Johnny had nothin' to do with him this long time. . . ."[3] not knowing that Johnny has sent him to his grave. When Captain Boyle, after the exhilarating news of the inheritance, tells Joxer: "Now an' agen we have our differ, but we're there together all the time,"[4] our misgivings about the Boyles' future welfare break in. The manner in which the "Paycock," Joxer and Mrs Madigan conduct themselves in Bentham's presence settles, as far as we can see, Mary's doom; though the poor girl little visualises what is to happen.

At times the irony is so subtle, and placed in a situation so comic, that it is difficult to comprehend its tragic significance. An excellent instance of this is in the beginning of Act III when the pains in the Captain's legs recur: an obvious indication that something has gone wrong with the Will. He gets into bed and asks Juno to give him a newspaper.

> MRS BOYLE [*getting the liniment and the stout*]: What paper is it you want—the *Messenger*?
> BOYLE: *Messenger*! The *News o' the World*![5]

Not in the least troubled by what is taking place in his own home, Boyle sets out to gather the news of the world! The *Messenger*? Ah, no; he will see no messengers now. Had not a messenger come into his life with the news which, as Juno had said, would give him the chance of his life, and then seduced his daughter and skulked away? But Boyle is not aware of the irony; and finally when he lets fall on the floor the "Wan single, solitary tanner left out of all [he] borreyed . . .,"[6] he attributes his drunken cataclysm to a world in anomaly: "I'm telling you . . . Joxer . . . th' whole worl's . . . in a terr . . . ible state o' chassis."[7]

Desmond MacCarthy, reviewing the play when it had started on its 202-nights run at the Royalty Theatre, London, wrote that at least the playgoer could say, "This play, thank

---

[3] *Juno and the Paycock*, Act I, p. 5. [4] *Op. cit.*, Act II, p. 37.
[5] *Op. cit.*, Act III, p. 64. [6] *Op. cit.*, p. 88.
[7] *Op. cit.*, p. 89. Mr Jack Daly, an old friend of O'Casey's now living in Oxford, told me that this phrase was first used by a newsagent called Billy Kelly during a conversation with him and O'Casey.

God, is not about us." "Integrity in self-criticism," he went on, "when it does not serve some immediate, definite, practical purpose, is not an English strong point."[8] How far self-criticism is an Irish strong point we shall see in O'Casey's next great play, *The Plough and the Stars.*

Mention may first be made of another one-act play, *Nannie's Night Out*, which preceded it. The play (which remains unpublished) was done at the Abbey Theatre as an after-piece to Shaw's *Arms and the Man* from 29 Sep. to 4 Oct. 1924.

Judging merely from what has been said about it, the play was better received than *Cathleen Listens In*. Holloway says that it drew in people to see Shaw's play,[9] while George Russell liked it for "the hint of the beautiful under all that disorder and drunkenness."[10] On the other hand Andrew Malone condemned both of O'Casey's one-act plays as negligible works "which should never have been staged,"[11] and which are unworthy of serious attention.

We may get some idea of the play from the following two criticisms in the Dublin press after its first performance. The critic of the *Evening Telegraph* wrote:

> At the expense of being thought irreverent, one might dare describe *Nannie's Night Out* as not a comedy, nor even a one act tragedy, but something much more akin to the revue. Mr. O'Casey takes as his mise-en-scene "the premises of the Laburnum Dairy," a perhaps not more than usually filthy huckster's shop, somewhere about the Coombe. We are here introduced to Mrs. Polly Pender, the proprietress of the "dairy"; her three decrepit lovers, a ballad singer, a gunman, a young girl, Irish Nannie, a methylated spirit-drinker on a "night out" from Mountjoy, and her son. It is out of a half-hour in the existence of these poor things that Mr. O'Casey creates his play.[12]

And the critic of the *Irish Independent* wrote:

> *Nannie's Night Out* presented the inside of a huckster's shop, in a back street where Nannie, a drinker of "spunk", made

---

[8] D. MacCarthy, *The New Statesman*, XXVI, 28 Nov. 1925.

[9] J. Holloway, MS. 1888, Jul-Sep. 1924, p. 650.

[10] Lady Gregory's *Journals*, ed. L. Robinson, p. 95.

[11] A. E. Malone, *The Bookman*, LXX, May 1926.

[12] *Evening Telegraph*, 30 Sep. 1924.

her voice incessantly heard. Three old humbugs were rivals for the hand of the widowed shopkeeper, and the humour of the farce lay mainly in their rambling talk—which rambled too long. . . . But the house laughed whole-heartedly.[13]

This second review accords with what Holloway wrote in his diary: "From the bits I saw, it seemed very rambling, go-as-you-please dialogue with little form or story," and, "the audience enjoyed the dialogue here and there very much. . . ."[14] As for the action dragging somewhat, O'Casey himself admitted this weakness in the play and told Holloway that he "thinks his piece a little too long drawn out. . . ."[15]

Without seeing or reading the play, it is difficult to know what O'Casey was attempting to bring out. Joseph Holloway praised him for his keen power of observation and strong characterisation, saying that "living in the midst of such life [he] is able to transfer it on the stage as no other dramatist possibly could, or at least, no other dramatist ever has."[16] From this we may infer that, like O'Casey's other Abbey plays, it is based on incidents and characters with which he was familiar. Many a Nannie may still be found in the *Blue Lion* pub, off O'Connell Street, a pub that O'Casey occasionally visited.

The Plough and the Stars has been the most popular play of O'Casey's in the Abbey repertoire. It has been revived seventy-six times at the Abbey Theatre between its first performance on 8 Feb. 1926, and the performance on 30 Oct. 1957; while *Juno and the Paycock* has been revived sixty times between its first performance and that of 20 Jul. 1957. This is a sort of paradox when one thinks of the hostility and hatred with which some of the Dubliners and critics greeted the première.

Lady Gregory noted in her journals on 23 Aug. 1925 that O'Casey worked on *The Plough and the Stars* for thirteen months.[17] This would mean that he sat down to write the play as soon as he had finished *Nannie's Night Out*. But that he had

[13] J. C. H., *Irish Independent*, 30 Sep. 1924.
[14] J. Holloway, MS. 1888, Jul.-Sep. 1924, p. 644-5.
[15] *Op. cit.*, p. 657.
[16] *Op. cit.*, p. 656.
[17] *Lady Gregory's Journals*, ed. L. Robinson, p. 86.

the plot in mind even earlier may be seen from what Holloway records on 20 May 1924:

> At Webbs I came across Sean O'Casey and I happened to mention something about stars and he said that is strange. I am thinking of writing a play called *The Plough Amongst the Stars* about Liberty Hall and Easter Week 1916.[18]

Either Holloway got the title wrong, or O'Casey later substituted "and" for "amongst." It is possible that O'Casey first thought of calling the play *The Plough Amongst the Stars*, for such a title would be strictly symbolic of the dramatist's central purpose: to contrast everyday realities by placing them amid ideal dreams, and thus to show how hard it is for the two to go together. The title itself is derived from the flag supposed to have been designed by A.E. (A.E. denied having designed it to O'Casey[19]) and adopted by James Connolly for the Irish Citizen Army.

The play has much in common with *Juno and the Paycock* and *The Shadow of a Gunman*. The background is again a disturbed period of Irish history—this time the 1916 Easter Rising. The important characters are again modelled on people whom the author had known: the rag-tag and bobtail of the Dublin slums. The greatest is Fluther Good, some of whose wildness O'Casey saw in himself[20] and whose name he sprawls all over his autobiographies. Holloway tells us that Fluther Good's real name was John Good, but that he got the name of Fluther by hitting a street-musician (a flautist) on the head with his own instrument.[21] Jack Clitheroe is drawn from Sean Connolly, who was killed in action in the Rising;[22] Mrs Gogan and Bessie Burgess were slum characters whom O'Casey introduced to the Abbey actress May Craig when she was rehearsing the part of Mrs Gogan;[23] Mollser was a basement-dweller in a tenement house, 422 North Circular Road, where O'Casey himself was then living. Rosie Redmond had her seed in "Honour Bright," a Dublin street-walker, who later

[18] J. Holloway, MS. 1886, Apr.-Jun. 1924, pp. 938-9.
[19] *Drums under the Window*, p. 271.
[20] *Inishfallen Fare Thee Well*, p. 290.
[21] J. Holloway, MS. 1900, Jan.-Mar. 1926, p. 431.
[22] My interview with Mr Frank Robbins on 3 Jul. 1958.
[23] My interview with Miss May Craig in Dublin on 4 Aug. 1958.

became the subject of a horrible murder case.[24]   The two Tommies are modelled on soldiers who took O'Casey prisoner during the Rising.

So far I have treated O'Casey's plays from the standpoint of characterisation because it is through his characters, rather than through his situations, that he speaks.   But in *The Plough and the Stars* I wish to lay greater stress on the theme.   In taking such a step I lay myself open to attack, for the play itself has been strongly criticised as lacking a definite plot.   The *Dublin Opinion* humorously commented that "Even the Government couldn't find a plot in Sean O'Casey's play."[25]   Starkie described it as a "chronicle play with very loose connection between the various scenes"[26]; and another critic called it "crude stuff," a "knock-about farce . . . not so much a play at all as four pictures of low Dublin life during the blackest chapter of Anglo-Irish history."[27]

These opinions have a certain amount of truth in them, though this defect does not spoil the play.   Starkie is right in describing it as a chronicle play with loose connections, and as the play is loosely connected it would be wiser to look at it act by act than to treat it as a whole.

The first two acts are set in a day in November 1915, and the last two during Easter week in 1916.   The tragedy, broadly speaking, is prepared in the first two acts, and reaches its culmination in the last two acts;   moving "to its tragic close through scenes of high humour and rich, racy fooling, about which there is something of Elizabethan gusto."[28]   It is interesting to note that O'Casey is most successful in his comedy scenes when they take place before a tragic background, as in the second act of *The Plough and the Stars*, or when they are strongly juxtaposed with tragedy, as at the conclusion of *Juno and the Paycock*.

The first act is set in the two-room tenement house occupied by the Clitheroes.   Through the conversation between Fluther Good, a rogue as large as life, and Mrs Gogan, the charwoman, O'Casey introduces Nora and Clitheroe to us.   We learn that

[24] Stephen Gwynn, *The Observer*, 14 Feb. 1926.
[25] *Dublin Opinion*, v, Mar. 1926.
[26] W. Starkie, *The Irish Theatre*, ed. L. Robinson, p. 160.
[27] E. S. A., *Spectator*, cxxxvi, 29 May 1926.
[28] James Agate, *The Contemporary Theatre*, p. 46.

Nora and Jack have not long been married, that little bickerings have arisen between them, that Jack has lost interest in the
Citizen Army because he wasn't made a Captain, that Nora
keeps grumbling about living in a tenement house and is out
to dress herself in finery. Here is Mrs Gogan complaining to
Fluther when a new hat arrives for Mrs Clitheroe:

> MRS GOGAN [*removing the paper and opening the cardboard box
> it contains*]: I wondher what's that now? A hat! [*She
> takes out a hat, black, with decorations in red and gold.*] God, she's
> goin' to th' divil lately for style! That hat, now, costs more
> than a penny. Such notions of upperosity she's gettin'.
> [*Putting the hat on her head*] Oh, swank, what! [*She replaces
> it in parcel.*][29]

This attitude of one woman towards another who tries to
improve her lot is also to be found in O'Casey's later plays,
but it is strongly underlined in his Abbey plays. Those of
O'Casey's heroines who attempt to rise above their grovelling
existence meet opposition from two sides: first, from the men
who evade their hardships by means of drink or flights of
imagination, leaving them to face the unpleasant realities;
and secondly, from other women themselves, women like
Mrs Grigson and Mrs Gogan, who are settled in their orbit
in the tenement universe and cannot bear to see any of the
satellites falling away.

As Mrs Gogan and Fluther converse, Peter Flynn, Nora's
uncle, enters. He is a typical O'Casey braggart. Dressed in
his Foresters' regalia he keeps far from the scene of action, and
spends the greater part of his time and energy cursing and
swearing at the Covey. The Covey is a fitter and a cousin to
Clitheroe, who has "a passion for Communism in the abstract
and a practical taste in plunder and loot."[30] Just as Fluther
constantly dwells on the words "derogatory" and "vice versa,"
in the same way the Covey keeps harping on a few catch-
phrases of socialism that he has memorised, winding up his
conversation by recommending "Jenersky's *Thesis on the Origin,
Development, an' Consolidation of the Evolutionary Idea of the
Proletariat.*" Without doubt O'Casey is poking fun at the

---

[29] *The Plough and the Stars*, Act I, p. 163.
[30] James Agate, *The Contemporary Theatre*, p. 46.

422 NORTH CIRCULAR ROAD
DUBLIN

The house in which O'Casey wrote all his plays from *Juno and the Paycock* to *The Plough and the Stars*. By courtesy of Gabriel Fallon, who took the photograph.

so-called Communists and Socialists, though he has said that he was a Communist at the time he wrote these plays. One may well wonder what sort of a Communist he was! Out of the four Abbey plays of his that are available, he has ridiculed the Socialists in three: Jimmy in *Cathleen Listens In*, Jerry Devine in *Juno and the Paycock*, and the Covey in *The Plough and the Stars*.

The scene that follows, and still more the scenes that are created by some of the characters and Bessie Burgess—a street fruit-vendor and a Loyalist with a son in the Dublin Fusiliers—consist mostly of knock-about farce. It is not till Nora and Clitheroe are left alone that the note changes and there is a touching love scene. In the original draft that O'Casey sent to the Abbey Theatre this scene may not have been so fine, for George O'Brien, the Government nominee on the Directorate of the Theatre Board, wrote to Yeats:

> The love scene between Clitheroe and his wife in Act I does not read true, and I am inclined to think that it could be easily improved. But even if it is let stand as it is there are a couple of phrases which I think would annoy the audience. These are:
>
> "You can; come on, put your leg against mine—there."
> "Little rogue of th' white breast."[31]

Yeats agreed that the "love scene in the first act is most objectionable . . . and does not ring true."[32] The scene must have been substantially modified, for the lines that O'Brien quotes are no longer in the play, and the scene as it now stands does not ring false.

The love scene comes to an abrupt end with the entry of Captain Brennan, who, to Clitheroe's surprise, addresses him as Commandant. When Clitheroe learns that Nora has burnt his letter of appointment all his tenderness vanishes, and after rebuking her fiercely he goes out with Brennan to take command of the battalion. Nora angrily hurls the truth at her husband:

CLITHEROE [*angrily*]: Why didn't you give me th' letter?

---

[31] Original letter dated 5 Sep. 1925, in the possession of Mrs W. B. Yeats.
[32] Lady Gregory's *Journals*, ed. L. Robinson, p. 89.

F

> What did you do with it? . . . [*He shakes her by the shoulder*]
> What did you do with th' letter?
> NORA [*flaming up*]: I burned it, I burned it! That's what I did
> with it! Is General Connolly an' th' Citizen Army goin' to
> be your only care? Is your home goin' to be only a place to
> rest in? Am I goin' to be only somethin' to provide merry-
> makin' at night for you? Your vanity'll be th' ruin of you
> an' me yet. . . .[33]

But Clitheroe has no eye for the truth, and O'Casey, doubting
if the audience have either, concludes the act by letting the
consumptive child Mollser ask Nora: "Is there anybody
goin', Mrs. Clitheroe, with a titther o' sense?"[34]

The second act transports us from the Clitheroe dwelling into
a commodious public house. Some people have objected to this
act, and have said that the play would have been better without
it. This is quite wrong, for the act is the very soul of the play.
True, it could be performed without this act, just as *The Silver
Tassie* could be staged without the symbolic second act, but
greatly to its disadvantage. It is not without meaning that
O'Casey has brought in this act which—it will be remembered
—was formerly a one-act sketch called *The Cooing of Doves* which
the Abbey rejected. Though in its present form it is an integral
part of the play, yet it can be treated as a one-act vignette of
the period.

One may ask why O'Casey set this act in a pub of all
places? Arland Ussher has described the pub as "the layman's
monastery,"[35] and so it is. I have myself seen an Irishman
making the sign of the Cross every time he entered a pub, and
when I asked him if he also crossed himself when he passed a
church he replied, "Dhat I leave to me wife!" Fantastic as it
may sound, I strongly believe that these public-houses played
a significant part in assisting the British rule in Ireland when
both its diplomacy and its civil service had failed miserably.
It was here that the patriotism of the lay Irishman bubbled
and puffed and puffed and bubbled and welled and swelled
and finally burst; so that when the time came, they failed to
support what they themselves deemed to be a "National Rising."

[33] *The Plough and the Stars*, Act I, p. 189.
[34] *Op. cit.*, p. 191.
[35] Arland Ussher, *Three Great Irishmen*, p. 17.

By bringing in this pub act, O'Casey gives the most significant cause for the failure of the Easter Rising. It is true that plans for the Rising went wrong from the start,[36] that even if the mass of the Irish had joined the rebels the result might have been the same. But all the same one cannot overlook the failure of the ordinary Irishman to support the Rising, for it was on the support of the public that Padraic Pearse, Commander-in-Chief of the Forces of the Irish Republic and President of the Provisional Government, depended. This is plain from the manifesto Pearse published a day after the Rising:

> All citizens of Dublin who believe in the right of their Country to be free will give their allegiance and their loyal help to the Irish Republic. There is work for everyone; for the men in the fighting line, and for the women in the provision of food and first aid. Every Irishman and Irishwoman worthy of the name will come forward to help their common country in this her supreme hour.[37]

Patriotic as the Irish are, many failed to come forward in Ireland's hour of crisis. Valiant in words but laggards in action, O'Casey's tenement Dubliners preferred cheering the rebels to fighting in their company, getting drunk and finally hitting out at each other. And this is exactly what the dramatist is anxious to bring out: to show that the snugs and their fond inmates played no mean part in the failure of the Rising.

Another reason why this act takes place in a pub is that only there can the various characters assemble: from visionaries like Clitheroe and Brennan to rogues like Fluther and the Covey; or a prostitute and pure pragmatist like Rosie Redmond. And they are all essential to the play, for the real protagonist of the drama is the crowd with its mean, selfish and divided aims.

Of the characters in this act, Rosie Redmond is the most important and the only one with whom the dramatist aligns himself. But quite a few Irish critics have failed to see this. Walter Starkie said, "There is no particular reason why she

---

[36] See T. A. Jackson, *Ireland Her Own*, pp. 379-82.
[37] Quoted in Dorothy Macardle, *The Irish Republic*, p. 171.

should be in the play,"[38] and George O'Brien protested to Yeats:

> My most serious objection is to Act II where, in my opinion, the introduction of the prostitute is quite unnecessary to the action. Of course the mere introduction of a prostitute as a character in the play is not objectionable but I think that the character as presented by Mr. O'Casey is objectionable. The lady's professional side is unduly emphasised in her actions and conversation and I think that the greater part of this scene should be re-written.[39]

But Yeats saw what O'Casey was aiming at and put his foot down. He replied to O'Brien:

> Now we come to the prostitute in Act II. She is certainly as necessary to the general action and idea as the drunkards and wastrels. O'Casey is contrasting the ideal dream with the normal grossness of life and of that she is an essential part. It is no use putting her in if she does not express herself vividly and in character, if her "professional" side is not emphasised.[40]

By "the normal grossness of life" Yeats means the sordid realities that are epitomised in the character of the prostitute. She alone remains aware of the daily toil and the struggle for existence, and is not swayed by any idealistic illusions as O'Casey's men are. This the dramatist brings out in the first few lines of the act which opens with a conversation between the Barman and Rosie:

> BARMAN [*wiping counter*]: Nothin' much doin' in your line to-night, Rosie?
> ROSIE: Curse o' God on th' haporth, hardly, Tom. There isn't much notice taken of a pretty petticoat of a night like this. . . . They're all in a holy mood. Th' solemn-lookin' dials on th' whole o' them an' they marchin' to th' meetin'. You'd think they were th' glorious company of th' saints, an' th' noble army of martyrs thrampin' through th' sthreets of paradise. They're all thinkin' of higher things than a girl's garter. . . .[41]

---

[38] W. Starkie, *The Irish Theatre*, ed. L. Robinson, p. 161.
[39] Copy of the letter, dated 5 Sep. 1925, in Mrs W. B. Yeats's possession.
[40] Lady Gregory's *Journals*, ed. L. Robinson, p. 89.
[41] *The Plough and the Stars*, Act II, pp. 192-3.

The conversation between the Barman and Rosie is cut short by the voice of the Man beyond the window—a brilliant conception—preaching his terrible doctrine of purification by blood sacrifice:

> It is a glorious thing to see arms in the hands of Irishmen. We must accustom ourselves to the thought of arms, we must accustom ourselves to the sight of arms, we must accustom ourselves to the use of arms. . . . Bloodshed is a cleansing and sanctifying thing, and the nation that regards it as the final horror has lost its manhood. . . . There are many things more horrible than bloodshed, and slavery is one of them![42]

This speech is taken, with slight changes, from Padraic Pearse's *The Coming Revolution*,[43] first published in November 1913. It is interesting to note that O'Casey omits one sentence from Pearse's speech, which if included would have prematurely exposed the plot of the play. The sentence he omits is: "We may make mistakes in the beginning and shoot the wrong people."[44] A mistake is made, but by the Tommies who shoot Bessie Burgess in the last act, taking her for a sniper.

As the figure moves out of sight and hearing, Peter and Fluther rush in. Their enthusiasm over what they have heard and seen contrasts poignantly with the cool-headed, calculating approach of Rosie:

> PETER [*hurriedly to the Barman*]: Two more, Tom! . . . [*To Fluther*] Th' memory of all th' things that was done, an' all th' things that was suffered be th' people, was boomin' in me brain. . . . Every nerve in me body was quiverin' to do somethin' desperate!
> FLUTHER: Jammed as I was in th' crowd, I listened to th' speeches patterin' on th' people's head, like rain fallin' on th' corn; every derogatory thought went out o' me mind, an' I said to meself, "You can die now, Fluther, for you've seen th' shadow-dhreams of th' past leppin' to life in th' bodies of livin' men that show, if we were without a titther o' courage for centuries, we're vice versa now!" Looka here [*He

---

[42] *The Plough and the Stars*, Act II, pp. 193-4.
[43] P. H. Pearse, *Political Writings and Speeches*, pp. 98-9.
[44] *Ibid.*

stretches out his arm under Peter's face and rolls up his sleeves.]
The blood was BOILIN' in me veins![45]

The voice of the Speaker is heard again paying mighty tributes
to blood sacrifice, and Fluther and Peter run out to hear him.
They soon return, however, followed by Mrs Gogan with her
baby in her arms. The clamour of their nationalistic fervour
is matched by its brevity; they are now no longer interested
in Ireland's destiny. Even the lip-service patriotism has
somehow disappeared. They are soon joined by the Covey
and Bessie Burgess. Bessie picks a quarrel with Mrs Gogan,
who has been worked up to a contentious state of mind with
drink. The two women rail, curse and hurl epithets at each
other, blaming the other for what they are guilty of themselves.
Their sound and fury has little meaning. When May Craig,
who was playing the part of Mrs Gogan, asked O'Casey what
certain lines meant, he replied: "They have no meaning . . .
a woman like she impersonates says anything when her temper
is roused."[46]

While the two women squabble and the Covey has his
prod at Peter, the dark figure of the Speaker is seen silhouetted
against the window for the third time:

> The last sixteen months have been the most glorious in the
> history of Europe. Heroism has come back to the earth.
> War is a terrible thing, but war is not an evil thing. People in
> Ireland dread war because they do not know it. Ireland has
> not known the exhilaration of war for over a hundred years.
> When war comes to Ireland she must welcome it as she would
> welcome the Angel of God.[47]

The impassioned call to duty and heroism contrasts bitterly
with the petty, meaningless bickering that is on the increase in
the pub. Fluther and Peter pay no heed to it now: the intoxication of the meeting outside has been replaced by that of strong
drink.

The verbal exchange between Bessie Burgess and Mrs
Gogan is about to turn into a physical bout when the Barman

[45] *The Plough and the Stars*, Act II, pp. 194-5.
[46] J. Holloway, MS. 1899, Jan.-Mar. 1926, p. 278.
[47] *The Plough and the Stars*, Act II, pp. 202-3. These lines are taken from the
speech "Peace and the Gael" published in Dec. 1915, and delivered by P. H.
Pearse. See P. H. Pearse, *Political Writings and Speeches*, pp. 216-7.

pushes them both out. In preparing for the fight, Mrs Gogan
has placed the child in Peter's arms, and this provides the
Covey with an opportunity for a few more jibes at Peter as the
latter rushes out to return the child to its mother. Fluther and
the Covey are the only two left in the snug when they are joined
by Rosie Redmond.

It is not long before the two men are insulting and hurling
threats at each other. Rosie, who is alone rooted to the facts of
her daily needs, supports Fluther against the Covey as there
appears a better chance of a night's business with him. The
Covey turns savagely at Rosie and calls her a prostitute. Her
spirited retort is worth a look:

> ROSIE [*wild with humiliation*]: You louse, you louse, you! . . .
> You're no man. . . . You're no man . . . I'm a woman,
> anyhow, an' if I'm a prostitute aself, I have me feelin's . . .
> Thryin' to put his arm around me a minute ago, an' givin'
> me th' glad eye, th' little wrigglin' lump o' desolation turns
> on me now, because he saw there was nothin' doin'. . . .
> You louse, you! If I was a man, or you were a woman, I'd
> bate th' puss o' you![48]

Rosie, though a prostitute, wins more sympathy from us than
any of the other characters assembled in the pub. In boldly
facing life and its grim realities, while the men trumpet and
swagger for a half-dream, she is the best instance of an O'Casey
heroine with her feet on the ground. It is strange that critics
turn to Juno and Nora when they wish to show how O'Casey's
heroines face the facts, and take no notice of Rosie Redmond.

Soon matters between Fluther and the Covey are at a pitch.
Fluther, after warning the Covey that he is tempting Providence
in tempting him, springs into the middle of the shop and begins
to paw the air. The Covey is about to accept the challenge
when the Barman pushes him out. Fluther, having routed his
foe, brags in his vituperative vocabulary that comes so naturally
to a Dublin slum-dweller:

> FLUTHER [*with proud complacency*]: I wasn't goin' to let meself
> be malignified by a chancer. . . . He got a little bit too
> derogatory for Fluther. . . . Be God, to think of a cur
> like that comin' to talk to a man like me!

---

[48] *The Plough and the Stars*, Act II, p. 210.

Rosie [*fixing on his hat*]: Did j'ever!

Fluther: He's lucky he got off safe. I hit a man last week, Rosie, an' he's fallin' yet!

Rosie: Sure, you'd ha' broken him in two if you'd ha' hitten him one clatther!

Fluther [*amorously, putting his arm around Rosie*]: Come on into th' snug, me little darlin', an' we'll have a few dhrinks before I see you home.[49]

Fluther is content to walk away with Rosie into the snug. Only an hour back he had said that "the blood was BOILIN' in me veins," and "th' shadow-dhreams of th' past leppin' to life in th' body of livin' men. . . ." But we cannot hold Fluther responsible for this sudden change: the intoxication of the meeting was a thing imposed, while that of drink came naturally to him. As he disappears with his arm round Rosie, his claim to serve Ireland keeps ringing in our ears

The act should have ended here. But O'Casey—either to relate this act with the act that is to follow, or to compare the intoxication outside with that in the pub—brings in Commandant Clitheroe, Captain Brennan and Lieutenant Langon after Fluther and Rosie have left. The voice of the Speaker is heard again: the words are those of Pearse delivered at the graveside of O'Donovan Rossa.[50] Roused, the three officers make their bold vauntings which unfortunately turn out to be prophetic:

CAPT. BRENNAN [*catching up The Plough and the Stars*]: Imprisonment for th' Independence of Ireland!

LIEUT. LANGON [*catching up the Tri-colour*]: Wounds for th' Independence of Ireland!

CLITHEROE: Death for th' Independence of Ireland!

THE THREE [*together*]: So help us God![51]

God helped them. Each paid the price he was so eager to pay.

O'Casey, having given us a scathing picture of these shiftless, jubilant tenement heroes who welcomed the idea of a rebellion as long as it was nowhere near, sets out to tell us how they conducted themselves when the unfortunate Rising did take place in Easter Week. The suspense and terror of the last

---

49 *The Plough and the Stars*, Act II, p. 212.
50 P. H. Pearse, *Political Writings and Speeches*, pp. 136-7.
51 *The Plough and the Stars*, Act II, pp. 213-4.

two acts are masterly and have rarely been excelled in dramatic literature. The play transcends the fate of individuals and becomes the tragedy of the whole race.

As the third act opens we learn from Mrs Gogan, who has a fiendish delight in the appurtenances of death and "last ceremonies," that Nora has gone out in search of her husband, and that Fluther has been away all night looking for her under heavy enemy fire. All this she relates with a ghoulish delight, connecting it with a dream in which poor Fluther lies a corpse. Fluther is the only male character in O'Casey's Abbey plays who shows any real courage and affection, though he is of a piece with the other characters in sharing with them their romantic illusions.

Fluther enters half leading, half carrying Nora. O'Casey now uses Nora to tell us about the men engaged in actual fighting. He does not scorn the ideals of men fighting for freedom, nor does he necessarily make them cowards. But he has a horror of warfare—for the price of war is death and destruction, the breaking of families and the ruining of hopes. Such a freedom to O'Casey, using a phrase of Rosie's, "wouldn't be worth winnin' in a raffle!"[52]

Here is Nora speaking to Mrs Gogan when she is asked if she was able to trace her husband. That they are O'Casey's views needs no proof:

> NORA [*wearily*]: I could find him nowhere, Mrs. Gogan. None o' them would tell me where he was. They told me I shamed my husband an' th' women of Ireland be carryin' on as I was. . . . They said th' women must learn to be brave an' cease to be cowardly. . . . Me who risked more for love than they would risk for hate. . . .
> What do I care for th' others? I can think only of me own self. . . . An' there's no woman gives a son or a husband to be killed—if they say it, they're lyin', lyin', against God, Nature, an' against themselves![53]

And this is what she says of her husband, and the courage of the men engaged in actual fighting:

> . . . Oh, I know that wherever he is, he's thinkin' of wantin' to be with me. I know he's longin' to be passin' his

---

hand through me hair, to be caressin' me neck, to fondle me
hand an' to feel me kisses clingin' to his mouth. . . . An'
he stands wherever he is because he's brave? [*Vehemently*]
No, but because he's a coward, a coward, a coward!

MRS GOGAN: Oh, they're not cowards anyway.

NORA [*with denunciatory anger*]: I tell you they're afraid to say
they're afraid! . . . Oh, I saw it, I saw it, Mrs. Gogan. . . .
At th' barricade in North King Street I saw fear glowin' in
all their eyes . . . An' in th' middle o' th' sthreet was
somethin' huddled up in a horrible tangled heap. . . . An'
I saw they were afraid to look at it. . . . An' some o' them
laughed at me, but th' laugh was a frightened one. . . .
An' some o' them shouted at me, but th' shout had in it th'
shiver o' fear. . . . I tell you they were afraid, afraid,
afraid![54]

The truth in what Nora tells Mrs Gogan we see for ourselves
when Clitheroe and Brennan enter with the wounded Langon.
Clitheroe's first words to Nora are, "My Nora; my little,
beautiful Nora, I wish to God I'd never left you."[55]   His
sentiments are human and natural and for a moment there is
a glow of hope that Clitheroe, before it is too late, has seen the
truth. But we are deceived. No sooner has Nora told him
that all through the night she had been searching for him at the
barricades than, instead of love, a foolish pride, possibly rooted
in cowardice, germinates in his mind. He rebukes her, not
for the risk she took in her love for him, but because her
actions might bring him shame:

They'll say now that I sent you out th' way I'd have an excuse
to bring you home. . . . Are you goin' to turn all th' risks I'm
takin' into a laugh?[56]

The risks taken, mind you, are not for Ireland's freedom alone.
There is a lot of truth in Fluther's drunken remark that "If
any o' them is hangin' at the end of a rope, it won't be for
Ireland!"[57]   Risks are being taken to feed a personal vanity,
and therefore the fear of a possible humiliation. Courage
requires a cause, not merely a personal ambition. Vanity
cannot make one brave, but it can still make one timorously
hold on to what one has already begun. And this is what

---

[54] *The Plough and the Stars*, Act III, pp. 221-2.   [55] *Op. cit.*, p. 232.
[56] *Op. cit.*, p. 235.   [57] *Op cit.*, Act II, p. 199.

happens to Clitheroe: Nora tries in vain to make him see his folly when Brennan fulminates at him for trying to act the renegade. Clitheroe goes out of the house after roughly pushing Nora away from him. She sinks to the ground in the street. Bessie Burgess, who till now has incessantly abused Nora, shows remarkable fellow-feeling and carries her in, and then rushes out to fetch the doctor.[58]

The scene between Nora and Clitheroe is the nucleus of the act. But O'Casey does not forget his jubilant tenement heroes who had earlier supported the fight for Ireland's freedom. Where are they all? Safe and sound in Clitheroe's house, gambling! When Bessie comes in with the things she has looted, the Covey exclaims:

> Th' selfishness of that one—she waited till she got all she could carry before she'd come to tell anyone![59]

Fluther and the Covey run out into the street to get their share in the plunder, the beer-thirsty Fluther bent on giving the pub a shake-up. Mrs Gogan too gets ready for business and is pushing a pram out when Bessie Burgess—who knows to what good use a pram could be brought—jumps at it. An excellent scene follows in which the two women appeal to each other's sense of dignity and honour, decrying loot and plunder from a battle fought for a holy cause. Before it is too late they strike a compromise and waddle off with the pram together. Only Peter remains behind in the fear that he may be "potted."

Historians have mentioned the looting and plundering on the part of the Dubliners during the Rising. O'Casey himself has written about it in *Drums under the Window* and from personal experience embodied it in the play. Padraic Pearse's visionary words that "When war comes to Ireland she must welcome it as she would welcome the Angel of God!"[60] are bitterly mocked at by the Covey's practical views on marauding, as "things God is givin' to His chosen people."[61]

After the third act O'Casey has little to say. Where heroic

---

[58] J. M. Synge intended to portray a woman like Bessie in a play he left in scenario form: a Protestant who risks her life for Catholics whose beliefs she has attacked. See D. H. Greene & E. M. Stephens, *J. M. Synge*, pp. 151-2.
[59] *The Plough and the Stars*, Act III, p. 225.
[60] P. H. Pearse, *Political Writings and Speeches*, p. 217.
[61] *The Plough and the Stars*, Act III, p. 230.

ideals clash against the unheroic deeds and actions of second-rate men; where dreams are used for the deception of others and more often of the dreamers themselves, death and tragedy are inevitable. And he leads us to it without any visible sign of terror and fear, without any philosophising or moralising, for he is leading us to that life in the midst of which he himself has lived.

The fourth act takes place in Bessie Burgess's two-room attic apartment. Fluther and the Covey are playing cards while in a coffin near them lie Mollser and Nora's still-born child. From their conversation—while they concentrate on the game to keep away "from th' sin o' idleness"—we learn that Clitheroe's home has been riddled with bullets, that half of Dublin is on fire, that Nora is going insane and the lot of them have taken shelter in Bessie's apartment. Their occupation is momentarily interrupted by the entry of Captain Brennan, who brings for Nora the news of her husband's death and the General's eulogy that "Commandant Clitheroe's end was a gleam of glory."[62] Nora appears, pale, her hair dishevelled, her eyes "glimmering with the light of incipient insantiy." At one moment she imagines herself walking through the countryside with Jack, and at another bewails the loss of her child and the absence of her husband. The General's tribute and Brennan's mulish contention that "Mrs. Clitheroe's grief will be a joy when she realizes that she has had a hero for a husband"[63] sound so much moonshine. Clitheroe's suffering for Ireland was not even a fraction of what Nora suffers in her love for him, and we are reminded of her words: "Me who risked more for love than they would risk for hate."[64]

Bessie takes Nora into the next room, and the card game begins in all earnestness. The door opens and Corporal Stoddart of the Wiltshires enters. The Corporal claims to be a Socialist and soon becomes involved in an argument with the Covey when the latter tells him that more die of consumption—in reference to Mollser's death—than are killed in the wars:

CORPORAL STODDART: Ow, I know. I'm a Sowcialist moiself, but I 'as to do my dooty.

---

[62] *The Plough and the Stars*, Act IV, p. 244. [63] *Ibid.*
[64] *Op. cit.*, Act III, p. 220.

THE COVEY [*ironically*]: Dooty! Th' only dooty of a Socialist is th' emancipation of th' workers.

CORPORAL STODDART: Ow, a man's a man, an' e' as to foight for 'is country, 'asn't 'e?

FLUTHER [*aggressively*]: You're not fightin' for your counthry here, are you?

PETER [*anxiously to Fluther*]: Ay, ay, Fluther, none o' that, none o' that!

THE COVEY: Fight for your counthry! Did y'ever read, comrade, Jenersky's *Thesis on the Origin, Development, an' Consolidation of th' Evolutionary Idea of the Proletariat?*[65]

O'Casey was extremely suspicious of the English Socialists[66] and this may be one of the reasons why he makes the Tommy talk of Socialism, which he understands no more than the Covey does.

Mrs Gogan comes in tearfully, but inwardly proud of being directly connected with death: "It always gives meself a kind o' thresspassin' joy to feel meself movin' along in a mournin' coach . . .,"[67] she had once told Fluther. The Corporal makes the men carry the coffin out, and when they return to play cards again he informs them that they are to be rounded up and locked in a Protestant church. Fluther, a true Catholic, is horrified at the thought of spending the night in a Protestant church, but when the Corporal suggests that he carry his pack of cards with him as there might be a chance for a game, his views change. O'Casey in *Drums under the Window* has given a vivid description of how he was arrested, locked up in a church for a night and later in a granary; how he struggled to read Keats through the little light that crept in through a crack in the shutters, while a few sat near him playing cards. He handles the scene with ease, for he is writing down his own experiences; he leaves little to imagination and therefore there is little chance of his going wrong.

As the three men are about to be led away Sergeant Tinley comes in. The Sergeant starts complaining that the rebels are not fighting fair and are "potting" them from behind roofs. Fluther who is unable to stand his countrymen being insulted

---

[65] *The Plough and the Stars*, Act IV, p. 249.
[66] See Desmond Ryan's *Remembering Sion*; and also O'Casey's article in *Irish Freedom*, Mar. 1913.
[67] *The Plough and the Stars*, Act I, p. 168.

bawls out, and the sentiments he expresses are those of O'Casey:

> Fight fair! A few hundhred scrawls o' chaps with a couple o'
> guns an' Rosary beads, again' a hundhred thousand thrained
> men with horse, fut, an' artillery . . . an' he wants us to
> fight fair! [*To Sergeant*] D'ye want us to come out in our skins
> an' throw stones?[68]

The odds were certainly far from fair. Less than a thousand
men with obsolete rifles held out for a week against 20,000
British soldiers armed with machine-guns, artillery and modern
weapons.[69]　G. B. Shaw, protesting against the executions
carried out by the British Government, said that it "was a fair
fight in everything except the enormous odds my countrymen
had to face."[70]　And O'Casey, through Fluther, reiterates this.

The play ends with Nora, now quite insane, appearing to
prepare tea for Jack, gently lilting the love song that he had
sung in their hour of joy. Recollecting for a moment the truth
about Jack and her baby she rushes to the window. Bessie in
her attempt to save Nora is shot by the soldiers who mistake her
for a sniper. Sergeant Tinley and Corporal Stoddart enter,
regret that they have shot a woman by mistake, and com-
placently settle down to drink the tea that Nora has prepared.

Splendid as the play is, there are a couple of weaknesses
that strike the reader when he arrives at it through a systematic
study of O'Casey's previous plays. There is a tendency to
repeat the methods employed in *Juno and the Paycock*. The
hymns, prayers and funeral in *The Plough and the Stars* are too
closely copied from the earlier masterpiece and so is the end.
"The magnificent audacity of the two beer-drinkers at the
end of one play should never have been repeated in the two
indifferent tea-drinkers of the other."[71]

Another weakness, as Nathan points out, is the excess of
tragedy piled into the last act:

> Again, as in *Juno and the Paycock*, the dramatist piles on the
> final woe to such an extent that a measure of persuasiveness is

---

[68] *The Plough and the Stars*, Act IV, p. 255.
[69] See P. S. O'Hegarty, *A History of Ireland Under the Union*, p. 709. For the
figures of casualties on both sides see John Devoy's letter to Laurence de Lacy in
Devoy's Post Bag, ii, edd. William O'Brien and Desmond Ryan, p. 505.
[70] G. B. Shaw, *Daily News*, 10 May 1916.
[71] Horace Shipp, *The English Review*, XLII, Jun. 1926

deleted from his work. His wholesale murder, sudden death and general desolation are Shakespearean in every way but the compensatory one of great poetry. The stage at the conclusion of his tragedy resembles nothing so much as the floor of a slaughter house. Those characters who haven't been shot and killed are either dead of tuberculosis, insane, in the last stages of alcoholism or being led off the stage for no good purpose.[72]

It may be because of this wholesale murder and chaos that another critic called it "horrible—far more horrible than *Juno and the Paycock*."[73] However, Nathan later modified his opinion and wrote that "*The Plough and the Stars*—to single out his best play—is one of the superbly fine things in modern drama,"[74] and in 1940 he described it as "one of the finest dramas in the modern world theatre. . . ."[75] Yeats in a letter described it as "almost our best play."[76] Why not the best? Perhaps because he thought *The Playboy of the Western World* deserved that place.

We may now turn to the reception of the play during its première run at the Abbey Theatre on 8 Feb. 1926. There is no need to dwell on the riots, accounts of which abound, and which O'Casey himself has described in *Inishfallen Fare Thee Well*. I shall only touch upon the salient features of the row, the reasons for the hostile attitude of a certain section of the Dublin public, and O'Casey's own reaction to their criticism of the play.

The play had aroused trouble in the Abbey and interest in the public even before its performance. Objections had been raised during rehearsals regarding the introduction of the prostitute, and certain other scenes in the play. Miss Eileen Crowe, who was initially given the part of Mrs Gogan, refused to speak the line "Ne'er a one o' Jennie Gogan's kids was born outside of th' bordhers of th' Ten Commandments," and F. J. McCormick refused to say the word "snotty."[77]

---

[72] G. J. Nathan, *Art of the Night*, pp. 189-90.
[73] S. R. Littlewood, *The Bookman*, LXX, May 1926.
[74] G. J. Nathan, *The Intimate Notebooks*, p. 194.
[75] G. J. Nathan, *Newsweek*, 29 Jan. 1940.
[76] To Ethel Mannin, postmarked 22 Aug. 1938. *The Letters of W. B. Yeats*, ed. Allan Wade, p. 914.
[77] *Inishfallen Fare Thee Well*, p. 300.

Ria Mooney was criticised for accepting the part of Rosie Redmond. Even when these differences were overcome the actors did not strive to swing themselves into the drama.[78]

Yeats, presumably for the sake of publicity, had announced while it was still in rehearsal that it was a "much finer play than *Juno and the Paycock*; more profound and more original, as much an advance on *Juno* as *Juno* is on the *Gunman*."[79] The poet did not forget to compare O'Casey with Dostoevsky, more, according to O'Casey, to impress others about his knowledge of the Russian novelist than for anything else.

With praise like that coming from Yeats, immense excitement was roused and the bookings broke all Abbey records. Joseph Holloway wrote in his diary:

> There was electricity in the air before and behind the curtains at the Abbey tonight when Sean O'Casey's play *The Plough and the Stars* was first produced. The theatre was thronged with distinguished people and before the door opened the queue to pit entrance extended past old Abbey Street—not quarter of them got in.[80]

The reaction of the audience and the critics did not live up to Yeats's estimation of the play, though most of the papers praised it highly. The Dublin *Evening Herald* and the *Daily Mail* denied that it surpassed *Juno and the Paycock*, while the *Irish Independent* predicted that it "will prove to be the most popular of Mr. O'Casey's works,"[81] as indeed it did in Dublin. The play was greeted with loud applause by the audience on the first three nights. The dramatist was called and was loudly cheered when he appeared on the stage to make his bow. Young ladies on the balcony besieged him for his autograph, and when a gentleman asked him to sign O'Casey replied that he "only did so for young and pretty girls."[82]

But trouble was secretly brewing. On the third night of

---

[78] Gabriel Fallon, who acted in all O'Casey's first nights at the Abbey, writes that Lennox Robinson was jealous of O'Casey and "Availing of his privilege as producer of the play and his position as Director of the Abbey Theatre, he insisted on putting most of the players in parts for which they were never intended." See *Modern Drama*, IV, Dec. 1961, p. 231.

[79] *The Irish Times*, 12 Jan. 1926.

[80] J. Holloway, MS. 1899, Jan.-Mar. 1926, p. 281.

[81] *Irish Independent*, 9 Feb. 1926.

[82] J. Holloway, MS. 1899, Jan.-Mar. 1926, p. 295.

the performance, Wednesday, 10 Feb., a sort of moaning sound was heard from the pit during the Rosie Redmond episode and when the Volunteers brought the flag into the pub. The management took little notice of it, but on the following night rioting broke out, the police were called, and the play progressed in pandemonium. Yeats, wild with rage, pranced on to the stage and hurled his contempt at the audience:

> I thought you had got tired of all this which commenced about fifteen years ago [the *Playboy* riots: see Yeats's *Autobiographies*]. But you have disgraced yourselves again. Is this to be an ever recurring celebration of the arrival of Irish genius? Synge first and then O'Casey. The news of the happening of the last few minutes will go from country to country. Dublin has once more rocked the cradle of a reputation. From such a scene in this theatre went forth the fame of Synge. Equally the fame of O'Casey is born here tonight. This is his apotheosis.[83]

This rhetorical outburst was perhaps not as spontaneous as most critics believe.

It appears that Yeats had come to the Abbey with a prepared speech, but as the row began he soon found that his words would be drowned in the protests of the audience. So he hastened to *The Irish Times* office and handed in the speech. On his return to the Abbey it became imperative for him to speak whether he could be heard or not, for in the morning *The Irish Times* would be coming out with his speech. And so Yeats spoke to an audience which couldn't catch a word of what he said.

The play was denounced by the rioters for bringing shame on the fair name of Ireland. They objected to the flag being shown in a public house, to certain of Rosie Redmond's utterances, to the characterisation of Clitheroe, Nora and Langon, and in general to the ridiculing of the men who had laid down their lives in Easter Week. Puerile as these objections may seem today they are not without their point. Most English and American critics have laughed at the Irishman's childishness in rioting over a play, quite unmindful of what Desmond MacCarthy could say even of a play like *Juno and*

---

[83] Quoted in P. Kavanagh's *The Story of the Abbey Theatre*, p. 137.

G

the Paycock: "This play, thank God, is not about us." That a public given to creating heroic stories about themselves and their past should shout down a play of this nature is not in the least surprising. Nathan shows astonishment at what the Dubliners could tolerate:

> As a surgical picture of the Irish, I know of nothing in drama or literature that comes anywhere near this play. That the Irish merely gave vent to catcalls and eggs when it was shown in Dublin is surprising; that they didn't bomb the theatre is even more surprising. O'Casey takes his people, themselves, their ambitions, their dreams, their pretences and their innermost philosophies, and doesn't leave a green thread in their chemises when he gets through. His clinical portrait is the most vicious thing in modern dramatic literature, but the viciousness is that of a deep understanding, a profoundly critical love and a prophylactic hair-brush swatting a turned-up child.[84]

The rioting was in fact an understandable reaction to the premature debunking of a national myth: a myth which came rather easily to the Irish mind, but of a kind nourished in most countries struggling for freedom. But at the same time we must not forget that some of the charges against O'Casey were without any foundation, while O'Casey, even at his worst, was giving them nothing but the truth as he saw it. This is best brought out in the two letters he wrote to defend himself and his play against an attack by Mrs Sheehy Skeffington in the *Irish Independent* of 15 Feb. 1926:

> They objected to the display of the tricolour, saying that that flag was never in a public-house. I myself have seen it there. I have seen the green, white and gold in strange places; I have seen it painted on a lavatory in "The Gloucester Diamond"; . . . but, perhaps, the funniest use it was put to was when it was made to function as a State robe for the Mayor of Waterford.
>   They murmur against the viewpoint of Nora Clitheroe, saying it did not represent the feeling of Ireland's womanhood. Nora voices not only the feeling of Ireland's women, but the women of the human race. The safety of her brood is the

---

[84] G. J. Nathan, *Art of the Night*, pp. 188-9.

true morality of every woman. A mother does not like her son to be killed—she does not like him even to get married.[85]

He also recalled the vanity of the men and how they gloated over the distribution of braids, tabs, Sam Browne belts etc. In his second letter he emphatically denied the charge that every character in the play connected with the I.C.A. was either a coward or a slacker:

> Mrs. Skeffington's statement that "every character connected with the Citizen Army is a coward and a slacker" is, to put it plainly, untrue. There isn't a coward in the play. [O'Casey forgets Peter Flynn.] Clitheroe falls in the fight. Does Mrs. Skeffington want him to do any more? Brennan leaves the burning building when he can do nothing else; is she going to persist in her declaration that no man will try to leap away from a falling building? Will she still try to deny that in a man (even the bravest) self-preservation is the first law? She may object to this, but, in fairness, she shouldn't blame me.
>
> Langon, wounded in the belly, moans for surgical aid. Does she want me to make him gather a handful of his blood and murmur, "Thank God that this has been shed for Ireland?" I'm sorry, but I can't do this sort of thing.[86]

Mrs Skeffington was not satisfied with O'Casey's arguments and challenged him to a debate which he, as he himself puts it, in "his pride, stupid pride," accepted. The debate took place on 1 Mar. at Mills Hall, and was attended by most of the actors and notables of Dublin. O'Casey was unwell and with great difficulty spoke a little, telling them "that he was not trying, and never would try, to write about heroes. He could write only about the life and the people he knew."[87] Four days later he set sail for London, leaving Mrs Skeffington and the rest to think and say whatever they liked.

As we have seen, the audience was not totally at fault in protesting against the play. They still thought of the Rising as a glorious event; the sacrifices, well made; the sufferings, creative. O'Casey's views on the Rising had changed in the course of time, but even in 1916 he had vehemently protested against an open battle with the English and had suggested guerilla warfare. Guerilla warfare was the only sort of fighting

[85] *The Irish Times*, 19 Feb. 1926.   [86] *Irish Independent*, 26 Feb. 1926.
[87] *The Irish Times*, 2 Mar. 1926.

that had a chance of success, and it would have prevented the
bloodshed of the innocent which forms an integral part of the
play. But the playgoers failed to see exactly what O'Casey
was trying to say: they thought he was ridiculing their ideals,
while in actuality he was holding up to ridicule the heroics of
second-rate men. And the second-rate men were among those
who most objected to the play.

Yeats, in a letter to John Quinn about *The Playboy of the
Western World*, said: "Nothing is ever persecuted but the
intellect, though it is never persecuted under its own name."[88]
How very true when one reads of the vicious attack on *The
Plough and the Stars* made by a number of aspirant writers
headed by the poet F. R. Higgins and the novelist Liam
O'Flaherty.[89] O'Casey's technique was accused of being
based on the revue, his theme the exploitation of the poor, his
humour that of the music-hall without its skill. But the play
quickly cut its way through the protests of a romantic audience
and the invidious criticisms of jealous writers, and established
for itself a popularity in Dublin that remains unrivalled.

We may end our study of the play by reiterating that
O'Casey remains a realist of the most uncompromising kind;
one who has sympathy in abundance for his characters, but
little for the audience; a dramatist who places life before us
just as he sees it, without any preconceived notions or ideas.

[88] *The Letters of W. B. Yeats*, ed. Allan Wade, p. 495.
[89] For attacks in *The Irish Statesman* see the following issues: 13 Feb., 20 Feb.,
27 Feb., 6 Mar., 7 Mar. 1926.

III

The Break with the Abbey Theatre and Exile

WITH *The Plough and the Stars* we come to the end of O'Casey's career as an Abbey dramatist. It is a fitting climax to what many consider to be the most fruitful period of his dramatic career. The play on the whole shows very little departure from his two other principal plays. The gist of the problem raised remains the same: "ideals are high but life is low; the theory is heroic and abstract, the actuality a mass of sordid or otherwise depressing particulars."[1] But still when we compare this play with those that went before, it is obvious that O'Casey has become more bitter about the evils of our civilisation, and that his vision has become broader, though he may still be looking out of a tenement window.

In the Abbey plays it was the "human content" that was O'Casey's chief concern. But the Abbey playgoers failed to see this, though they are not wholly to be blamed. Their minds got confused by O'Casey's magnificent juxtaposition of tragedy and comedy: opposite emotions followed so fast on each other's heels that they laughed and cried at the wrong moments. Bertha Buggy, admitted:

> And the worst of it is, that if we go on allowing him to make us laugh and cry together in this hysteric manner, we may end up insisting that he is a genius.[2]

Another reason why the "human content" got lost was because of a change in the Abbey audiences. O'Casey with his plays brought the general public into the theatre, which till then had been patronised mostly by people who had a strong interest in literature. The crowds who came to enjoy his plays were too often not aware of the comedy in their lives. And as there is a wealth of comedy on the surface of O'Casey's plays it is not surprising that they took to it heartily and lost the deeper,

[1] Eric Bentley, *In Search of Theatre*, p. 337.
[2] Bertha Buggy, *The Irish Statesman*, III, 18 Oct. 1924.

tragic significance that lay beneath it. That the meaning was missed can be seen from this letter to the editor of *The Irish Statesman*:

> Dear Sir,
>
> That the psychology of the audiences at the Abbey Theatre has changed in some curious way, is very evident to anyone who attends the theatre from time to time. It is possible to go to humorous plays. . . . But any discerning member of an Abbey audience is driven to murderous inclinations by the repeated bellows of stupid and prolonged mirth which punctuate plays like *The Shadow of a Gunman* or *Juno and the Paycock*. The habit of laughter seems to have seized the Abbey audiences, and even in the most poignant moments of Mr. O'Casey's plays, a meaningless titter will set your nerves on edge.[3]

It is commonly believed that O'Casey was the first Irish dramatist to bring the Dublin slums on to the stage. This is not true though without doubt he is the greatest. Other slum plays staged at the Abbey before the advent of O'Casey were A. P. Wilson's *The Slough*, Gogarty's *Blight* which O'Casey saw and liked,[4] and Daniel Corkery's *The Labour Leader*. But these plays had little in common with O'Casey's masterpieces; they were serious plays not written with the intention of making the audience laugh. It was left for O'Casey to "discover the comedy of distress in its own setting,"[5] to dig deep beneath the surface of official Ireland to the slum-dwellers of Dublin, to reveal another Ireland, hitherto forgotten. And this he achieved with a genius no less than Synge's.

It is paradoxical that though the Abbey Theatre was the offspring of Yeats's Neo-Romanticism, yet its greatest achievements consisted of realistic plays, and that its naturalistic masterpieces were written at a time—the early nineteen-twenties—when there was a vogue for Expressionism in the theatre world. Of the realistic writers of the Abbey Theatre, O'Casey best realised the inadequacy of writing about gods and goddesses and thus shelving the pressing problems of the present. Peasant naturalism had reached its peak with the

---

[3] Mac., *The Irish Statesman*, iii, 20 Sept. 1924.
[4] J. Holloway, MS. 1877, Apr.-Jun. 1923, p. 743.
[5] Micheál MacLiammóir, *Theatre in Ireland*, p. 7.

plays of J. M. Synge; it was left for O'Casey to raise urban naturalism to a similar apex. This he achieved with his "Gorky-Chekhovesque" plays, giving the Abbey Theatre a turn which, says Edmund Wilson, "Yeats never contemplated or desired."[6]

There are many reasons for O'Casey's remarkable success. Of these the most important are his acute sensitivity of mind and shrewd insight into his characters, coupled with a detestation of the Dublin slums and the determination to be a great dramatist. He had made his first attempt at playwriting as far back as 1911[7] and since then he had starved, sweated and struggled to see the Abbey curtains go up on his plays. All this was treated in my first chapter: it now remains for us to see what part the Abbey played in discovering him, his personal story at this period, what brought about the schism between him and the Theatre and the reasons that led to his exile.

Contradictory opinions have been expressed on the part that the Abbey Theatre played in discovering O'Casey. When I asked Lennox Robinson if there could have been an O'Casey without the Abbey Theatre, he replied: "No. But you mustn't tell him that, for he thinks that there could be no Abbey Theatre without him."[8] Ria Mooney, the actress, told me that O'Casey's services to the Abbey have been somewhat exaggerated, and that George Shiels did far more for the theatre though his plays never commanded the crowd as O'Casey's did.[9] Richard Findlater avers that:

> It is possible that O'Casey might have become a dramatist had the Abbey never existed, but not, I think, probable. The Abbey played the same part in the creation of O'Casey's drama as the Vedrenne-Barker management in the work of Galsworthy, the Independent Theatre for Shaw, the Arts Theatre for Fry, the Scottish National Theatre for Bridie, the Canterbury Festival for Eliot, and so on, however far he may have gone beyond the original matrix, and however bitterly in his old age he may turn upon its sponsors.[10]

---

[6] Edmund Wilson, *Axel's Castle*, pp. 42-3.
[7] Letter to me from O'Casey, postmarked 23 Oct. 1958.
[8] My interview with Dr Lennox Robinson on 3 Sept. 1958.
[9] My interview with Miss Ria Mooney on 17 Jul. 1958.
[10] R. Findlater, *The Unholy Trade*, p. 172.

On the other hand we have Gabriel Fallon reminding us that it would be more correct to say that Sean O'Casey discovered the Abbey than that the Abbey Theatre discovered O'Casey.[11] This perhaps is too bold a claim, though Yeats said almost as much when rejecting *The Silver Tassie*:

> I had looked forward with great hope and excitement to reading your play, and not merely because of my admiration for your work, for I bore in mind that the Abbey owed its recent prosperity to you. If you had not brought us your plays just at that moment I doubt if it would now exist.[12]

Where does the truth lie? Perhaps somewhere between these two extremes. Just as Yeats discovered Synge, rather in the same way Lady Gregory discovered O'Casey. And let us not at this moment forget Lennox Robinson's very accurate observation that "Lady Gregory was—is—the Abbey Theatre."[13] Thus, whatever O'Casey owed to Lady Gregory or her copartner Yeats, he owed to the Abbey Theatre; and this is what he himself said to Lady Gregory:

> I owe a great deal to you and Mr. Yeats and Mr. Robinson, but to you above all. You gave me encouragement. And it was you who said to me upstairs in the office—I could show you the very spot where you stood—"Mr. Casey, your gift is characterisation." And so I threw over my theories and worked at characters and this is the result.[14]

To discover a new dramatist is not an easy thing. This is especially true of Ireland. John Alldridge writes: "For the honour of being played at the Abbey, Ireland's 3,000 playwrights—that is a conservative estimate—submitted 300 new plays last year [1947]."[15] The number of plays sent in during the nineteen-twenties must have been less, but still one can conceive the magnitude of the task. Such a task becomes all the more difficult when a writer persists, as O'Casey did, in sending in manuscripts "written in a difficult long-hand, on poor

---

[11] G. Fallon, *Theatre Arts*, Jan. 1950.
[12] *The Letters of W. B. Yeats*, ed. Allan Wade, p. 740.
[13] Lady Gregory's *Journals*, ed. L. Robinson, p. 53.
[14] *Op. cit.*, p. 75.
[15] John Alldridge, *The Irish Digest*, Feb. 1948.

paper with bad ink."[16]   Lady Gregory and Lennox Robinson puzzled through these manuscripts, and gave him whatever encouragement or advice they could.   This provided O'Casey with the necessary impetus to keep struggling with his pen till he wrote *The Shadow of a Gunman*—a play which Lady Gregory, more than anybody else, helped him to launch on the Abbey stage.

O'Casey brought to the Abbey Theatre a popularity it had never known before.   For almost the first time in its history the theatre was thronged to the doors, and the authorities were compelled to turn away crowds night after night.   And all this came at a time when the Abbey was facing bad days.   But to say that the theatre would have closed down had O'Casey not appeared is stretching the Abbey's debt to O'Casey too far. It would amount to repudiating the hard struggle of the Abbey Theatre for over twenty years, and forgetting plays by dramatists of considerable talent like Lady Gregory, Lennox Robinson, T. C. Murray, Seumas O'Kelly, Padraic Colum, Brinsley Macnamara, George Shiels, St John Ervine and others.   It was fortunate for the Abbey Theatre that O'Casey turned up with his plays at a time when its funds and popularity were low; it was equally fortunate for O'Casey that Lady Gregory and others took to him and helped him to see where exactly his genius lay, namely in portraying the life and character-istics of the tenement-dwellers whom he understood so well.

What exactly O'Casey did to make a living from 1922 till the time of the London success of *Juno and the Paycock*—the play brought O'Casey £80 a week during its run—is rather hard to make out.   O'Casey does not tell us in his auto-biographies what work he did to keep himself alive during these years.   Hannen Swaffer writes that he gave up manual work after *The Shadow of a Gunman* was accepted,[17] while James Lansdale Hodson writes that it was after the success of *Juno and the Paycock*.[18]   Lady Gregory recorded in her journal on 8 Mar. 1924 that when she asked O'Casey to tea he replied that he was working with cement and couldn't come.[19]   When

[16] Lennox Robinson, *Curtain Up*, p. 138.
[17] H. Swaffer, *Who's Who*, pp. 17-18.
[18] J. L. Hodson, *No Phantoms Here*, p. 151.
[19] *Lady Gregory's Journals*, ed. L. Robinson, p. 74.

I asked O'Casey where the truth lay, this is what he wrote:

> Worked at demolition of one old house and the building of two new ones. Fact I wasn't working when Lady Gregory put the question to me. She very kindly asked me if I'd care for her and her friends to seek a more suitable job than laboring work for me. I emphatically answered that I would not care for that; that I couldn't take any post furnished by favor. You see I was determined to stand alone on my own feet, without help from anyone. You will find another example of this rejection of help in Batt O'Connor book—*The Irish Brigade*, I think it is called [*Sic*. The book is *With Michael Collins in the Fight for Irish Independence* (1929)]. Batt was a friend of M. Collins; and, at that time, of Sean MacDermott. He offered me a couple of sovereigns in *Irish Freedom* Office for a pair of boots, seeing the ones I then wore to be tattered and torn. I refused them. He records incident in his book.[20]

The early years of success were years of poverty, hardship and struggle. He felt no great sense of pride at his achievement and continued to live the humble life that he was accustomed to in his tenement room in 422 North Circular Road: "a tall, gloomy house, dirty grey, with peeling plaster, and stone passage—the sort you find in any slum."[21] In this one room he slept, ate, worked and lived his life; cooking his own meals, which normally consisted of a piece of bacon and a few potatoes. He spent the greater part of what little he earned purchasing books which he crammed into home-made bookshelves. He devoted his time to writing plays, making "no divisions of day and night,"[22] though his eyes were so weak that he had to hold the manuscript three inches from his nose to read it. He wrote in penny school exercise books and then typed and retyped it till he got it right. He concentrated on the three-act play which took a long time and needed a great many ideas, though sometimes he would write a one-act play as a diversion.

Now that he was famous, newspaper correspondents tramped the long North Circular Road seeking interviews

[20] Letter to me from O'Casey, postmarked 23 Oct. 1958.
[21] J. L. Hodson, *No Phantoms Here*, p. 148.
[22] J. W. Cunliffe, *Modern English Playwrights*, p. 233.

which he abhorred. Letters came asking him for his autograph, people in the streets begged him for his signature on
scraps of paper, the influential and the rich sought him for
At Homes. All this would have turned the head of a lesser
man but it passed him by without affecting him. This is what
Holloway records a year before the success of *Juno and the
Paycock* in London:

> I was speaking to O'Casey at theatre—he usually wears a
> cloth cap and trench coat, and looks anything but a successful
> writer. His successes have passed him by without enlarging
> his head in any way, and he remains the same unassuming,
> observant and human he always has been.[23]

And at the time of the play's success in London:

> Success ruins many, but O'Casey is not the pattern. He only
> hopes that some day his talents may make it possible for him
> to rest after all the weary years of toil and keeping the body
> and soul together by the merest thread of existence.[24]

Though O'Casey avoided all those who wished to flatter him,
he responded to the friendly advances of Lady Gregory. From
the start she had been mindful of the spark of genius in his
writing and had kept encouraging him, but she did not actually
meet him till 1923.[25] Unlike Yeats, who was at times so
unworldly, she believed in the crowds, and O'Casey was the
first dramatist to satisfy this desire of hers. Reading her
journals one may well get the impression that nothing pleased
the old lady more than the sight of a long queue at the pit and
not one fourth of them being able to get in.

There are many reasons why O'Casey became so attached
to Lady Gregory. He knew what the Abbey Theatre owed
to her, the significant part that she had played in making him
a dramatist, that she and Yeats alone stood above the petty
intrigues and jealousies of the back-stage and the green-room.
But more than all this, he found in Lady Gregory one who
could play the part of a mother to him, someone to whom he
could give his trust and unburden his innermost thoughts and

[23] J. Holloway, MS. 1889, Oct.-Dec. 1924, p. 736.
[24] *Op. cit.*, MS. 1898, Oct.-Dec. 1925, p. 1084.
[25] Letter to me from O'Casey dated 31 Mar. 1959.

feelings. He discovered that, like his mother, she was courageous, that she had a fine sense of humour, that by some devious ways she—though belonging to the aristocracy—had come close to the common people. He opened his heart to her and told her the story of his early struggles, his likes and dislikes, which she attentively listened to and jotted down. She took him for a short holiday to Coole Park, her home in Galway. Here, for the first time, he had the blessings of comfort. During the day he would roam through the Seven Woods of Coole, and at night he would stretch himself on a deep settee while Lady Gregory read to him Hardy's *Dynasts*, Melville's *Moby Dick* and Hudson's *The Purple Land*.

The affectionate friendship with Lady Gregory lasted till her death. Though she had her share of responsibility in the rejection of *The Silver Tassie* he did not feel any bitterness towards her. However, it is sad to learn that when Lady Gregory asked to see him in October 1929 he refused to meet her, for he feared that he would speak bitterly of Yeats and others and that this might hurt her. The last opportunity to see Lady Gregory was lost. She died in 1932.

Another friendship which perhaps was of even greater significance to his mental and literary development was with a beautiful Catholic girl called Maura.[26] He met her for the first time in 1919[27] at the starting of an amateur drama club, though he had often seen her in the past as she hurried to a Catholic elementary school where she was training to become a teacher. This girl gave O'Casey what he describes as "the fullest experience of feminine good companionship he had had so far."[28] He would wander with her through the lonely country lanes, through the "sun-dappled meadows" and the green fields. He would read to her verses from Milton, Burns, Keats and Shelley, and talk to her about Dumas, Tolstoy,

[26] O'Casey has described his intimate friendship with her in the chapter "The Girl He Left Behind Him" in *Inishfallen Fare Thee Well*. He writes of her under the name Nora Creena. She is still alive and got married for the second time in 1958. I tried to get some information on O'Casey from her but failed in my attempt. This is what she wrote to me in a letter dated 8 Jul. 1958: "After mature consideration and having regard to the lapse of time since my friendship with Sean O'Casey, I have come to the conclusion that I can be of no assistance to you in the matter in which you are so interested."

[27] Letter to me from O'Casey dated 3 March 1959.

[28] *Inishfallen Fare Thee Well*, p. 232.

Thackeray and Shaw.[29] He wrote songs and poems in which
her influence appears. He published some of these in the
section "First Fall" in *Windfalls*. The most arresting of them
is "A Walk with Eros," which runs to sixty-nine stanzas. It
is written in the pastoral tradition and shows influences from
Wordsworth, Coleridge, Shelley and Oscar Wilde. It embodies
his passionate love for Maura, with whom he wishes to escape
from mankind to nature. The poet's emotion varies from
extreme happiness to extreme misery, the mind shifts rapidly
from the beauties of nature to the dust-clad streets of Dublin
and back again. Though the poem ends on an optimistic
note, the death-knell of the poet's love is sounded earlier in
lines such as these, that stand out ruggedly against the sensuous
cynicism of the other verses:

> When we come back to city streets,
> Drab-fac'd and gable-spir'd,
> Eros' visions lose their beauty,
> Where the herds of men are byr'd;
> For 'tis only in the city that
> His tireless feet are tir'd.

> A curse upon the state of life,
> That life for long has led,
> For life oft seeks escape from life,
> By seeking out the dead;
> Not that life of life was weary.
> But because life needed bread.[30]

The poem is O'Casey's offering of the beautiful to his beloved.
But love cannot live on songs alone and Maura warned him
that he must earn a name for himself in six months or their
sweet alliance would end for ever. Even before that he had
come to realise that she was scantily equipped to travel the
hard road with him, that she could never defy the stern
respectability of her middle-class family, never cease to believe
in "the tinselled glory of religion's parade, in supernatural
nursery-tale of hell, and folk-invention of cherubim and
seraphim that merged with the devil's face grinning from the
show's centre, amid the coloured candle-light of religious

---

[29] Information supplied by a very close friend of Maura's.
[30] "A Walk with Eros," *Windfalls*, pp. 17-18.

fear."[31] He had tried in vain to bring her to his way of thinking, had even written verses attacking Catholic belief, such as:

> Let those who will dream heaven's dreams,
> Or fear a pictur'd hell,
> Who answer Nature's outcries with
> The Church's blatant bell:
> But we can worship only where
> Sweet Nature's Beauties dwell.[32]

And

> Pale superstition paints her waning face
> With gaudy hue,
> And charms with fetters all the human race,
> All, but the few:
> Who fearless stand, and live the life that's true,
> Tho' ston'd down to the dead, or rob'd in rue.[33]

But it was of no use, none whatsoever. Maura was not willing to stand against the rebukes of her family and the resentment of the priests. The happy days were over—

> The days with gentle Mary spent,
> Like lightning flashes sped;—[34]

and once again he was lonely, though in the presence of Nature he felt he could never be alone.

O'Casey must have cherished an intense feeling for Maura, and for a long time. He dedicated *Juno and the Paycock* "To Maura and the Abbey Theatre," openly acknowledged her influence in the poems included in the section "First Fall" in *Windfalls*, made her the heroine of his play *Red Roses for Me* and devoted a whole chapter to her in *Inishfallen Fare Thee Well*. There is undoubtedly something of bitterness mixed with scorn in the last two works, but nowhere does he ridicule her. Maura's strict religious outlook, her lack of courage and her belief in what he regarded as superstitions were the cause of much grief to him. Yet in his Abbey plays he does not acrimoniously make women weak or superstitious as one might

[31] *Inishfallen Fare Thee Well*, p. 233.
[32] "A Walk with Eros," *Windfalls*, pp. 18-19.
[33] "Sunshadows," *Windfalls*, p. 26.
[34] "A Walk with Eros," *Windfalls*, p. 18.

expect from a writer who had been a victim to these very qualities. Though Maura proves herself weak, his heroines are strong; it is the men who are superstitious, worthless liars and cowards. Moreover he does not laugh at superstition in his Abbey plays. In *The Shadow of a Gunman*, Seumas Shield's fear about the "tappin' on the wall," and, in *Juno and the Paycock*, Johnny's concern about the "votive light" turn out to be true. It is only in some of his later plays that he makes fun of superstition, and even then chiefly in relation to men. This is strange, for on the whole women are more superstitious than men.

It is a wholly mistaken belief that O'Casey was a regular Abbey-goer and that he learnt his technique by watching the plays at the Abbey Theatre. There is little in common between his plays and those of the other Abbey dramatists that would warrant such a conclusion. Besides, he is quite outside the Abbey tradition—if such a phrase can be used—and in this particular art of playwriting owes nothing to anything except his innate genius. In a letter to me dated 31 Mar. 1959 he writes:

> You are quite right—the books are all mistaken badly.[35] . . . I went with Nora Creena to see a two-acter, *Blight*, and, I think a one-act, *The Jackdaw*; a friend, Jack Daly, living then in Dublin, now in Oxford, brought me to see Shaw's *Androcles and the Lion*; with a one-act done from a short story by James Stephens. These all I saw before production of *Gunman*. I learned by acting on Abbey stage before, long before, it became Abbey, in Boucicault's *The Shaughraun*, and going to the melodramas done in the Queen's, where the Abbey is now.

O'Casey began to visit the Abbey Theatre regularly from 1923 onwards. He soon became popular with the actors and actresses and would spend long hours talking to them, but never about himself. He was fond of arguments, and when engaged in one he would bring his face near the other fellow's and keep poking him in the chest with his forefinger as he spoke.[36] This soon became a joke in the green-room. But

[35] O'Casey means books which say that he learnt his technique at the Abbey, such as Stanley J. Kunitz, *Living Authors*; A. E. Malone, *The Irish Drama*; Stephen Gwynn, *Irish Literature and Drama*.

[36] My interview with Mr Tony Quinn on 26 Aug. 1958.

his popularity was a short-lived one, and the tide silently turned against him at the most unexpected hour—after the success of *Juno and the Paycock* in Dublin. O'Casey then knew nothing about it, and even if he had, he could have done little to prevent it, for the fault (if it be one) was a part of his character: candidly expressing his opinions even when they were not wanted.

Until the production of *Juno and the Paycock* O'Casey's career as a dramatist was insecure, for his second play *Cathleen Listens In* had been a failure. But *Juno and the Paycock* decided his future as that of a dramatist. Hyperbolic praises poured in. O'Casey suspected the intentions of his admirers and thought they were out to flatter him. Tony Quinn told me that once when a person said to O'Casey, "How true to life your plays are," O'Casey retorted in anger: "How the hell do you know —you have never lived in a slum!"

Although this attitude of O'Casey's was resented, he did not stop here. Having now been intimate with the Abbey community for a good while, he took them as old friends and began openly expressing his views on the works of other dramatists, and also on the plays that were produced in the theatre. Holloway warned him to be careful:

> He [O'Casey] thinks Robinson has too many irons in the fire—his *Never the Time and the Place* is but poor stuff. He read it over last night and it confirmed his judgement. He liked his *Crabbed Youth and Age*. I said, "He'd never be forgiven if he dispraised a piece of Robby's." "And why not, if one has an opinion, be allowed to express it?" he queried, and I replied: "I don't know but such is the case when the Abbey group is concerned. They never forgive those who criticise their work adversely".[37]

O'Casey could not have thought much of Holloway's advice for soon afterwards he was criticising what he thought to be a very poor rendering of Shaw's *Man and Superman*, produced by Michael J. Dolan. This time he was up to the neck in trouble not only with Dolan, but also with the actor F. J. McCormick, who came up to him and said: "I hear you've been criticising our rendering of Shaw's play. You've got a

[37] J. Holloway, MS. 1886, Apr.-Jun. 1924, p. 940.

bit of a name now, and you must not say these things about an Abbey production. If you do, we'll have to report it to the Directors; so . . . try to keep your mouth shut."[38]   A few nights after this incident O'Casey was crossing the stage on his way to the green-room when the scene painter, Sean Barlow, stopped him and told him not to pass that way any more.   The Abbey clique had disowned him; he saw it and never again set foot on the Abbey stage or in the green-room.   Denis Johnston gives O'Casey's quarrel with Barlow as the cause of his exile,[39] which decidedly is not the whole truth.

In *Inishfallen Fare Thee Well* O'Casey listed his grievances against Dublin and the Abbey Theatre, and reading it one would come to the conclusion that his exile was a planned and premeditated act.   This was not so, though later on recollection of past bitterness did help him to give up Dublin for good.   There is ample evidence that in the beginning he had no intention of exiling himself, and that when he did go to London on J. B. Fagan's request (Fagan was presenting *Juno and the Paycock* at the Fortune Theatre and wanted O'Casey to be there so as to give the play publicity) it was only for a short visit.   Gabriel Fallon tells us that O'Casey accepted the invitation reluctantly;[40] and the actor Tony Quinn told me that when he went to see O'Casey off at Westland Road Railway Station, O'Casey remarked: "I'll see you tomorrow night, Tony."

O'Casey left Dublin for London on 5 Mar. 1926 and attended the first night of *Juno and the Paycock* at the Fortune Theatre with Lady Gregory three days later.   He gave many interviews to Press correspondents, from which it is clear that he had not the faintest wish to settle in London.[41]   But London was to capture him soon.   As he hesitantly fell under her charm he realised that Dublin had very little to offer him. "Here I'm being lionised," he told Ria Mooney when she met him in London.   "If I return to Dublin they'll tear me to pieces."[42]   He had made friends with Bernard Shaw and

[38] *Inishfallen Fare Thee Well*, p. 194.
[39] D. Johnston, *Irish Writing*, Dec. 1950.
[40] G. Fallon, *The Irish Digest*, Nov. 1946.
[41] For instance he told the *Daily Sketch* (24 Mar. 1926) that although he liked London and the English, he could not live there and would soon be returning to Dublin to work.   [42] My interview with Miss Ria Mooney on 17 Jul. 1958.

Augustus John and was revelling in the glories of the art galleries. He saw no point in returning to Dublin.

But something was to bind him to London even more closely than literary and artistic ties. Not long after his arrival he met Eileen Carey, a beautiful Dublin girl, and fell in love with her. He took a flat in Chelsea for three years and the *Daily Sketch* announced on 7 Jul. 1926 that Sean O'Casey was forsaking Ireland for good. He married Eileen Carey on 23 Sep. 1927 in the Church of All Souls and the Redeemer in Chelsea.

O'Casey's marriage led him to choose London as his workshop for the next few years, if not for ever. This did not mean that he would stop writing for the Abbey Theatre. In fact he wanted to remain an Abbey playwright and precisely for this reason he sent *The Silver Tassie* to the Abbey Theatre. Had the Abbey accepted the play it would not have lost its finest dramatist, and perhaps at some future date O'Casey would have returned to Dublin. But the rejection of the play, and the methods adopted by the Abbey to harass him with regard to a production of *Juno and the Paycock* by Sinclair completed the break between him and the theatre. This side of the story is so little known that many critics in their ignorance have blamed O'Casey for turning bitter against a theatre that sponsored his early plays, and helped him to establish his reputation.

Arthur Sinclair wanted to produce *Juno and the Paycock* and *The Plough and the Stars* in Belfast and in Cork, and as O'Casey had no connexion with the Abbey Theatre after the rejection of *The Silver Tassie* he gladly gave his consent. The booking and theatrical manager wrote on behalf of Arthur Sinclair to ask the Abbey solicitors for permission to perform the plays. The Abbey solicitors replied that the right to perform these plays in Ireland rested with the Abbey Theatre, as the result of an agreement with O'Casey, and that their clients were unwilling to relinquish their rights.[43] Sinclair immediately contacted O'Casey who wrote to the Abbey asking them why they were preventing Sinclair from producing his plays when he had given him permission. The Abbey solicitors replied, pointing out that he had signed an agreement with the Theatre

---

[43] Messrs Whitney Moore and Keller to Mr Percival W. Selby, 17 Jul. 1929. Copy of the letter in Mrs W. B. Yeats's possession.

in August 1928 for *The Plough and the Stars* and *Juno and the Paycock* with the right of extension for another year if one month's notice was given, and that the Abbey Theatre had given him this due notice.[44] O'Casey sent a long letter saying that he had not received any notice for the renewal of the agreement, that the Abbey's claim was therefore null and void, and that they should be asked to stop prejudicing his rights. His letter is of interest to us, not because of the legal justification of his stand but because it reveals what exactly he felt about the way the Abbey was treating him. He wrote:

> So not being satisfied with the fine pleasure of an insult given some time ago, they now seek the coarser satisfaction of a pleasure through an attempted injury. After what was done in the refusal of *The Silver Tassie* which was sent to them as a first offering, contrary to business advice here,—which no other dramatist would do, except, perhaps, one conscious of a good reason for faithfulness, it's a bit thick for the Abbey to believe that Sean O'Casey would singing a song, chain himself to the Abbey for the sole production of his plays over in Ireland. . . .
>
> The Abbey theatre has had *The Plough and the Stars* for three years, and, as far as I know, never proposed playing it in Belfast till they heard it was to be played there by the Irish Players. They have had *Juno and the Paycock* for four years, and are thinking of playing it in Cork, because a production there has been planned by the Irish Players. This sudden interest in the two plays seem to me more significant than generous.[45]

The Abbey solicitors saw that O'Casey was adamant and that they had no right to stop Sinclair from carrying out the Belfast and Cork performances. The tone of their letters to O'Casey suddenly changed: they now humbly claimed to have sent a notice for the renewal of the agreement with a cheque of four guineas which, they said, must have gone astray.[46] O'Casey's answer shows how bitter he felt against the Abbey:

Dear Sirs,

Yes, cheques have an unaccountable way of going astray,

---

[44] Messrs Whitney Moore and Keller to O'Casey. Letter dated 23 Jul. 1929.
[45] O'Casey to Messrs Whitney Moore and Keller.
[46] Letter dated 30 Jul. 1929.

and always when it is necessary they shouldn't.   Only a short
time ago, a cheque owed to me from Ireland, was asked for
from him who owed, to hear that it had already been sent to
me, and had unaccountably gone astray.   They are behaving
now like sheep and Christians—all cheques, like sheep, have
gone astray—you know the quotation from the Koran.

Permit me to repeat that the Abbey Theatre had neither
moral or legal right to the claims they have made.   The
permission given in July and in August of last year was an act
of generosity.   The question then was (in the circumstances of
your clients' refusal of *The Silver Tassie*) not whether I should
give them the exclusive right for Ireland, but whether I should
separate from them altogether;   and, probably, this latter way
would have been chosen but for the appeals of G. B. Shaw,
Mrs. Shaw and St. John Ervine. . . .

Your clients have given me a lot of pain and trouble and
whether they can have permission for Dublin performances
cannot be decided yet by me: at present my inclination, for
my own peace of mind, is to finally cut away from them
altogether.[47]

The Abbey went on pressing O'Casey for the rights of the
play so that finally he had to appoint Messrs McCracken &
McCracken of Dublin as his solicitors.   An agreement was
eventually reached through the intervention of Lady Gregory;
the Abbey confining its claim to Dublin for another year,
while Sinclair was allowed to proceed with his plans.

Though expatriation has been the badge of the Irish writer,[48]
none has been so harshly criticised for leaving Ireland, or for,
as most critics consider, losing some of his force after exiling
himself.   Sean O'Faolain calls O'Casey's exile "an error, not
of the judgement but the emotions," and goes on to say that
"never was exile more foolishly and unprofitably self-imposed
than by this man who mistook two theatre directors for a whole
people, and thereby deprived himself of an inspiration, of an
audience, and of a home."[49]   Frederick Lumley writes that in

[47] Letter dated 1 Aug. 1929.
[48] Daniel Corkery in *Synge and Anglo-Irish Literature*, p. 4, has drawn up a
list of over thirty living Irish writers of that time who had exiled themselves,
showing that it would be impossible to draw up a list a quarter as long of Irish
writers staying at home.   St John Ervine in *Oscar Wilde*, pp. 62-4, also points out
how all notable Irish authors have in some way or the other chosen exile.
[49] Sean O'Faolain, *The Commonweal*, XXII, 11 Oct. 1935.

"his new home his genius turned to bitterness, his poetry to politics, his nationalistic hopes became hopes for a Communist International and his 'darlin' son' was born a Red Commissar."[50]   Richard Findlater emphatically asserts:

> With his departure the holy fire abated in O'Casey's work, and his subsequent plays—whatever their streaks of genius— are ultimately unsuccessful.   For he was trying to create a new drama in an alien country out of his own head, and he had the imagination but not the intellect to do so.[51]

Dogmatic as these views seem there is some truth in them.   A highly personal writer, O'Casey lost some of his force after he exiled himself.   He also lost contact with those characters among whom he had lived, and on whose portrayal his fame rested.   So far he was the poorer for his exile.   But there was much that he gained in breaking away from the provincial Dublin atmosphere.   Before we pass any judgment of our own as to whether O'Casey was right or wrong in exiling himself, we must carefully study his later plays.   We shall turn to them now.

[50] F. Lumley, *Trends in Twentieth Century Drama*, p. 208.
[51] Richard Findlater, *The Unholy Trade*, pp. 174-5.

IV

The Silver Tassie: Controversy and Play

"PERSONALLY, I think it is the best work I have yet done. I have certainly put my best into it, and have written the work solely because of love and a deep feeling that what I have written should have been written,"[1] wrote O'Casey to Lady Gregory, but "Dublin's Gods and Half-Gods"[2] thought differently, and almost unanimously decided to reject it (Walter Starkie was away in Spain and thus his criticism, in which he supported the performance of the play, arrived too late). The rejection of *The Silver Tassie*, coupled with Yeats's pompous advice as to what constitutes a good play and how he could best get rid of this bad one, led to a heated controversy which even today makes virile reading. The controversy aroused an unprecedented interest, and, having delighted the Dublin audience, it crossed the Irish Channel and wafted itself across the Atlantic. Soon the British and the American papers were carrying the story, and many of them hinting to O'Casey that the name and reputation of Yeats were of greater consequence than his arguments.

As the controversy preceded the publication of the play (12 Jun. 1928), and its first London performance at the Apollo Theatre on 11 Oct. 1929, and since neither the dramatist nor the play has been able to shake off the effect of the opinions that Yeats left behind, I shall go into the controversy first, presuming that the reader knows what the play is about. In a letter to the editor of *The Irish Statesman* dated 30 May 1928, O'Casey wrote:

> Dear Sir, Questions are beginning to fall on top of me about the Abbey's production of *The Silver Tassie* which I find impossible to answer *in toto absolutium questionarii*, and to place

---

[1] Lady Gregory's *Journals*, ed. L. Robinson, p. 104.
[2] O'Casey's term for Yeats, Lady Gregory, Robinson and others, used in *Inishfallen Fare Thee Well*.

before all who may be interested, the full circumstances surrounding the rejection of the play by the Abbey directorate. I shall be glad if you could kindly publish the enclosed correspondence. . . . The publication would, I'm sure, save me a lot of toil and trouble, fire-burn and cauldron bubble.[3]

Cauldron bubble! It was even rumoured that O'Casey had challenged Yeats to a duel. No sooner was the correspondence in its entirety published than the Abbey enthusiasts saw that a good broth had been cooking, and that the *Sunday Independent* had seen rightly: "that whatever else may come of *The Silver Tassie* there is brewing in it a storm much more exciting than that which ordinarily rages in theatrical teacups."[4]

O'Casey had seen the fallacy of Yeats's denunciation of his play. Confident that they were attacking him at his strongest, all his past bitterness against the Abbey welled up in his mind. He must reply, come what may. Cochran's determination to produce the play, and Macmillan's willingness to publish it even after having read Yeats's criticism, reassured him as to its merit. He now set out to "send a salvo of words that would shake the doors of the Abbey and rattle the windows,"[5] but with Yeats on guard the Abbey doors stood firm and silent, though a "salvo of words" did get in through the window and Lady Gregory sighed: "Very, very sad, the whole matter."[6]

Though *The Irish Times* treated the skirmish with literary contempt, the event was of sufficient importance to bring two letters from Shaw. Both these letters are important as they rightly sum up the strength in O'Casey's play, and the weakness in Yeats's criticism which was the ultimate cause of its rejection. Writing to Lady Gregory, Shaw said:

Why do you and W.B.Y. treat O'Casey as a baby? Starkie was right, you should have done the play anyhow. Sean is now *hors concours*. It is literally a hell of a play; but it will clearly force its way on to the stage and Yeats should have submitted to it as a calamity imposed on him by the Act of God, if he

[3] *The Irish Statesman*, x, 9 Jun. 1928. Part of the correspondence was already appearing in the *Irish Independent*, and had been published in *The Observer* (London) on 5 Jun. 1928.

[4] *Sunday Independent*, 3 Jun. 1928.

[5] *Rose and Crown*, p. 34.

[6] Lady Gregory's *Journals*, ed. L. Robinson, p. 109.

could not welcome it as another *Juno*. Besides, he was extra-ordinarily wrong about it on the facts. The first act is not a bit realistic; it is deliberately fantastic chanted poetry. This is intensified to a climax into the second act. Then comes a ruthless return for the last two acts to the fiercest ironic realism. But that is so like Yeats. Give him a job with which you feel sure he will play Bunthorne and he will astonish you with his unique cleverness and subtlety. Give him one that any second-rater could manage with credit and as likely as not he will make an appalling mess of it. He has certainly fallen in up to the neck over O'C.[7]

And to O'Casey himself Shaw wrote:

My dear Sean, what a hell of a play! I wonder how it will hit the public. Of course the Abbey should have produced it as Starkie rightly says—whether it liked it or not. But the people who knew your uncle when you were a child (so to speak) always want to correct your exercises; and this was what disabled the usually competent Yeats and Lady Gregory. Still it is surprising they fired so very wide, considering their marksmanship. . . .[8]

This was O'Casey's first victory over Yeats's literary reputation, and Shaw has been well rewarded by O'Casey for his timely support. Many others were to take up a similar stand years later.

Yeats while rejecting the play wrote to O'Casey:

I am sad and discouraged. You have no subject. You were interested in the Irish Civil War, and at every moment of those plays wrote out of your amusement with life or your sense of its tragedy; you were excited, and we all caught your excite-ment; you were exasperated almost beyond endurance by what you had seen or heard as a man is by what happens under his window, and you moved us as Swift moved his contemporaries. But you are not interested in the Great War; you never stood on its battlefields or walked its hospitals, and so write out of your opinions, . . . there is no dominating character, no dominating action, neither psychological unity nor unity of action, and your great power of the past has been the creation of some unique character who dominated all about

---

[7] Lady Gregory's *Journals*, ed. L. Robinson, pp. 110-1.
[8] *Rose and Crown*, pp. 42-3.

him and was himself a main impulse in some action that filled
the play from beginning to end. The mere greatness of the
World War has thwarted you; it has refused to become mere
background, and obtrudes itself upon the stage as so much
deadwood that will not burn with the dramatic fire.[9]

In thus asserting that O'Casey was not interested in the Great
War, Yeats not only laid himself open to a devastating attack
but also left a gap which showed on what weak foundations
his whole criticism was based. Those acquainted with
O'Casey's life are aware of the interest with which he followed
the course of the Great War. Yeats must have known nothing
about this; he had not the same kindred feeling for O'Casey
that he had for Synge. But that is no excuse, and O'Casey,
after pointing out his interest in the Great War, goes on to ask
Yeats:

> . . . And now will you tell me the name and give me the
> age and send me the address of the human being who, having
> eyes to see, ears to hear and hands to handle, was not interested
> in the Great War?
>
> I'm afraid your statement (as far as I am concerned) is not
> only an ignorant one, but it is a silly statement too.
>
> You say "you never stood on its battlefields." Do you
> really mean that no one should or could write about or speak
> about a war because one has not stood on the battlefields?
> Were you serious when you dictated that—really serious, now?
> Was Shakespeare at Actium or Philippi? Was G. B. Shaw in
> the boats with the French, or in the forts with the English when
> St. Joan and Dunois made the attack that relieved Orleans?
> And someone, I think, wrote a poem about Tir na nOg who
> never took a header into the land of youth. And does war
> consist only of battlefields?[10]

In giving the reasons for his disapproval of *The Silver Tassie*
Yeats reached certain conclusions, regarding the background
to a play and about the "author's opinions" being consumed
by the dramatic action, which were even stranger than his
criticism of the play. Yeats wrote:

> Dramatic action is a fire that must burn up everything but
> itself; there should be no room in a play for anything that does

---

[9] *The Irish Statesman*, x, 9 Jun. 1928.
[10] *Ibid.*

not belong to it; the whole history of the world must be
reduced to wallpaper in front of which the characters must
pose and speak. Among the things that dramatic action must
burn up are the author's opinions; while he is writing he has
no business to know anything that is not a portion of the action.[11]

O'Casey's reply is a study in his power of retaliation with which
we are familiar through his autobiographies and critical
writings:

> I have pondered in my heart your expression that "the history
> of the world must be reduced to wallpaper," and I can find
> in it only the pretentious bigness of a pretentious phrase. I
> thank you, out of mere politeness, but I must refuse even to
> try to do it. That is exactly, in my opinion (there goes a
> cursed opinion again), what most of the Abbey dramatists
> are trying to do—building up, building up little worlds of
> wallpaper and hiding striding life behind it all. . . .
> It is all very well and very easy to say "that dramatic action
> must burn up the author's opinions." The best way, and the
> only way, to do that is to burn up the author himself. . . .
> And was there ever a play, worthy of the name of a play, that
> did not contain one or two or three opinions of the author that
> wrote it. And the Abbey Theatre has produced plays that were
> packed skin-tight with the author's opinions—the plays of
> Shaw, for instance.[12]

It is not surprising that O'Casey found Yeats's arguments
chimerical. If Yeats were to have followed his own injunctions
strictly, he would have had to reject many of the plays performed
at the Abbey, as well as his own nationalistic plays *Countess
Kathleen* and *Cathleen Ni Houlihan*. To be consistent he should
have rejected the earlier plays of O'Casey as well, for though
there is a dominating character in all of them, the history of
the world is decidedly not reduced to wallpaper.

Strictly speaking it is hard to wedge any O'Casey play
into the narrow confines of Yeats's dramatic conclusions. In
The Silver Tassie Harry Heegan, though not as dominating as
his earlier heroes, is a moving figure: but Yeats had failed to
grasp what O'Casey was trying to achieve. "It is all too
abstract, after the first act," he wrote to O'Casey. "The second
act is an interesting technical experiment, but it is too long

[11] *The Irish Statesman*, x, 9 Jun. 1928.   [12] *Ibid.*

for the material; and after that there is nothing."[13] "Really
nothing?" asked O'Casey, "Nothing, nothing at all? Well,
where there is nothing, where there is nothing—there is God."[14]
Ironic words for they are Yeats's own ("Where there is nothing,
where there is nothing—there is God!" is said by Martin
Hearne in Yeats's *The Unicorn from the Stars*). If Yeats's theory
were applied as an acid test we should have to do away with
some of the best plays on record; among those that remained
there would be his *Four Plays for Dancers*, *The Words upon the
Window Pane* and *Purgatory*.

From Yeats's letter we can assume that the play was
rejected because he thought it, rightly or wrongly, unsuitable
for an Abbey performance. This would have been the right
moment for us to turn to the play and judge for ourselves, but
for O'Casey's insinuation in *Rose and Crown* that more personal
issues were involved. He tells us how, while he was working
on the last act of *The Silver Tassie*, Lennox Robinson, and later
Yeats, paid him a hurried visit to ask if he would give his new
play to the Abbey as there were rumours in Dublin that he
was not going to do so. Rumours? O'Casey couldn't believe
it; if there were any he ought to have heard about them. He
was puzzled.

Once the play was rejected, O'Casey took no pains to
conceal his suspicions. He wrote:

> Sean could not but believe that the play's rejection had been
> decided upon before the play had been sent. To answer
> Yeats would be a dangerous thing to do. Yeats in his greatness
> had influence everywhere, and the world of literature bowed
> before him. But answered he must be, and answered he would
> be, even though the strife meant the end of Sean.[15]

That O'Casey sincerely believed that a dirty trick had been
played upon him by the Abbey Directorate is plain from the
various retorts he made in the Press defending his play. Answer-
ing George Russell's criticism that the play had been rejected
so as to save his reputation,[16] O'Casey said:

> The concern for O'Casey's reputation vanishes with its tail
> down when we remember that the replies to the Abbey's

---

[13] *The Irish Statesman*, x, 9 Jun. 1928.   [14] *Ibid.*
[15] *Rose and Crown*, p. 34.   [16] *The Irish Statesman*, x, 21 Jul. 1928.

criticisms showed that O'Casey was prepared to risk his reputation, which was all his own business and none of theirs, to which they refused to respond by producing the play to show whether their opinions were right or wrong; by the fact that the one favourable criticism from the Abbey was hidden till the last moment; that strenuous efforts were made to prevent the publication of the criticisms, and then, when those efforts failed, by the tremendous threat of a legal action [by the Abbey] through the Society of Authors.[17]

In his letter to Lennox Robinson, O'Casey said that the rejection of the play was not unexpected, that he had a bet with his wife that it would be rejected, and that in his opinion the play had been rejected because it was a good one.[18] Though O'Casey does not make any definite charge of bad faith against the Abbey we cannot lightly pass over his insinuations. O'Casey has his case and it is further strengthened because of certain inconsistencies on the part of Lennox Robinson and Walter Starkie. But it is extremely unlikely that actual dishonesty was involved as O'Casey suspects. Though Starkie and Robinson's were also Directors at this time, the control really rested in the hands of Yeats and Lady Gregory. Yeats's intellectual uprightness cannot be challenged and Lady Gregory's love and sympathy for O'Casey are beyond question. Robinson's and Starkie's position, however, is not altogether free from inconsistency. Robinson in his letter to Lady Gregory dated March 1928 did not give his opinion as to whether the play was worthy of a performance or not. He spoke highly of the first two acts, but wished that the second half was better.[19] After learning from Lady Gregory that she agreed with his criticism, he wrote to her:

> I was very relieved to get your letter to-day and to find that you agreed with me about O'Casey's play. If you had disagreed with me I should have suspected myself of all sorts of horrid subconscious feelings.[20]

He added that the cause of the haphazard nature of the last two acts might be hasty writing, since "everybody was beginning

[17] *The Irish Statesman*, x, 4 Aug. 1928.
[18] *Op. cit.*, 9 Jun. 1928.
[19] *Ibid.*
[20] Lady Gregory's *Journals*, ed. L. Robinson, p. 104.

to say he [O'Casey] would never write a play again." Whom he means by "everybody" we do not know.

It was only after Yeats and Lady Gregory had rejected the play that Robinson took a positive stand. Some days later, when Lady Gregory had got Yeats to agree to performing *The Silver Tassie* at the Abbey, and relations with O'Casey could have improved, Robinson put his foot down: "No. It is a bad play."[21] Of course, it is only too likely that he was outraged because O'Casey had exposed the correspondence to the public. When I asked O'Casey if he had a feeling that Lennox Robinson had a strong hand in the play's rejection, O'Casey replied: "More than a feeling: I'm sure he was responsible for the rejection of the *Tassie*."[22]

Walter Starkie wrote to Yeats on 30 Apr. 1928, soon after his return from Spain, that he had read *The Silver Tassie* "several times very carefully"[23] and that the play should be produced. But Lady Gregory recorded in her journals on 4 May:

> Starkie at the Abbey last night. . . . He has but read a part of *The Silver Tassie*—began saying that he didn't care for it, but I said he must not judge it till he has read it through.[24]

What are we to make of it? There are discrepancies everywhere. There is a curious passage in Yeats's letter to O'Casey of 20 Apr. 1928 where he says: "Enclosed with it [*The Silver Tassie*] were the opinions of my fellow-directors, but those opinions I shall not read until I have finished this letter; the letter, however, will not be posted unless their opinion concurs with mine."[25] He may have written this for two reasons. Either he already knew what the opinions of the other Directors were likely to be, and was therefore keen to arrive at an independent judgment. Or he was aware of the nature of the play and had already decided to reject it, knowing that there was, at least, a good possibility of it being thrown out.

In all this rather tangled exchange there was clearly some

[21] Lady Gregory's *Journals*, ed. L. Robinson, p. 110.
[22] Letter to me from O'Casey dated 31 Mar. 1959.
[23] *The Irish Statesman*, x, 9 Jun. 1928.
[24] Lady Gregory's *Journals*, ed. L. Robinson, p. 106.
[25] *The Irish Statesman*, x, 9 Jun. 1928.

justification for O'Casey's suspicion. But the real cause for the rejection of *The Silver Tassie* was that Yeats thought it to be a poor play, and this he maintained till his death,[26] though he allowed a performance of the play a few years later. How far Yeats was justified in his criticism of the play is happily beyond the scope of this book, but we may here consider a couple of the prejudices that blurred his judgment. We have already seen that Yeats considered the love scene in Act I of *The Plough and the Stars* "most objectionable" in its original draft, and not true to life. Yet all along in his earlier plays O'Casey shocks us with an almost superhuman insight into his characters: a realism that amounts to libel. But Yeats was judging from very different premises, and though he had a clearer vision than most of his contemporaries, his prejudice and his belief in his own estimation of the play led him to write to Lady Gregory:

> I did not think it tactful to say in my letter that he [O'Casey] has left his material here in Dublin and will in all likelihood never find it anywhere else, because he cannot become a child and grow up there. I did not say that to him, because I thought he might suspect me of exaggerating some of his faults in order to lure him back.[27]

O'Casey's retort to Walter Starkie, when the latter surmised that O'Casey had lost the power to see intensely, is as much a reply to Yeats's complaint:

> In the first place, it would be impossible to lose in two years the impressions of forty; in the second place, a good deal of those two years have been infused into the production of my own plays, and the rest of the time has been spent in the writing of *The Silver Tassie* so that about a lunar month remains in which I must have lost the power to see intensely.[28]

Coupled to his dramatic theory, his prejudices, his pedantic conception of duty towards O'Casey and a concern for O'Casey's reputation was, as Hone points out, Yeats's "distaste for O'Casey's approach to certain special subjects, which he considered spiritually unprofitable."[29] What these special subjects

---

[26] My interview with Mrs W. B. Yeats on 29 Apr. 1958.

[27] *The Irish Statesman*, x, 9 Jun. 1928.

[28] O'Casey, *The Nineteenth Century*, civ, Sep. 1928.

[29] Joseph Hone, *W. B. Yeats, 1865-1939*, p. 389.

were one can see from the comment Yeats made in his diary on the London performance of *The Silver Tassie*:

> It would seem from its failure in London that we were right, upon the other hand Mr. Shaw's and Mr. Augustus John's admiration suggest that it was at least better than we thought it, and yet I am certain that if any of our other dramatists sent us a similar play we would reject it. We were biased, we are biased by the Irish Salamis. The war as O'Casey has conceived it is an equivalent for those primary qualities brought down by Berkeley's secret society, it stands outside the characters, it is not part of their expression, it is that very attempt denounced by Mallarmé to build as if with brick and mortar with the pages of a book. The English critics feel differently. To them a theme that "bulks largely in the news" gives dignity to human nature, even raises it to international importance. We on the other hand are certain that nothing can give dignity to human nature but the character and energy of its expression. We do not even ask that it shall have dignity so long as it can burn away all that is not itself.[30]

Yeats's refusal to give *The Silver Tassie* an Abbey performance was the chief cause of the skirmish between him and O'Casey, though other factors played their part in ensuring that it would be no mean fight. Yeats having poured the oil in his first letter, set it on fire by his second. In his letter to Lady Gregory of 25 Apr. he suggested that O'Casey could withdraw his play and give out to the Press that he himself had become dissatisfied and had withdrawn it for revision. Yeats expected that Lady Gregory would write and make this suggestion in her own way; but she, instead, enclosed a portion of Yeats's letter in her own letter to O'Casey. "This was a serious mistake," said Mrs Yeats to me. "W.B. never wanted it like that." The first letter of Yeats to O'Casey was enough to infuriate him, this one turned it into a question of honour. Writing to Lennox Robinson, O'Casey said:

> If W. B. Yeats had known me as faintly as he thinks he knows me well, he wouldn't have wasted his time—and mine— making such a suggestion; I am too big for this sort of mean

---

[30] W. B. Yeats, *Pages From a Diary Written in Nineteen Hundred and Thirty*, pp. 57-8.

and petty shuffling, this lousy perversion of the truth. There is going to be no damned secrecy with me surrounding the Abbey's rejection of the play. Does he think that I would practise in my life the prevarication and wretchedness that I laughed at in my plays?[31]

To this must be added the haste with which the Directors' views were forwarded to him, due to "an excess of consideration" on Lady Gregory's part, as he was correcting the proofs and she thought he would like to be able to make alterations. Starkie's absence was another misfortune, for had Yeats seen his letter he would not have forwarded his own to O'Casey ("the letter, however, will not be posted unless their opinion concurs with mine"). Mrs Yeats told me that she felt O'Casey might not have reacted so violently had not the rejection of the play coincided with the birth of his son and his financial exigencies.[32]

Whatever the case, the consequences, though minor and temporary for Yeats (he complained in a letter to Olivia Shakespear of O'Casey having sent up his blood pressure), were disastrous for O'Casey. He writes:

> Yeats's denunciation of *The Silver Tassie* had done Sean's name a lot of violence. The Nobel Prize winner, the Leader of English Literature was a judge against whom there was no appeal for the time being. Sean's flying start had been rudely curtailed of its fair proportions, and he would have to start over again, and fight the battle anew.[33]

It was like starting again. The play was financially a failure: it only ran for eight weeks in London and did not pay its expenses. O'Casey had hoped that it would bring in enough to live on for one year, but all that it brought was extreme poverty. He was soon forced to sell the amateur rights of his Abbey plays to Messrs French and Sons for £300. Shaw advised him against it, but there was no alternative.

All this must be taken into account or we are likely to misconstrue large portions of his autobiography as the work of a monomaniac. Actually, we need not be in the least surprised at O'Casey's constant harping on *The Silver Tassie*, for to this

[31] *The Irish Statesman*, x, 9 Jun. 1928.
[32] My interview with Mrs W. B. Yeats on 29 Apr. 1958.
[33] *Rose and Crown*, pp. 77-8.

11.5.28

19, WORONZOW ROAD,

ST JOHNS WOOD,

N W e

You seem, Mr Yeats, to be getting beautifully worse; you astonish me more & more. There seem to be shallows in you of which no one ever dreamed.

What have packed houses, enthusiastic (cheering, says Mr Robinson) audiences for "The Plough" got to do with your contention that "The Silver Tassie" is a bad play? Perhaps this thought is due, as a journalist might say, to your delightful sense of Irish humour. Farewell

Sean O'Casey

SEAN O'CASEY'S LETTER TO W. B. YEATS

Dated 11th May 1928. By courtesy of Mrs W. B. Yeats, who owns the original.

day has he not been able to wash away the stain of Yeats's criticism. How O'Casey would have fared had Yeats accepted the play is a matter for conjecture. That temporarily the play would have been a success is certain: even Yeats admitted that in his letter to Olivia Shakespear: "Of course if we had played his play, his fame is so great that we would have had full houses for a time."[34] But in a very honest attempt to protect O'Casey's name he did him much harm. A break between Yeats and O'Casey was inevitable for it was based on no mere clash of opinions, but on a deep-rooted conflict between men of different convictions and temperaments. We may conclude the controversy with Eric Bentley's words:

> Yeats was under no obligation to make a success story of Mr. O'Casey's career; he was under no obligation to like *The Silver Tassie*. But, all other questions aside, we may judge his famous rejection of it in terms of the consequences. Yeats did more than any other man to deflect from the theatre one of its two or three best playwrights.[35]

Since Yeats looked upon O'Casey's exile as the cause for what he considered to be faults in *The Silver Tassie*, it may be worthwhile to see whether O'Casey began writing the play before or after his arrival in London. From Eric Bentley's defence of O'Casey—"Mr. O'Casey observes plaintively that his residence in England was held accountable for the faults of a work which was conceived and begun before he left Ireland"[36] —it would appear that *The Silver Tassie* was begun while he was in Dublin. On the other hand if one relies solely on the account that O'Casey gives in *Rose and Crown*, of how in a London office he heard a business man hum a "riotous and romantic song" and decided to give the title of the song to his next play,[37] it would seem that he took to writing the play after he had been in London for a while. Of course it is possible to begin a play and later on clap a title to it, but in this case the title is so highly symbolic and so woven into the play that I am inclined to think that it must have come first. This,

---

[34] *The Letters of W. B. Yeats*, ed. Allan Wade, p. 743.
[35] Eric Bentley, *The Dramatic Event*, pp. 44-5.
[36] *Op. cit.*, p. 44.
[37] The song is by Robert Burns. The accepted title is "A Farewell" and not "The Silver Tassie."

I

however, does not rule out the possibility that the dramatist had decided while in Dublin that his next play would be about the Great War. In fact we have reason to believe that soon after he had finished writing *The Plough and the Stars* he had decided upon a war theme for his next play. This inference is based on an entry in Lady Gregory's journal on 10 Jan. 1926, that O'Casey was thinking of using a character from *Lizzie's Night Out* (*Nannie's Night Out*) for his new play, *The Red Lily*.[38] A play with this title never appeared and the mystery would have remained unsolved but for what J. L. Hodson has recorded:

> I asked him [O'Casey] where the *Red Lily* was, and what he was working at? He laughed that I had been taken in. There never had been a *Red Lily*, he said, nor was there ever such a play in his intention. He had told people that to put them off —they were always pestering him those days.[39]

This clears up much confusion. It was in Dublin that O'Casey first planned to experiment with a new play in a new manner. He wanted to keep this a secret—he remembered how Liam O'Flaherty in private conversation had praised *The Plough and the Stars* and had later attacked it in the Press—and so gave it out that he was engaged on a play called *The Red Lily*. It is evident that Lady Gregory and Yeats were taken in and this was largely responsible for the shock they received.

Having seen that *The Silver Tassie* was conceived in Dublin and written in London, we may now turn to the play. So much has been said about it, and such diverse views have been expressed, that one is apt to lose one's personal reaction in the swim of critical opinions. The most singular thing about the plot is that O'Casey should have considered it "something unique."[40] The whole of it can be found in a short poem called "Disabled" by Wilfred Owen. Town, in the poem, is the prototype on whom O'Casey modelled his hero Harry Heegan. There is the same football match, the victory and the fun of being "carried shoulder high," all the joy of youth and the love of women. Then the War, and the thoughtless

[38] Lady Gregory's *Journals*, ed. L. Robinson, p. 95.
[39] J. L. Hodson, *No Phantoms Here*, p. 153.
[40] O'Casey in his letter to Yeats. See *The Irish Statesman*, x, 9 Jun. 1928.

and evanescent reasons that carry him off to pour his strength "down shell-holes"; the return home as a cripple in a wheel-chair, envying the pleasures of those who are sound; noticing the eyes of the women turning from him to those who are whole; knowing that: "Now he will never feel again how slim Girl's waists are, or how warm their subtle hands."[41]

The first act of the play is in the typical O'Casey vein and delighted the Abbey Directors—Yeats told a friend that O'Casey had surpassed himself. The setting is not dismal: the few ribbons and decorations and a half-pint bottle of whiskey manage to lift it above the tenement level. The play opens with Sylvester Heegan, a docker, and his friend Simon Norton, a checker on the docks, engrossed in recalling the feats of his son Harry Heegan. Susie Monican, a shapely, attractive and God-fearing girl stands nearby putting the fear of God into the hearts of these two men. The scene is cut short, after it has gone on for a bit too long, by the appearance of Mrs Foran, a top-flat neighbour, who is delighted at the prospect of her husband Teddy departing the same night to the battle front. She is soon chased out by Teddy who learns of her secret joy at his departure. Harry Heegan and Jessie Taite arrive, carried on the shoulders of their admirers and followed by Barney Bagnel. Harry is drunk with youth and joy at having scored the goal that brings the cup for the third successive year to the Avondale Football Club. Harry, Barney and Jessie celebrate the victory, the lovers drinking from the silver tassie. The ship's siren is heard and Harry, Barney and Teddy are hustled off to the boat.

The second act transplants us immediately from the familiar Dublin scene to the ruins of a monastery. Nothing is familiar save a figure of the Virgin, a life-size crucifix and a placard or two, one marked HYDE PARK CORNER standing at the base of a howitzer. The characters are no longer individuals as they were in the first act; only Barney is still referred to by name. Their identity is lost, they act and move like automata, chanting out their thoughts in unison: "a kind of mass sub-consciousness expresses itself directly in the choruses."[42] It may be noted that O'Casey's purpose here is to give us a brief

---

[41] Wilfred Owen, "Disabled," *Poems*, pp. 32-3.
[42] Una Ellis-Fermor, *The Frontiers of Drama*, p. 122.

impression of modern warfare and its effect on the human mind. No tragedy is shown except the tragic waste that lies around before the curtain rises. No sooner does the attack begin than O'Casey breaks off, knowing that the impression of the horror and indecency of war will wear off, or turn into fake heroism, if actual fighting is shown.

The act opens with the Croucher intoning his blasphemies, followed by the soldiers complaining of their miserable lot. A pompous visitor comes to survey the scene, proud to penetrate into danger wherever he is sure there is none. Now and again a Staff Officer hops in to read some stupid orders, while the stretcher-bearers and the wounded chant alternately as they move towards the Red Cross Station. When the attack begins and the curtains descend, the soldiers group round the howitzer, "the only object of veneration, the only help in the hour of death and destruction, the only strong unbroken thing."[43] Even the Croucher rises and joins the soldiers' choric response —"We believe in God and we believe in thee"—to the Corporal's prayer to the howitzer:

> Hail, cool-hardened tower of steel emboss'd
> With the fever'd, figment thought of man;
> Guardian of our love and hate and fear,
> Speak for us to the inner ear of God!

> Dream of line, of colour, and of form;
> Dreams of music dead for ever now;
> Dreams in bronze and dreams in stone have gone
> To make thee delicate and strong to kill.[44]

The third act takes us to a hospital to witness the aftermath of war. Sylvester and Simon are apparently suffering from minor ailments, but Harry Heegan is paralysed from the waist down. Sylvester and Simon have been forced into the ward by O'Casey for the simple reason that he wishes to provide comic relief after the sombre second act. Their presence in the hospital, their happy-go-lucky attitude and their sound physique contrast bitterly with the mood, now tranquil, now one of demoniac rage, of the crippled Harry. Susie Monican has shed her narrow religion which had its origin in her

---

[43] A. G. Macdonnel, *London Mercury*, XXII, Dec. 1929.
[44] *The Silver Tassie*, Act II, p. 54.

frustrated love for Harry; she has now found her hero in
Surgeon Maxwell, a character who is strongly reminiscent of
the doctor in Wilfred Owen's poem "The Dead-Beat." Harry
is to be operated upon, and his mother and Mrs Foran come to
see him. From them we learn with surprise that Barney has
earned a V.C. for saving Harry's life. Harry waits for Jessie
to come, but in vain. Barney brings Harry's ukelele and a
bunch of flowers from Jessie, lays them on his bed as if he
were laying them on a grave, and departs. The act ends with
the sisters singing the hymn *Salve Regina*, and Harry's bitter
cry: "God of the miracles, give a poor devil a chance, give a
poor devil a chance!"[45]

In the final act O'Casey goes to show that no poor devil
was given a chance. An emasculate and crippled Harry is
carried to the scene where he had gloried in his former strength
—the Avondale Football Club. Almost all the characters in
the play are present, Harry and Barney decorated with their
medals and ribbons. Jessie has deserted Harry for Barney, and
as she twirls round and makes merry with him, Harry follows
her in a wheelchair, a pathetic figure, now and again throwing
himself into a paroxysm of hysterics. Surgeon Forby Maxwell
and Susie try to calm him. Finally they manage to get him
out after he has had a drink from the tassie, Maxwell lamenting
that they have already wasted too much time. Harry having
departed with Teddy, his comrade in arms who has been
blinded in the War, the dance begins again, Maxwell's song
being an ironic but appropriate conclusion to the play:

> Swing into the dance,
> Take joy when it comes, ere it go;
> For the full flavour of life
> Is either a kiss or a blow.
> He to whom joy is a foe,
> Let him wrap himself up in his woe;
> For he is a life on the ebb,
> We a full life on the flow![46]

The Silver Tassie was not written to provide entertainment.
O'Casey had already done enough to entertain his audiences

[45] *The Silver Tassie*, Act III, p. 79.
[46] *Op. cit.*, Act IV, p. 103.

and now he wanted them to swallow some of his bitter pills. He makes his purpose very clear:

> He would set down without malice or portly platitude the shattered enterprise of life to be endured by many of those who, not understanding the bloodied melody of war, went forth to fight, to die, or to return again with tarnished bodies and complaining minds. He would show a wide expanse of war in the midst of timorous hope and overweening fear; amidst a galaxy of guns; silently show the garlanded horror of war.[47]

That the play is highly pacifist in scope is axiomatic. Opinions vary, however, as to how far O'Casey has succeeded in his purpose. Harold Clurman says that "as an anti-war play *The Silver Tassie* is almost foolish. The true theme of the play lies in O'Casey's feeling for the Irish people."[48] Richard Jennings describes it as "a lugubrious blunder, almost incredibly crude in its emotional emphasis; painful, in no profitable sense, with its rubbing-in of points presented by the dreadful theme of a wounded body derided by its surviving rivals in health and strength."[49] These two views clash with John Gassner's opinion that it is "one of the most trenchant pacifist protests of the generation,"[50] and with J. C. Trewin's appreciation of what he describes as "the compelling certainty of the *Tassie* in which O'Casey knew exactly what he wishes to say and said it, not in the common form of the theatre, but in a medium that seemed to wed flame and ice."[51]

However much opinions may differ on the result, it is certain that the play will reveal its full significance only when we keep the author's purpose firmly before us. The first act, of which the Abbey Directors spoke so highly, is important in so far as it shows the course of a normal family life cut short by the havoc of war. The jokes are laboured, the antics of Sylvester and Simon border on the farcical—the two clowns are feeble echoes of the "Paycock" and Joxer. Susie's religion is as narrow as it is false, and Mrs Heegan's anxiety that Harry

---

[47] *Rose and Crown*, pp. 29-30.
[48] H. Clurman, *New Republic*, CXXI, 19 Sep. 1949.
[49] R. Jennings, *Spectator*, CXLIII, Oct. 1929.
[50] John Gassner, *Masters of the Drama* (3rd edn.), p. 570.
[51] J. C. Trewin, *The Theatre Since 1900*, p. 189.

should be back from the football match in time to catch the boat since otherwise she would lose her separation money is unreal because of its exaggeration. It is not till Harry arrives that the play really moves. O'Casey describes him as one who "has gone to the trenches as unthinkingly as he would go to the polling booth."[52] He is pulsating with joy and energy, holding high the silver cup "as a priest would elevate a chalice."[53] The cup is symbolic of his youth and strength. It also signifies the consecrated chalice of the Mass. His drinking from it in lust is a sacrilege for which he atones later by being injured in the war. But at this stage there is nothing that hints of the tragedy that is to follow, except perhaps in Mrs Heegan's sigh of satisfaction as Harry hastens to catch the boat: "Thanks be to Christ that we're after managin' to get the three of them away safely."[54]

O'Casey gave us a more vivid picture of the Boyle family in the first few pages of *Juno and the Paycock* than he does of the Heegans in a whole act. Why? Because in *Juno and the Paycock* he was not faced with the problem of making the first act a mere background, he was free to proceed and develop the action of the play. All the acts being in the naturalistic vein, he had the additional advantage of spreading his material from one act to another so as to maintain a balance. In *The Silver Tassie* this could not be done, for the second act was to be wholly expressionistic. Thus he was forced to devote the whole of the first act to portraying a background, which he could have accomplished in a short scene. Therefore it drags: the act has to be filled up with the tomfoolery of Sylvester and Simon, with Susie Monican's constant harping on religion, with Mrs Heegan's monotonous chiming about her government money. Harry Heegan could have saved the situation, but he has to be kept off stage till the end so that his abounding vitality and exuberance have no time to flag and can contrast strongly with the disaster that is about to overtake him. Not a shadow of evil must cross his path at the moment, for that would weaken O'Casey's attempt to drive home his trenchant hatred of war by means of his maimed hero. Thus far he sacrifices his art to his purpose—a thing Yeats would have never done.

[52] *The Silver Tassie*, Act I, p. 25.
[53] *Ibid.*   [54] *Op. cit.*, p. 34.

Granville-Barker said of the second act, that O'Casey broke loose "under the spell of a greater theme and his own deeper passion, into that remarkable second act of *The Silver Tassie*, where he employs symbolism of scene and character, choric rhythms of speech and movement, the insistence of rhyme, the dignity of ritual, every transcendental means available in his endeavour to give us, seated in our comfortable little theatre, some sense of the chaos of war."[55] To this "spell of a greater theme and his own deeper passions" must be added the consummate skill with which he moulds this act; a little surprising, for O'Casey wrote in a letter to Kenneth Frederick Howse: "I dont know what Expressionism means. I never did anything to perpetrate it in any play of mine."[56] However this may be, O'Casey has succeeded in driving home his "purpose" as insistently as does Wilfred Owen in his poems or Ernst Toller in *The Swallow Book* or *Letters from Prison*.

The whole act is a vast canvas totally devoid of those elements normally required for a successful play; namely plot, character and action. O'Casey's first love was painting not playwriting, and here he has painted one of the most compelling pictures of war, showing not its results in physical dilapidation (this he reserves for the next two acts) but the mental paralysis it has caused in the soldiers. The soldiers' chant, where each picks up what the other has said and chants it with a reversion of the order of words, brings this out:

> 1st SOLDIER: Cold and wet and tir'd.
> 2nd SOLDIER: Wet and tir'd and cold.
> 3rd SOLDIER: Tir'd and cold and wet.
> 4th SOLDIER [*very like Teddy*]: Twelve blasted hours of ammunition transport fatigue!
> 1st SOLDIER: Twelve weary hours.
> 2nd SOLDIER: And wasting hours.
> 3rd SOLDIER: And hot and heavy hours.
> 1st SOLDIER: Toiling and thinking to build the wall of force that blocks the way from here to home.
> 2nd SOLDIER: Lifting shells.

---

[55] Harley Granville-Barker, *On Poetry in Drama* (The Romance Lecture), p. 25.
[56] Letter dated 29 Jan. 1951. See *The Plays of Sean O'Casey* by K. F. Howse, p. 144. See also *The Dramatic Practice and Theory of Sean O'Casey* by H. R. Nordell, p. 58.

3rd SOLDIER: Carrying shells.
4th SOLDIER: Piling shells.
1st SOLDIER: In the falling, pissing rine and whistling wind.
2nd SOLDIER: The whistling wind and falling, drenching rain.
3rd SOLDIER: The God-dam rain and blasted whistling wind.[57]

The Visitor has been brought in to point the contrast between the soldiers in their deplorable plight and those who have stayed at home and think of war as a glorious event. His parallel can be found in the character of the Professor in Toller's *Transfiguration*, or even more poignantly in the character of the Father in Paul Raynal's *The Unknown Warrior*. In all these instances we see that the men who have stayed behind, and to whom war figures mainly as news, are unable to visualise its sordid meanness. The Visitor is symbolic of the inane pot-bellied people at home, ever anxious to "penetrate a little deeper into danger," viewing the stealing of a cock belonging to a friendly state as "Infra dignitatem," and putting the nervous irascibility of the soldiers down to: "Too much time to think. Nervy. Time to brood, brood; bad."[58]

This total inability to grasp what war means to those who fight is most poignantly brought out when the Second and Third Soldiers receive parcels from home. The Third Soldier, opening his parcel, looks forward to its being a bundle of cigarettes, but to his astonishment it turns out to be a prayer-book. The Second Soldier is more fortunate. His parcel contains a coloured ball with a note which reads: "To play your way to the enemies' trenches when you all go over the top."[59] Soon the soldiers are dribbling the ball across the stage. The truth is that neither the prayer-book nor the ball is going to help them in their hour of need, though the ball is the better present of the two.

There are a few things in this act that seem to defy explanation. Why is Barney singled out, and why is he the only character referred to by name? Why should the killing of an "Estaminay" cock be brought in? The Fourth Soldier is "very like Teddy," but we cannot trace Harry. Why is Harry kept out of this act? Taking Barney first, the only reason that I can see for O'Casey giving him a separate identity is that he

[57] *The Silver Tassie*, Act II, pp. 37-8.
[58] *Op. cit.*, p. 47.   [59] *Op. cit.*, p. 51.

wants to focus our attention on him. He wishes to hint that
Barney is the one character who has not fused into this mass
subconsciousness, the only character thus likely to escape
uninjured and mould the destiny of the play. The story of
Barney choking an "Estaminay" cock and being punished for
it is based on fact. O'Casey in his letter to Yeats tells how a
soldier, Barney Fay, got field punishment No. I for stealing
poultry in France. Besides, poultry thieving is a common sport
at the front and O'Casey probably felt the necessity of giving
a little realistic touch to his high-fantasy act. But this is not
the main reason. O'Casey here wants to show that Barney's
stealing of the cock, belonging to a citizen of a friendly state,
is symbolic of his stealing his friend's girl.

There is no satisfactory explanation why Harry alone should
be left out of this act. The one reason I can think of is that
which I have already suggested: O'Casey is keeping him
away from all harm and hardship so as to add force to his
suffering when the time comes. He wants to take us unawares—
to show a life vibrating with joy suddenly consumed by fire. He
wants us to preserve in our minds the last happy glimpse of Harry
that we had, and he sees no reason for introducing him in an
act which is impersonal and to which he can contribute nothing.

When Shaw wrote that "the hitting gets harder and harder
right through to the end,"[60] he was commending the last two
acts. Professor Allardyce Nicoll pays the play a high tribute
when he says that "Nothing greater or finer in the modern
theatre has been done than the majestically bitter chants at
the altar of the gun or the restless, agitated movement of the
third act of this play."[61] The beauty of the third act is undeniable, but how far does it further O'Casey's overall aim of
condemning war? Judged from this standpoint only it is a
failure. It is even unnecessary to the action of the play, and
to some extent destroys the very thing O'Casey wishes to bring
out—the sudden reversal in the fortune of his hero. The right
thing would have been to move straight from the second to the
fourth act, thus making *The Silver Tassie* a three-act play. The
third act as it stands now augurs what is to follow, and only
succeeds in lessening the excruciating horror of the last act.

[60] Quoted by John Gassner in *Masters of the Drama*, p. 570.
[61] A. Nicoll, *British Drama* (4th edn.), p. 484.

Dwelling on trivialities and so lengthening a play was a weakness that O'Casey had from the very start. *Juno and the Paycock* had another act, the shooting of Johnny Boyle, wisely cut by the Abbey Directors, and *The Plough and the Stars* in its original draft was longer almost by half its present length.[62]

But we cannot dismiss the act as lightly as all that. We must try to see what made O'Casey bring it into the play. The second act was a fantasy, an adventure in the realm of symbolism of which O'Casey then knew little. By the time he completed it he felt uprooted and was keen to return to solid earth again, and to be once more amid scenes and people he had known. He had not forgotten the failure of *Cathleen Listens In*, and was aware that his fame as a dramatist rested on the delineation of familiar situations and characters. The fourth act, though sketched in his earlier realistic manner, could not provide him that opportunity, as it dealt with a theme and passion which he had not suffered or known. Therefore he includes the third act in the hospital, where he takes us back not only to realism but also to his personal experiences. In his letter to Yeats, O'Casey wrote:

> But I have walked some of the hospital wards. I have talked and walked and smoked and sung with the blue-suited wounded men fresh from the front. I've been with the armless, the legless, the blind, the gassed and the shell-shocked; one with a head bored by shrapnel who had to tack east and tack west before he could reach the point he wished to get to; with one whose head rocked like a frantic moving pendulum.[63]

In *Drums Under the Window* O'Casey has given us a full account of his hospital experiences when he was admitted for a tubercular swelling on the right side of his neck. It is this hospital experience which is largely responsible for the third act, and now and again we see him portraying people and incidents which were familiar to him. To point a few instances: the character Sylvester can safely be traced to that of Den Duffy, a docker, who was in for an operation and dreaded it. Harry may partly have his origin in Cock Duffy, brother of Den Duffy, one of the best football backs Dublin has ever

---

[62] G. Fallon, *Sunday Independent* (Dublin), 24 Dec. 1950.
[63] *The Irish Statesman*, x, 9 Jun. 1928.

known. The nuns appearing at the end of the act perhaps owe their origin to a nun who had dropped on her knees in the middle of the ward in St Vincent's Hospital to honour the Angelus.

The meandering, agitating third act moves to its sombre conclusion as the curtain goes up for the last time. The War and the hospital having made a good job of Harry, he is now returned to his pre-war surroundings—the Avondale Football Club. As the crippled Harry wheels about, tormented by Jessie's desertion and his own helplessness, the futility and horror of war breaks through the crimson and black striped curtains of the Avondale Club; the atmosphere of festivity adds to the tragic situation of Harry. O'Casey does not side with any particular character, for he has already sided with an issue; he shows no sympathy for Harry, for it is through Harry's sufferings that he must speak. And he speaks in a language of piercing beauty. Instances abound all through the act and we can do little more than pick out a couple of them. See how Harry speaks when Barney asks Jessie whether she will have red wine or white:

> HARRY: Red wine first, Jessie, to the passion and the power and the pain of life, an' then a drink of white wine to the melody that is in them all!
> JESSIE: I'm so hot.
> HARRY: I'm so cold; white wine for the woman warm to make her cold; red wine for the man that's cold to make him warm!
> JESSIE: White wine for me.
> HARRY: For me the red wine till I drink to men puffed up with pride of strength, for even creeping things can praise the Lord![64]

Perhaps the most pathetic utterance comes from Harry when Surgeon Maxwell asks Mrs Heegan to take her son home. Tired in body and spirit he gives in to his destiny, but not before he has flung the tassie to the ground. The cup that once, in its fullness, was symbolic of his youth and strength, now, battered shapeless, symbolises his defeated hope and fate:

> HARRY: Dear God, this crippled form is still your child.
> [*To Mrs. Heegan*] Dear Mother, this helpless thing is still

---

[64] *The Silver Tassie*, Act IV, pp. 81-2.

your son. Harry Heegan, me, who, on the football field, could crash a twelve-stone flyer off his feet. For this dear Club three times I won the Cup, and grieve in reason I was just too weak this year to play again. And now, before I go, I give you all the Cup, the Silver Tassie, to have and to hold for ever, evermore. [*From his chair he takes the Cup with the two sides hammered close together, and holds it out to them.*] Mangled and bruised as I am bruised and mangled. Hammered free from all its comely shape. Look, there is Jessie writ, and here is Harry, the one name safely separated from the other. [*He flings it on the floor*] Treat it kindly. With care it may be opened out, for Barney there to drink to Jess, and Jessie there to drink to Barney.[65]

As if this alone was not painful enough, O'Casey uses other devices. Teddy is shown groping in the darkness, and finding his sole satisfaction in drink. There is the demand for Harry to sing his Negro spiritual to the ukelele which, as Wilson Knight observes, arouses a "nostalgic barbarism."[66] This great footballer, once sound in body and mind, is now fit only to pluck out a few notes on the ukelele for the amusement of others. Just as Maurice Tabret, "a born flyer," in Somerset Maugham's *The Sacred Flame*, excels in chess, so does Harry excel at the ukelele—all that is left for him to excel in. It is perhaps this and the helpless state of Harry which led Kappo Phelan to refer to him as a "one-dimensional baby from start to finish."[67] If Harry remains a one-dimensional figure it is because he is not meant to develop—the war has deprived him of his dimensions even before he was aware of them. Besides, *The Silver Tassie* is not a tragedy of the soul but of the flesh. Harry's longing for Jessie is physical rather than spiritual, and the force that drives him forward is not love, but jealousy and spurned passion. To lift Harry to unselfish heights would be to make him a martyr; it would perhaps make him a more interesting character, but it would thwart the dramatist's purpose and lessen the revulsion against war.

The play ends on a note of calm. What is wrong is that

---

[65] *The Silver Tassie*, Act IV, pp. 101-2.
[66] G. Wilson Knight, *Christ and Nietzsche*, p. 58. It may be noted that a similar barbarism is aroused by the "twang of the banjo" in a short story "The Banjo" by H. E. Bates.
[67] Kappo Phelan, *Commonweal*, L, 7 Oct. 1949.

the calm is forced upon us, that the spirit of resignation is not in keeping with Harry's character or with the development of the tragedy to its climax. A play which, like Christopher Fry's *A Sleep of Prisoners*, can be described as "a drama full of the naked friction of wills,"[68] is finally resolved into a noble-minded oration.

The play which comes closest to *The Silver Tassie* is not *A Sleep of Prisoners*, but Ernst Toller's *Hinkemann*, written in the prison-fortress of Niederschoenfeld in 1921-2. An incomplete English translation appeared under the title "Hobbleman" in the periodical *Germinal* in 1923; and it is possible that O'Casey might have come across the play, for the tragedy that overtakes Harry has close resemblance to the tragedy that falls on Eugene Hinkemann. Eugene's cry, "The world has lost its soul and I have lost my sex"[69] could well have been Harry's. Both heroes are left emasculated by the War and both lose the object of their affection to men who have nothing to offer but their virility. There is also considerable anti-war propaganda in both plays. The last words of Susie in *The Silver Tassie* and of Eugene in *Hinkemann* are worthy of comparison, though those spoken by Eugene are more moving. Here is Susie speaking to Jessie who feels sorry for Harry:

> SUSIE: Oh nonsense! If you'd passed as many through your hands as I, you'd hardly notice one. [*To Jessie*] Jessie, Teddy Foran and Harry Heegan have gone to live their own way in another world. Neither I nor you can lift them out of it. No longer can they do the things we do. We can't give sight to the blind or make the lame walk. We would if we could. It is the misfortune of war. As long as wars are waged, we shall be vexed by woe; strong legs shall be made useless and bright eyes made dark. But we, who have come through the fire unharmed, must go on living.[70]

And here is Eugene lamenting over the dead body of his wife who has committed suicide:

> GENE: . . . Leave me alone. Leave me alone. Leave me alone with my wife. . . .
> [*Beseeching.*] Please.
> [*The people leave the room*].

[68] Derek Stanford, *Christopher Fry*, p. 21.
[69] Ernst Toller, *Hinkemann*, *Seven Plays*, p. 191.
[70] *The Silver Tassie*, Act IV, p. 103.

She was strong and sound. And she broke the net. And here I stand—here I stand—monstrous—ridiculous. In all ages there'll be men like me. But why me? Why should it fall on me? It doesn't pick and choose. It hits this man and that man. And the next and the next go free. What can we know about it? Where from? Where to? Any day the kingdom of heaven may arise, any night the great flood may come and swallow up the earth.[71]

The Silver Tassie, though magnificent in its own way, does not reach the tragic heights of *Hinkemann*. The suffering of Eugene is greater than that of Harry because Eugene's is of the soul. This does not mean that Harry fails to hold our attention. Harry's suffering is best revealed when we place him beside some of the other emasculate heroes in plays and novels. Maurice Tabret in *The Sacred Flame* is dead when the second act opens. The first act gives us an opportunity to see the pain and gloom under the surface stoicism of his character. His part in the play is to set the ball rolling, and it rolls very much faster after he is gone. Sir Clifford Chatterley in *Lady Chatterley's Lover* is portrayed with a different intention: he is not asked to command sympathy. D. H. Lawrence says in his "A Propos of Lady Chatterley's Lover" that he "recognised that the lameness of Clifford was symbolic of the paralysis, the deeper emotional or passional paralysis." Thus as a character he is the very opposite of Harry, for Harry's paralysis has gone to sharpen his emotional life. In *The Silver Tassie* the tragedy falls on Harry; in *Lady Chatterley's Lover*, it falls not on Clifford but on Connie. In Ernest Hemingway's novel *The Sun also Rises*, Jake loves without the feeling of sex, while Brett cannot do without sex where she loves. Thus Jake is not so tragic or helpless a character as Harry, for he is able to give compassion and protection to Brett in spite of his impotence.

Among the war plays written in English, perhaps its only rival is R. C. Sherriff's *Journey's End*. No two plays on a similar theme could be more different. O'Casey has referred to *Journey's End* as a play of "false effrontery," and has quoted G. J. Nathan that it "apparently needed only a butler to convert it into a polite drawing-room comedy."[72] Whatever

---

[71] Ernest Toller, *Hinkemann, Seven Plays*, p. 193.
[72] *Rose and Crown*, p. 128.

O'Casey might think, *Journey's End* remains a fine play, though
not so moving in its impact as *The Silver Tassie*. And yet the
history of *The Silver Tassie* has been one of failure. To the
best of my knowledge it has not had in the last thirty years as
many productions by professional companies as *Journey's End*
has had in a single day.[73] It is ironic that *Journey's End*,
though a lesser play, brought the firm which produced it a
profit of £50,000,[74] while Cochran who produced *The Silver
Tassie* ran into a loss. It is even more ironic that Sheriff should
have made over £300,000 from his play, which is perhaps more
than O'Casey has earned from all his plays put together.

It is not within the scope of this study to go into the story of
a play's performance, but *The Silver Tassie* is among those plays
which reveal its full significance only when produced. Starkie
was among the first to realise that the merit of the play could
not be judged merely from reading it, for as early as August
1928 he wrote of the second act:

> It is difficult to imagine such scenes when we read the play,
> but in a production they would no doubt flog up the excitement
> of the audience. The chanting in the scene of the trenches
> would be more striking on the stage where the author wishes
> to make it all seem like a fantastic echo of the grim vision of
> war.[75]

Other critics were to voice a similar opinion later, after they
had seen the play performed. Of the few productions that
The Silver Tassie has had, the most significant from the author's
angle was at the Apollo Theatre, London. It was more or less
unanimously acknowledged by the critics that the play, in spite
of its faults, was worthy of an Abbey production, and that the
Abbey had done wrong in rejecting it. To some extent this
helped to restore the reputation that O'Casey had lost in the
literary duel with Yeats. But when it was finally produced at
the Abbey Theatre from 12 Aug. 1935, the play was attacked
from every quarter of the Irish Press. O'Casey has described
the uproar at length in *Rose and Crown*. The chief grounds for
attack, which surprisingly nobody had thought of when it was

---

[73] At one time there were nearly twenty companies playing *Journey's End*
somewhere every night. See Ashley Dukes, *The Scene is Changed*, p. 148.

[74] R. Findlater, *The Unholy Trade*, p. 117.

[75] W. Starkie, *The Nineteenth Century*, CIV, Aug. 1928.

produced in London, was that the play was a travesty of the Mass, that it was an insult to the Christian faith and its proudest possessions, and that it was full of indecent language. The Catholic papers such as *The Tablet, The Irish Rosary, The Cross, The Eagle, The Irish Catholic, The Standard* and the *Evening Herald* were most vocal about it. The *Evening Herald* quoted a member of the audience saying that the play was "a series of slaps in the teeth," and itself added that "Mr. O'Casey's vulgarity is neither clever nor funny."[76] The critic of the *Irish Independent* wrote: "It is cheap. Where there is an attempt at humour it is cheap farce relying largely on vulgarity for its effect . . ." and "there is tragedy behind the farce—the tragedy of the author. There is also the tragedy of our best players having to consent to appear in such a jig-saw nightmare."[77]

The attack continued for some weeks, even after the play had been called off. The most startling criticism was published by the *Irish Independent* under the caption "Revelation by a Director of the Theatre." Mr Brinsley Macnamara, one of the Abbey Directors, denounced the play, the actors and the audience, and justified his own position and the conditions under which he had reluctantly agreed to the play's performance:[78]

> I did not see the play until the second night of its production, and my immediate feelings were that an outrage had been committed. . . . The audience of the Abbey Theatre has for more than ten years shown a wholly uncritical, and, I might say, almost insane admiration for the vulgar and worthless plays of Mr. O'Casey.[79]

This statement came as a shock to the other members of the Abbey Directorate. A meeting was called, at which W. B. Yeats, W. Starkie, Dr Richard Hayes and the poet F. R. Higgins (Ernest Blythe was absent from the meeting but concurred with the decision taken by the Directors) issued a

---

[76] *Evening Herald* (Dublin), 13 Aug. 1935.

[77] *Irish Independent*, 13 Aug. 1935.

[78] Mr Macnamara told me that he objected to the play's production because he knew that it would hurt Catholic sentiments. My interview with Mr Macnamara in Dublin on 26 Sep. 1958.

[79] *Irish Independent*, 29 Aug. 1935.

K

statement blaming Macnamara for "an obvious breach of
confidence."[80]   Macnamara immediately resigned.

Though Yeats did not jump to O'Casey's defence as he had
done during *The Plough and the Star* riots, a few intelligent
people came forward when they saw the excess with which the
dramatist was being attacked. The strongest defence of O'Casey
was made by the famous actor Robert Speaight. He summed
up the campaign against *The Silver Tassie* in these words:

> The play is an outcry from a passionate and embittered mind.
> But it is much nearer to Christianity, because it is nearer to
> life, than the complacent criticisms levelled against it. The
> soul of the bourgeoisie has betrayed itself. This surely is the
> essence of the bourgeois mind—that it cannot look tragedy
> in the face; for O'Casey has seen into the heart of the horror
> of war, and wrenched out its dreadful secret; that the co-heirs
> with Christ destroy one another in the sight of the Son of Man.[81]

The attack is important for two reasons. First, it established
firmly the attitude of the Roman Catholic Church and the
Irish people towards Ireland's greatest dramatist; second, it
embittered and angered O'Casey and led him thereafter to
direct his talents to ridiculing the Church and its devoted
followers. In *The Silver Tassie* O'Casey had no intention of
having a stab at religion and if he did use Biblical phrases and
reverse their meaning, it was because he wanted the play to
be a kind of ritual. He could, of course, have written something of his own which conveyed the same meaning, but it
would not have been easy to achieve the force and the beauty
of the Bible.

What had O'Casey to say to the two major charges that
Catholic Ireland framed against him: that a travesty of the
Mass is to be found in the play, and that it is full of indecent
language? He has given his answer in "A Stand on *The Silver
Tassie*" which he sent to W. B. Yeats with a covering letter on
23 Nov. 1935:

> You may remember when I had the pleasure of being with you
> in your home in Terenure, I suggested that I should send you a
> few words on the controversy about *The Silver Tassie*, which

---

[80] *Evening Herald* (Dublin), 3 Sep. 1935.
[81] Quoted in *Rose and Crown*, p. 58.

was to include some passages from the Bible giving expression to "indecent" words. I enclose with this note what I have written, and you will see that even the Lord God of Israel Himself has said a mouthful!

You can do as you wish with the article, print it whole or in parts, or ignore it altogether. It might be useful if you were again to put on the play.[82]

To the best of my knowledge Yeats did not get it published. He was old and in poor health and the Abbey was no longer the passion of his life as it had been till the nineteen-twenties. A more important reason might be that nearly two and a half months had passed since the play's performance, and the controversy in the Irish papers had died down, or had taken other directions.[83] He was never sufficiently interested in *The Silver Tassie* to fight for it, he himself had never considered it a good play, and he may have thought it best to let sleeping dogs lie. As O'Casey's "A Stand on *The Silver Tassie*" is with Mrs Yeats and not yet published, and as it is absolutely necessary that the reader should acquaint himself with O'Casey's defence of his play, I quote the whole article here. It is mainly a reply to the attack on him by the Abbey Director, Brinsley Sheridan Macnamara, Father Gaffney, the Catholic dramatist, and Mr J. Murphy, Professor of Religion at Galway.

The most serious objection alleged against *The Silver Tassie* is that a travesty of the Mass is to be found in some nook or cranny of the play. Mr. Macnamara has been particularly vocal about it, but, like Father Gaffney, he hasn't told anybody where the travesty is to be found. Is it to be found in the first, second, third, or fourth act of the play? And will Father Gaffney or Mr. Macnamara tell us what part or passage in the play forms the travesty of the Sacred Office? There is no travesty of the Mass in the second act of the play. As far as I know, and I ought to know, there is no travesty of the Mass, stated clearly or furtively implied, from one end of the

---

[82] Letter in Mrs W. B. Yeats's possession.

[83] Louis J. Walsh attacked *The Silver Tassie* in *The Irish Rosary* of Sep. 1935, under the heading "The Defiance of the Abbey." The attack was repeated in the October number, under the title "A Catholic Theatre for Dublin," Mr Walsh arguing that such a theatre would restore Catholic principles. This question was taken up by Gabriel Fallon in the November number and the cry against O'Casey was soon lost in the demand for a Catholic theatre.

play to the other.   The murmuring or singing of part of the
Service in the second act was put in by me to imply the sacred
peace of the Office compared with the horrible cruelty and
stupidity of war, and constitutes the only irreverence in the play
as touching the Sacred Office of the Mass.   If the portrayal of
the infinite peace and mercy implied in the Sacrifice constitutes
an irreverence to the Catholic Faith as conceived by Father
Gaffney and Mr. Macnamara, then it is an irreverence and
it will remain an irreverance; for I refuse to take my conception of the Catholic Faith from the conception held tight in the
minds of Father Gaffney and Mr. Macnamara, now, or in any
hour of the time to come.   Perhaps the travesty of the Mass
may, in the mind of Father Gaffney, be associated with the
words spoken by the crippled Harry Heegan in the last act
of the play.   They are these: "No, white wine, white, like the
stillness of the millions that have removed their clamours from
the crowd of life.   No, red wine; red, like the blood that was
shed for you and for many for the commission of sin."   Now
the last sentence is taken—with an alteration of one word—
from the Anglican Rubric of the Service of Holy Communion,
and so cannot be a travesty of the Mass.   The Eastern Rite of
the Mass is recognised by the Catholic Church, but the Anglican
Rite is not so recognised, and so the sentence cannot be an
insidious insult to the Mass.   Let us say here that, neither
directly nor indirectly, is the quotation meant to be a stab at
the Anglican Rite of Holy Communion.   The sentence was
introduced in an effort to convey a suitable symbol of the
anguished bitterness that the unhappy Harry might conceiv-
ably feel for what he thought to be the fell waste of the
war.

     Father Gaffney tells us that he "cannot give an adequate idea
of the play's deliberate indecency and its mean mocking
challenge to the Christian Faith."   What is the Christian
faith?   Isn't it to be found summarised in the creeds, the
Athanasian Creed, the Apostles' Creed, and that Creed that
particularly expresses the faith of the Catholics.   Now is there
one phrase in the play from the start to the finish that in
any way, directly or indirectly, challenges any part of the
Catholic Faith as expressed by the Creed of Pope Pius?   If
Father Gaffney had said that the play was a challenge to the
faithful rather than the Faith, he would have been nearer the
mark.   Let me suggest to Father Gaffney that the Faith is a
perpetual challenge to the faithful.

Father Gaffney says that "plain etiquette will not tolerate indecency or blasphemy on or off the stage." This is nonsense. He has his job cut out for him if he thinks plain etiquette will banish indecency or horror off the stage or out of life. There are many indecent things in life outside of sex, things more seriously indecent than the common language of the streets and the workshops. There are indecent things in politics, in home life, in business, even in religion, that we never or rarely hear a word about. Plain etiquette won't do very much to soften them down. The Seven Gifts of the Holy Ghost and the Twelve Fruits of the Holy Spirit have to do with mightier things than the paltry things he calls plain etiquette. If I were a Christian priest I should put more trust in the Sword of the Spirit than I would put in Father Gaffney's Etiquettical Catechism.

There were some who raved about a few naughty words in the play that were peculiar to the characters that spoke them. Some of them are to be found in the Bible, naked and unashamed. Turning to the Second Book of Kings, the Eighteenth Chapter and the Twenty-seventh Verse, we find this: "But Rab-Shakeh saith unto them, hath my master sent me to thy master, and to thee, to speak these words? Hath he not sent me to the men which sit on the wall, that they eat their own dung and drink their own piss with you?" We find this, almost word for word in the Gaelic of Bedell's Irish Bible. In the First of Samuel, Twenty-fifth Chapter, Twenty-second Verse: "So and more also do God to the enemies of David, if I leave off all that pertain to him by the morning light any that pisseth against a wall." And let all concerned have a squint at the Seventh and Tenth Verse of the Fourteenth Chapter of First Kings. Here is written, "Thus saith the Lord God of Israel, . . . I will bring evil upon the house of Jeroboam, and will cut off from Jeroboam him that pisseth against the wall." Each, of course, appearing in the Irish Bible as translated by Bishop Bedell. Hot and biting words indeed. What do the two chancellors of the spoken word think of them? But there is something more to come: in a play called *The Satin Slippers* [*sic*], written by a well-known Catholic, the words, bastards, son of a bitch, and arse, are flaunted in our faces. Worse still, these are translated from the French by a Catholic priest, the Reverend Fr. John O'Connor, and the book is published by a Catholic firm, Messrs Sheed and Ward. What have Father Gaffney, Mr. Brinsley Sheridan Macnamara, Red Handed

Cu Uladh, or the Doxological Professor of Galway, Mr. J. Murphy, got to say to me now, and what have I to say to them? I have only to say this:

What to such as they, anyhow, such a poet as I? Therefore leave my works,
And go lull yourself with what you can understand, and with piano tunes,
For I lull nobody, and you will never understand me.

The lines that O'Casey quotes in the first paragraph of the above article are said by Harry in Act IV of the play when Simon asks him if he would have "red wine or white?" Though only one word is altered, "commission" being substituted for "remission," the entire meaning of the phrase is changed. Thus O'Casey's plea that only one word has been altered is not much of an answer, but then the criticism that a travesty of the Mass has been made is not much of a question. O'Casey attempted here, and very successfully, to give us a picture of what the crippled Harry suffers.

Similar parodies are even more noticeable in the opening lines of the second act where the Croucher is chanting his blasphemies. The effect is heightened by the voices heard from the monastery, singing the blessings of the Lord, in between the Croucher's cry of despair. The passages are taken from the Book of Ezekiel and their meanings reversed. They are the following:

And the hand of the Lord was upon me, and carried me out in the spirit of the Lord, and set me down in the midst of a valley
And I looked and saw a great multitude that stood upon their feet, an exceeding great army.
And he said unto me, Son of man, can this exceeding great army become a valley of dry bones?[84]

And I answered, O Lord God, thou knowest. And he said, prophesy and say unto the wind, come from the four winds a breath and breathe upon these living that they may die.[85]

---

[84] *The Silver Tassie*, Act II, p. 36. Reversal of Ezekiel, xxxvii: 1-3.
[85] *Op. cit.* Reversal of Ezekiel, xxxvii: 9.

And I prophesied, and the breath came out of them, and the sinews came away from them, and behold a shaking, and their bones fell asunder, bone from his bone, and they died, and the exceeding great army became a valley of dry bones.[86]

O'Casey's parodies in themselves do not constitute a travesty of religion, but the singing of a part of the Service between the Croucher's intonations does make a mockery of worship; the more so as the Croucher's prophecy is nearer credibility and more likely to be granted by God than the prayer of the faithful.

O'Casey's purpose in writing *The Silver Tassie* was to awaken in the minds of men a feeling against the horror and indecency of war. To the London audiences he succeeded in conveying his passionate hatred of warfare, but to his own people and in his own country he failed to make himself understood. They ignored his aim and attacked him for the means that he had employed to convey his message. In his attempt to teach, he learnt that his cry against war was a lone and forsaken one; that before wars could be done away with, the world must free itself from superstition and blind reverence; that above all it must learn to face the truth, however bitter that truth might be.

We may conclude our study of *The Silver Tassie* by briefly observing some of the respects in which the play is a departure from his previous ones. This is necessary, for it stands as a transitional play between the Abbey plays and the one that follows. The first thing that strikes our attention is that the scenes are no longer all laid in Dublin, and that nearly half the characters are not Irish. Though the major characters are of proletarian background, no emphasis is laid on depicting slum life. Irish national struggles and politics are ignored; war, that had so far constituted only a background, now becomes the leading motif. In matters of technique the departure is even greater. In addition to the juxtaposition of tragedy and comedy, which is not very expertly handled, O'Casey has juxtaposed acts written in very different manners. The symbolic second act is indeed one of the finest things that O'Casey has written and is the very soul of the play, but how far it

---

[86] *The Silver Tassie*, Act II, pp. 36-7. Reversal of Ezekiel, xxxvii: 8, 10.

combines successfully with the diametrically opposed form of dramatic expression of the other acts is hard to say. However this may be, O'Casey, here, was experimenting with the possibilities of symbolic drama; and having satisfied himself, he proceeded to write a totally expressionistic play, *Within the Gates*.

V

The Exile Plays : I

What exile from his country ever escaped from himself.

HORACE

*T*HE SILVER TASSIE, as we have seen, was conceived in Dublin though written in London. For all its departures with regard to technique and setting, it was written to suit the Abbey stage. But *Within the Gates* owed nothing to Dublin nor was it meant for the Abbey Theatre, which could hardly have accommodated the play's action. Here there is a deliberate attempt on the dramatist's part to break away from anything that is Irish. The play is set in Hyde Park and the stage is packed with characters, but there is not a single Irishman on the scene: a strange omission, for in real life a large number of the soap-box speakers are either Irish or of Irish descent. Yet there is much that is Irish about the play. Though most of the characters speak cockney, "the cadences of dialogue are the cadences of Irish speech that were brought into the theatre by Synge and Mr. Yeats."[1] The Dreamer has something in common with Donal Davoren and more with O'Casey himself; the Young Woman's frustration and desire to "die game" are more Irish than English, and finally the Bishop and his sister—though they may frequent Hyde Park as often as they like—would have found themselves more at home in Dublin's St Stephen's Green or Phoenix Park. O'Casey's English characters are never really English as Shaw's are. At the best they are naturalised Englishmen who betray their Irish descent or mannerisms at one moment or another of their lives.

Not long after O'Casey's arrival in London a visit to Hyde

---

[1] Derek Verschoyle, *Spectator*, CLII, 16 Feb. 1934.

Park suggested to him a dramatic source yet untapped. He told Beverley Nichols:

> Yesterday . . . was the happiest day I've spent since I came to England. It was in Hyde Park that I spent it, and I stood there listening to the speakers. I felt almost drunk at the end of it—the characters up there are so rich in comedy.
>
> *What are your dramatists doing to neglect Hyde Park?* . . . Why, young man, it's the finest field of character you'll ever know. The people I saw there last night. You listen. . . . There was a man with a bald head, and little glistening eyes, who spoke of Jesus. There was the light of madness in his eyes, and as I watched him I saw right deep into him, and I knew that he would have killed anybody who refused to be led to Jesus—killed him and thanked his God for the opportunity. . . . There was every sort of religious mania, dietetic mania, political mania, personal mania. And there it all goes on, night after night, under the trees. But nobody seems to notice it. None of those characters is ever put on to the stage. Why? Tell me why?[2]

O'Casey decided to weave a play round the flotsam of Hyde Park. He had first thought of doing it as a film script and calling it *The Green Gates*, but he soon discovered that the film magnates were more interested in things that didn't happen in Saragossa and Honolulu than in what happened under their noses.[3] So he turned the idea for a film into an idea for a play. Here too he was beset with difficulties. If he was to bring contemporary London on to the stage with "its life, its colour, its pathos, its pattern; its meaning to the rest of England,"[4] he would have to put many varied characters into the play; and the more he put in, the less chance it had of a good production in England. What was he to do? Intellectual and creative honesty, coupled with a disregard for the general public's reactions to his plays, were the hall-marks of his character. He followed his own judgment. The play was published in 1933 and had its first performance at the Royalty Theatre, London, on 7 Feb. 1934. Financially it was a failure. O'Casey was left with less than £20 to call his own after various expenses

---

[2] B. Nichols, *Are They the Same at Home?*, pp. 273-4.

[3] "No Flowers for Films," *The Green Crow*, pp. 174-5. The article first appeared in *The Leader Magazine*, 19 Feb. 1949.

[4] *Op. cit.*, p. 174.

had been paid. Later the play had a run of 101 nights at the National Theatre, New York.

The play does not submit to a summary in terms of plot. At its barest it is a picture of contemporary London; in its wider symbolic significance it is a "microcosm of human life,"[5] a "microcosm of modern civilization,"[6] a "dramatization of the Waste Land of the post-war world."[7] It is multi-directional. Themes social, political and religious interlace into a pattern and converge into "a pervasive conflict between the false life that has death's canker in it and the springing life—fierce, passionate, inevitable, beyond reason—which survives the winter of man's corruption."[8]

The action of the play centres round the Dreamer, the Bishop, the Young Woman, Jannice, and her mother the Old Woman. But to say that the play is principally concerned with these four characters is to say very little, for the theme of the play is life itself—life consisting of religion, politics, scientific thought, lust, joy, despair, clashing against each other in a heedless frenzy and then moving apart; the good alone mingling with nature, which continues its seasonal change uninterrupted.

Within the Gates is a symbolic drama both in setting and in characterisation. Symbolism was never wholly absent in O'Casey's plays: he was interested in it from the very beginning of his dramatic career. In *The Shadow of a Gunman* the bag left by Maguire remains on the stage from the beginning, increasing in significance as a symbolic answer to Davoren's question to himself: "And what danger can there be in being the shadow of a gunman?"[9] The one-act fantasy *Cathleen Listens In* was a wholly symbolic play. In *Juno and the Paycock* the red votive light flickers, burns brightly and finally goes out before Johnny is shot. In *The Plough and the Stars* the dark figure of the Speaker silhouetted against the window and his revolutionary words can be symbolically interpreted. We have already discussed the second act of *The Silver Tassie*. But not till *Within the Gates* does O'Casey exploit symbolism to its maximum capacity.

[5] Desmond MacCarthy, *Drama*, p. 351.
[6] Ernest Reynolds, *Modern English Drama*, p. 155.
[7] Florence Codman, *The Nation*, cxxxviii, 25 Apr. 1934.
[8] *The Times* (London), 28 Nov. 1933.
[9] *The Shadow of a Gunman*, Act I, p. 124.

That he was out to liberate the creative spirit by breaking the shackles of naturalism is obvious from his statement on the play on offering it to the public: "I am out to destroy the accepted naturalistic presentation of character; to get back to the poetic significance of drama."[10] That O'Casey did get back to the poetic significance of drama cannot be questioned, but whether he was able to free himself wholly from the dictates of naturalism is rather doubtful. Though symbolism governs the main features of the play there are broad sweeps into naturalism and some of the dialogues, especially between the Bishop and the Old Woman, are on the naturalistic plane rather than the symbolic. The greater part of the glow and fire of O'Casey's poetry is to be found in the outbursts of Jannice and her mother, the Old Woman; and it is these two and not the Dreamer who voice the social criticism of the play.

Since the play is multi-directional and the theme is human life in its different aspects, O'Casey avoided descriptive titles such as "Tragedy" or "Tragi-comedy" and simply called it "A Play of Four scenes in a London Park."[11] To bring a sense of order and to increase the symbolic meaning, he has knit the loose themes and rambling dialogues into a design of Morning, Afternoon, Evening and Night. These in their turn are made to fuse with the seasonal changes which are shown by changing the colours of flowers and trees. The dominant features of a morning on a spring day are "a clear, light-blue sky," trees dotted with green, yellow and red buds; the colours for a summer noon are mainly "golden glows, tinged with a gentle red"; the sky of an autumn evening is "a deep rich crimson," faintly touched with golden yellow; and finally the sky on a winter night is a "deep black," tinged with rich violet and purple hues.

As far as possible everything in the play is stylised. "An artistic serenity rules all the minor conflicts, ordering and composing various essences into one settled design. This moves with a noble ritualistic dignity, whether pagan as in the festivity symbolism of the first chorus and the coloured maypole, or

[10] *The New York Times*, 26 Mar. 1934. For O'Casey's attack on Naturalism see: "Green Goddess of Realism," *The Flying Wasp*, pp. 111-127; and "O'Casey's Lively Credo," *The New York Times* (international edn.), 10 Nov. 1958.
[11] 1933 edition.

Christian in the dominating Cross of the Bishop."[12]   There is
significance implicit in chosen moments of sunshine and bird-
song: human action, wherever symbolic of the author's design,
is related to the seasonal moods.   The four seasons correspond
to the four stages of human life: childhood, manhood, old age
and death.

The play is as musical as it is colourful.   O'Casey has
successfully used the technique of musical comedy to express
philosophic tragedy.   Human life and struggle in its entirety is
symbolised in the songs, choruses and antiphonal chantings.
From this standpoint the key to the first scene is in the opening
chorus of boys and girls representing nature:

> Our mother the Earth is a maiden again, young, fair,
>   and a maiden again.
> Our mother the Earth is a maiden again, she's young,
>   fair, and a maiden again.[13]

This feeling of joy is sustained in the song of the Gardener, in
which the crowd of couples join in:

> A fig for th' blossoms th' biggest vase can hold,
> The flow'rs that face the world shy, the ones that face
>   it bold.[14]

The tragedy of the Young Woman has no definite place in the
scheme so far, and the distant sombre drumbeat of the Down-
and-Outs is the shadow of death—a shadow only, lurking in
the distance.

The keynote to the second scene is in the chorus sung by the
people:

> Ye who are haggard and giddy with care, busy counting your
>   profit and losses, . . .
>
> Bellow good-bye to the buggerin' lot'n come out
> To bow down the head 'n bend down the knee to the bee, the
>   bird, 'n the blossom,
> Bann'ring the breast of the earth with a wonderful beauty![15]

Here is Youth's idealistic affirmation to meet the onslaught of
a materialistic civilisation and to defend its childhood heritage.
That it must fail in the end is brought out by the chant of the

---

[12] Unpublished study of *Within the Gates* by Prof. G. Wilson Knight.
[13] *Within the Gates*, Sc. I, pp. 118.
[14] *Op. cit.*, p. 136.   [15] *Op. cit.*, Sc. II, p. 149.

Down-and-Outs which can be heard in the near distance. The problem of sex is prominently introduced, the tragedy of the Young Woman takes root, and the means offered for escape seem to be through love and a zest for life as apprised in the Dreamer's song "Jannice."

The song in the third scene sung by the Man wearing a Straw Hat

> London Bridge is falling down, falling down, falling down,
> London Bridge is falling down, my fair lady[16]

suggests the fall of all that is good and beautiful in life. The Young Woman's fierce reply, "Let it fall to pieces then," is acceptance of the inevitable end. She makes a feeble attempt to recover the past by singing softly the Dreamer's song "Jannice," but soon becomes breathless. Her attempts to be merry and her song to the tune of "Little Brown Jug" are stifled and frozen by the chanting of the Down-and-Outs who make their first appearance:

> We challenge life no more, no more, with our dead faith,
>   and our dead hope;
> We carry furl'd the fainting flag of a dead hope and a dead
>   faith.
> Day sings no song, neither is there room for rest beside
>   night in her sleeping;
> We've but a sigh for a song, and a deep sigh for a
>   drum-beat.[17]

The last song of the scene is the hymn "There were Ninety and Nine." The stray sheep is the Young Woman who has forsaken the "tender Shepherd's care" for the tender care of the Dreamer, or rather the vision of the future for the reality of the present.

Death is the theme of the songs in the last scene; from the Old Woman's song to her "Irish Dragoon" to the final chant of the Down-and-Outs. The Dreamer's vigorous song at the end of the play is both a challenge and a concession:

> Way for the strong and the swift and the fearless:
> Life that is stirr'd with the fear of its life, let it die;
> Let it sink down, let it die, and pass from our vision for ever.[18]

The song of the Dreamer sums up O'Casey's philosophy.

16 *Within the Gates*, Sc. II, p. 181.   17 *Op. cit.*, p. 196.
18 *Op. cit.*, Sc. IV, p. 230.

The Drum-beat and Chant of the Down-and-Outs is the principal motif of this work. O'Casey introduces them with a gripping technique: they are first heard far off, then a little nearer, then silhouetted—a part of their chanting heard to the monotonous tap of the drum-beat—and finally they take up the stage. The Down-and-Outs are symbolic of the death-force, the absolute Evil that can only be resisted through a desire for life. Its victims are, as O'Casey points out, the living dead. It is the scavenger which sweeps away the scum of life.

Within the Gates is an extremely controversial play and the impression left varies considerably with each reader. James Agate, who had called O'Casey's Abbey plays the greatest in the English theatre since the days of the Elizabethans, called this play "pretentious rubbish."[19] Joseph Wood Krutch called it "Mr. O'Casey's Charade,"[20] and J. M. Brown wrote: "Those who are happiest and most impressed in the presence of what they cannot understand will undoubtedly put up with its pretentiousness and salute it as the masterpiece it most assuredly is not."[21] On the other hand, Professor Wilson Knight thinks it is O'Casey's greatest and most comprehensive play,[22] and Horace Reynolds, after admitting its apparent faults, says: "it is a wonderful play, Elizabethan in its youthfulness, intensity, language, and, to some extent, its structure."[23]

The hostility of certain critics has perhaps been due to their inability to appreciate the symbolic meaning of the play. The play has been attacked for being anti-moral and anti-Christian; also for the cheap irony of making the Bishop the father of the Young Woman. Nothing could be further from the truth. *Within the Gates* is the most Christian of O'Casey's plays and the one that shows how religious he is. The play is not written to reprove religion, but to attack those superficial and indurate ostentations which are often displayed as true religion.

Take the structure of the play. In its patterning it closely follows the Breviary and the Missal. The four seasons, which are further reduced to the component parts of a single day— Morning, Noon, Evening and Night—are parallel at the

---

[19] James Agate, *First Nights*, p. 271.
[20] J. W. Krutch, *The Nation*, cxxxix, 7 Nov. 1934.
[21] J. M. Brown, *Two on the Aisle*, pp. 129-30.
[22] In conversation.
[23] H. Reynolds, *Saturday Review of Literature*, x, 3 Mar. 1934.

religious level to the Canonical Hours of the Breviary. The Spring and Summer choruses are a variation on the psalms of the morning hours, Matins and Lauds. The Winter scene, set in violet, purple and black, symbolises the traditional liturgical colours for penitence and death.

The play, like Christianity, concerns itself with human life. The action takes place at the foot of a war memorial, a statue of a soldier—"the head bent on the breast, skeleton-like hands leaning on the butt-end of a rifle."[24] On the rational plane the statue is an effective reminder of human folly. On the religious plane it connotes Christ crucified a second time; helpless, and full of shame and sorrow at what Man and Church have made of God.

The emphasis laid on Biblical phraseology is strong. In most cases the meaning is reversed, as in *The Silver Tassie*. These parodies are by no means a travesty of religion: they are introduced to convey the agonising bitterness of some of the characters. A splendid example of this is in the Young Woman's defiant reply to the Bishop when he asks her what will she do when night comes and youth has departed:

> When youth has gone, when night has fallen, and when the heart is lonely, I will stand and stare steady at a God who has filled the wealthy with good things and has sent the poor empty away.[25]

This is an adaptation from the Magnificat. Again her outburst, mocking people reading crime news—

> Let us pray! Oh, Lucifer, Lucifer, who has caused all newspapers to be written for our learning—stars of the morning and stars of the evening—grant we may so read them that we may always find a punch in them, hot stuff in them, and sound tips in them; so that, outwardly in our bodies and inwardly in our souls, we may get closer and closer to thee![26]

parodies two Collects in the Missal. Such instances abound and feature even more prominently in his next play, *The Star Turns Red*.

To appreciate the play and its religious significance best, we must turn to the four principal characters: the Dreamer,

[24] *Within the Gates*, Sc. I, p. 117.   [25] *Op. cit.*, Sc. III, p. 197.
[26] *Op. cit.*, p. 182.

the Bishop, the Young Woman and the Old Woman. The Dreamer and the Bishop hold views which appear to be diametrically opposed. O'Casey brings this out by his masterly juxtaposition of pagan feeling and Christian thoughts; consistently hinting that between these two poles the gulf is not so wide as official religion supposes. To achieve this, he makes both the Dreamer and the Bishop noble, honest and dignified. Both believe in God but differ in their manner of approaching Him. The Dreamer's approach to God is through a "song" and a "dance," the Bishop's approach through "sigh" and "repentance." As these two characters are bound to clash, he seldom brings them together, but allows their beliefs to have their effect on the mind and actions of the Young Woman. She is used as a highly sensitive instrument to weigh the two points of view, and although throughout the play the scales appear to be weighted on the side of the Dreamer, in the end they are balanced.

That the Dreamer is O'Casey's ideal character is plain from his explanation of the symbols included in the programme of the play when it was performed at the National Theatre, New York:

> *The Dreamer*, symbol of a noble restlessness and discontent; of the stir in life that brings to birth new things and greater things than those that were before; of the power realizing that the urge of life is above the level of conventional morality; of ruthlessness to get near to the things that matter, and sanctify them with intelligence, energy, gracefulness and song; of rebellion against stupidity; and of the rising intelligence in man that will no longer stand nor venerate, nor shelter those whom poverty of spirit has emptied of all that is worth while in life.[27]

Not only is this explanation abstruse, but it expresses more than any one symbol can hold. Moreover, the Dreamer does not live up to what he is meant to symbolise. His question to the two Chair Attendants: "When are you going to die?" or his prayer: "Kill off the withered mind, the violently-stupid, O Lord. . . ."[28] can hardly be looked upon as coming from a

---

[27] Quoted in Jules Koslow, *The Green and the Red*, p. 70.
[28] *Within the Gates*, Sc. I, pp. 120, 132.

L

"rising intelligence." His pocketing a pound note out of the three that the Bishop had left for the Young Woman, and then offering this very pound to her for a gay time is far from commendable. He attaches himself to the Young Woman because she is beautiful and has a zest for life. But he suggests no means by which she could make a living, and at his best is able to offer her only "another month of gay and crowded life."[29] His advice to her to "transmute vague years of life into a glowing hour of love"[30] sounds all very good, except that the vague years still remain vague years.

I am not attacking the Dreamer: he remains an admirable character, but he does not symbolise all that the dramatist demands of him. He stands only for "the urge of life." This means freedom from false fears and superstitions; a desire to live intensely and wrench out of life every joy; and, when death approaches, to "dance to His glory, and come before His presence with a song!"[31] God through a dance or a song is the very quintessence of the play, and the whole idea is to be found in the poem of Ernest Toller:

> The miracle is here!
> The miracle!
> The miracle!
> Dance, my swelling breast,
> Dance, my weary imprisoned eyes,
> Dance! Dance!
> Only in dance do you break your fetters,
> Only in dance do you shout with the stars,
> Only in dance comes the quiet of God.
> Dance! Dance!
> In dance is dreamed the holy song of the world.[32]

This is O'Casey's Christianity: pagan not heathen, human not divine; and for all its lapses into the sensuous, many people might regard it as nearer to Christ than that of our Churches.

The Bishop is the protagonist and the only character in the play that sufficiently develops, though O'Casey refers to him as "simply a symbol."[33] He is not a caricature or an

---

[29] *Within the Gates*, Sc. III, p. 200.   [30] *Op. cit.*, Sc. II, p. 170.
[31] *Op. cit.*, Sc. IV, p. 228.
[32] E. Toller, *The Swallow Book*, tr. Ashley Dukes, p. 10.
[33] *Flying Wasp*, p. 49.

object of contempt.　O'Casey, replying to Agate's criticism, said:

> The Bishop was never contemplated by me as either oily or as
> a scoundrel.　He is good-natured, well-intentioned, religious,
> and sincere; but he is timid, mistaking good-nature for the
> fire of the Holy Ghost, and life has passed him by.[34]

Too much has been made of the fact that the Young Woman is the illegitimate daughter of the Bishop.　That the Bishop in his student days should have fallen for a woman who "would make a man long for something to 'appen" is not astonishing but natural.　O'Casey is not attacking the Bishop.　If he is attacking anything it is the celibacy that is involved in a Catholic ministry: a celibacy which did not exist in the first three centuries when the Church was nearest to its Master. Celibacy may lead men to glorify divine love but it makes the clergy extremely suspicious of sexual love.　"O'Casey's satire is not directed against Christianity but against a Church which has failed in the Herculean task of relating Christianity to sexual energies."[35]　The Bishop's failure to acknowledge publicly that he has fathered the Young Woman is, at its worst, timidity rather than wickedness.　And, short of admitting that, he does everything in his power and runs considerable risks to help her.　He turns down her request that he should ask her employer to reinstate her in her job, because this is not a bishop's function, and also because his religious authority would be spurned by an irreligious man.　He is equally right in refusing money to the two Chair Attendants who plead in the name of the Church, but are far removed from it.　His apologetic suggestion to the Young Woman that she should spend a couple of years in a pious Sisterhood is harsh but sound advice. The irony lies in this: the Bishop does not know that her present plight and her distrust of religion are the result of such an institution, where "the terrors an' dangers of hell became the child's chief enjoyment!"[36]

The Bishop's kindness, generosity, self-sacrifice and humanity are brought out in every scene of the play.　He is a

[34] *Flying Wasp*, pp. 48-9.
[35] Unpublished study of *Within the Gates* by Prof. G. Wilson Knight.
[36] *Within the Gates*, Sc. I, p. 123.

tragic figure, insulted by every character in the play but never
directly by the Dreamer, except perhaps in the last scene when
the Dreamer tells the Young Woman in his presence:

> Turn your back swift on the poor, purple-button'd deadman,
> whose name is absent from the book of life.[37]

The remark is most unfair and all our sympathies go to the
Bishop.   Often the Bishop scores over the Dreamer in an
argument.   Here is a fine instance:

> DREAMER [*to the Bishop*]:   Not God, but a poet speaking of
>   Spring, sir.   Render to God the things that are God's and
>   to the poet the things that are his.
> BISHOP [*to the Dreamer—smilingly*]:   God is in all, and God is
>   all things, sir.[38]

Note the respect that these two characters have for one another.
Also note how just O'Casey is in that he gives each character a
fair part to play.   The mere fact that he aligns himself with the
Dreamer does not prevent him from seeing the Bishop's point
of view, nor does it hinder him from pointing out the Dreamer's
faults.

Though the Bishop differs from the Dreamer, he is not the
chief adversary to the Dreamer's concept of life.   The opponent
is the crowd with its mean, sickening, deadened soul.   The
Dreamer's regard for the Bishop is brought out in the very
opening of the play when he reprimands the two Chair
Attendants for "fawning on the bishop and on every good
coat that sits down on a chair."[39]   The Bishop shares with the
Dreamer his love and enthusiasm for the coming of spring, the
budding of flowers, and the singing of birds.   His words that
the birds are "Facing out life with a song"[40] could have well
been said by the Dreamer.   His admiration of the Young
Woman's pretty face and shapely legs, which stir in him an
"old interest," are to his credit.

Because of his attempt to get closer to the common people,
and in his silent forbearance, the Bishop at times appears
nobler than the Dreamer.   He suffers indignity, humiliation,
rebuffs, but never for a moment does he give up the struggle to

---

[37] *Within the Gates*, Sc. IV, p. 228.   [38] *Op. cit.*, Sc. I, p. 128.
[39] *Op. cit.*, p. 121.   [40] *Op. cit.*, p. 130.

bring the Church nearer to the masses. "Get them to talk
with us; laugh and joke with us; and then we can expect them
to pray with us,"[41] he remarks to his sister. He tells the two
Chair Attendants that "the Church isn't altogether so solemn an
institution as many people seem to think—she can laugh, sing,
and skip—at a suitable time."[42] If his efforts come to naught,
one of the reasons is that the layman suspects some hidden
motive in every move on the part of the clergy. This is brought
out in Scene IV, where even the religious fanatic—Man wearing
Trilby—questions the Bishop's intention in running after the
Young Woman:

> 'Ere 'e is agine! Like 'Amlet's ghost. Wot interest 'as 'e in
> the girl, I wunner?[43]

If the Bishop fails in his purpose he is not wholly to be blamed.
His goodness and good intentions are revealed in the numerous
assertions that he makes throughout the play. Here are a few
of them, isolated from their context:

> In this life, we have to forgive many things.[44]

> You have forgotten God for a few moments, but He sends
> you His help in time of trouble; and, through me, unworthy
> messenger, a share of His sympathy and love.[45]

> My child, the sinner is always nearer to God than the sinner
> dares to think.[46]

> A human soul is not a trivial thing.[47]

> Not hers, but our souls, I'm afraid, are the trivial things in the
> sight of God, and in the minds of brave men. (*Fiercely*) But
> mine's going to be trivial no longer! I go to seek her, and
> don't follow me.[48]

> Being too sensible has been my curse all along. By trying to
> save my honoured soul, I am losing it.[49]

But the most significant utterance is at the climax of the play
when the Young Woman spurns his offer of peace for a reckless

---

[41] *Within the Gates*, Sc. I, p. 133. [42] *Op. cit.*, Sc. II, p. 156.
[43] *Op. cit.*, Sc. IV, p. 204. [44] *Op. cit.*, Sc. II, p. 153.
[45] *Op. cit.*, Sc. III, pp. 187-8. [46] *Op. cit.*, p. 190.
[47] *Op. cit.*, Sc. IV, p. 205. [48] *Ibid.*
[49] *Op. cit.*, p. 206.

and defiant dance with the Dreamer, as the Down-and-Outs close in on them from all sides. The Bishop prays:

> O Lord, who taketh pleasure in Thy people, let this dance be unto Thee as a merry prayer offered by an innocent and excited child![50]

Here indeed is the victory of the Dreamer over the Bishop, but still more it is the victory of the Bishop over himself. By putting these words into the mouth of the Bishop, and also, "she died making the sign of the cross,"[51] O'Casey brings the blessing of the Christian Church on his unrepentant Young Woman. The end might also suggest that it is not the Young Woman who has strayed away from the flock, but the Christian Church that has cut itself off from Christ. The lost sheep is the Church which has found its way to God by both accepting and blessing the Young Woman for coming before His presence with a song.

This is but one way of looking at it. The play can be interpreted as O'Casey's attempt to relate the physical union between man and woman to Christianity. Unlike Huxley, he does not hold sexual union to be an impurity from which we must free ourselves in our search for God. To O'Casey sexual love is an experience that ought to be rejuvenated by the Church. He is one with V. V. Rozonov, Nicolas Berdyaev and others in asking for a vigorous sex-life and exposing the hypocrisy of the Church in matters of sex. This conflict between the sex instinct and Christianity may be traced in O'Casey faintly even from the first, but it features recurrently in his later plays.

The Young Woman is used as a highly sensitive instrument to weigh and react to the opinions expressed by the Dreamer and the Bishop. The horrors of Hell implanted on her mind by the nuns in a Church institution, followed later by the drunken outbursts of her mother who looks upon her as a child of sin, have landed her on the street. The urge for life and mother-hood draws her towards the Dreamer, the fear of Hell and the need for salvation pull her towards the Bishop. She is closer to the Dreamer than to the Bishop, but on the whole remains rootless. Her cry: "I'll go, go game, and I'll die dancing,"[52] is

---

[50] *Within the Gates*, Sc. IV, p. 229.   [51] *Op. cit.*, p. 231.
[52] *Op. cit.*, p. 228.

not sufficient consolation for her as it lacks conviction; and she finally seeks the Bishop's blessing: "Guide the hand you hold into making the sign of the cross, that I may whisper my trust in the golden mercy of God!"[53]   The last utterance of the Dreamer, as the curtain comes down on the final scene, indicates the dramatist's own feelings: "You fought the good fight, Jannice; and you kept the faith."[54]   This faith is an integral part of O'Casey's life; its absence is the root of all tragedy.

O'Casey's explanation of the symbol of the Old Woman as "one of those who stand still, think the little world round was born to serve them, and that when they die, life dies too"[55] is no explanation at all.   She is unpleasant to the eye: "pale and haggard, and vicious lines harden the look of her mouth."[56] Still she commands a large share of our sympathy for, like her daughter, she is the innocent victim of forces she cannot comprehend.   A demoniac, rampageous woman, she is constantly delirious with drink; and it is in her utterances rather than those of the Dreamer that we have the real fire of O'Casey's poetry.   She tells the Bishop the story of her seduction:

> Your voice has a strange echo in it.   Behind that [the Bishop's] wizened face is hidden a look of the first young man who conquered me on a Sunday night, after the ora pro nobis people had pulled down their blinds and were slinking into sleep.   There under a yellow moon, among the shadows by a grove of birch trees, on a bed of flattened bluebells, one of the prettiest fillies that ever wore a skirt was jockeyed into sin, and out of the rapture and the risk came this girl who dares to fancy men more than she does her own mother.[57]

Both the Old Woman and her daughter fear religion: the dread of Hell has taken the place of the love of God, and therefore both perish.   A similar fate overtakes the two Evangelists who are constantly haunted by the fear of death and judgment. The moral seems to be, using the Dreamer's words, that "courage in the hearts of men and women is what God needs

---

[53] *Within the Gates*, Sc. IV, p. 230.
[54] *Op. cit.*, p. 231.
[55] Quoted in Jules Koslow, *The Green and the Red*, p. 71.
[56] *Within the Gates*, Sc. II, p. 164.
[57] *Op. cit.*, pp. 165-6.

most."[58]   In other words we must free ourselves from false fears and live bravely.   To do this we must forgive our own sins, for the greatest sin in the eyes of God is—the fear of God.

The numerous other characters in the play need no special mention.   Individually they sum up the different types of men with their different outlooks, thoughts and arguments; as a body they symbolise the vast stream of human life flowing on, unmindful of seasonal changes and personal tragedies.   Mighty and foolish arguments are shown, taking the reader nowhere and leaving the disputants none the wiser.   In this panorama of opposite views, O'Casey rarely takes sides, but ridicules all demonstrations of religious and atheistic fanaticism.   He is, however, more tolerant towards the Atheist—who is a friend of the Dreamer—than towards any other disputant.   The reason is to be found in O'Casey's explanation of what the Atheist symbolises: one "of those who, trying to get rid of God, plant Him more firmly on His throne."[59]   The Atheist, unknowingly, is doing service to God, and O'Casey's leniency towards him reveals his love of God.   The real atheist in the play is the Man with the Stick, and he is the character that is held up to maximum ridicule.

These characters provide plenty of amusement on the stage.   They are all real people picked up straight from Hyde park,[60] where they assemble every evening to probe into the problem of the Almighty.   As they talk or sit down to read newspapers showing absurd headlines of "Murder," "Rape," and "Suicide," they come nearer to a "Londoner's typical experience than anything found in a theatre."[61]   It is O'Casey's remarkable feat to have brought these characters on to the stage, just as they are to be found in life, and to have given them a symbolic significance without destroying their respective individuality.

The play has its faults.   Some may agree with Stark Young that "its final sum, taken seriously, is likely to be adolescent,"[62] or with Granville Barker that a writer who has not the impartial

---

[58] *Within the Gates*, Sc. IV, pp. 229-30.
[59] Quoted in Jules Koslow, *The Green and the Red*, p. 70.
[60] My interview with Mr O'Casey on 6 Apr. 1959.
[61] Unpublished study of *Within the Gates* by Prof. G. Wilson Knight.
[62] S. Young, *The New Republic*, LXXX, 7 Nov. 1934.

magnanimity of the gods should not use characters as "the counters and symbols by which to illustrate some moral plan."[63] Others may rightly feel what Professor Wilson Knight alone observes, that if the play lacks anything, it lacks intensity: "the resolution and catharsis is not wrenched out, crushed like wine, from the tragic action itself."[64] To these may be added other charges such as violence of phrase, fragments of hysteria, use of the music and rhythm of words rather than their meanings to create effect, and so on.

Still, the play remains a very rare thing in our theatre: a morality play that is also a work of art. There is nothing weak or feeble about it. In O'Casey's own words, it is a "cry for courage, decency, and vitality in life."[65] It is not an attack on religion but on the organised Church that has cut itself off from the teachings of Christ. O'Casey exposes the hypocrisy, fear and false compromises of the Church by attacking it at its most vulnerable spot: its failure to relate Christianity to sexual urges. The failings of the Church are not entirely brought out in the shortcomings of the Bishop, as commonly supposed, but in the inadequacy of the Salvationists, the Evangelists and even society at large, which worships God from fear—not from love.

After *Within the Gates* there was a long hiatus in O'Casey's dramatic career. It was not till 1940 that his next two full-length plays, *The Star Turns Red* and *Purple Dust* appeared. In the interim O'Casey gave to the public his *Windfalls* (1934), *The Flying Wasp* (1937) a vigorous attack on the London theatre, and his first autobiography, *I Knock at the Door* (1939). Of these *Windfalls* alone is of immediate interest to us.

The poems included in *Windfalls* come under three sections. Those in the section "First Fall" were written when he was an impoverished Dublin labourer. All these poems show the influence of the Catholic girl Maura. The most ambitious of these is "A Walk with Eros," which I have already referred to. The others deserve no special mention: they are mostly imitations of the Romantic poets, and are on the whole amateurish. Of the three poems included in the section

---

[63] H. G. Barker, *On Poetry in Drama* (The Romance Lecture), p. 26.
[64] Unpublished study of *Within the Gates* by Prof. G. Wilson Knight.
[65] *Rose and Crown*, p. 258.

"Second Fall," "Gold and Silver Will not Do" and "The Dreamer Dreams of God" are written in prose but are essentially poems. Both are offshoots from his plays. The verses bear close resemblance to lines spoken by Davoren in *The Shadow of a Gunman* and by the Dreamer in *Within the Gates*. The third poem, "She Will Give Me Rest," is probably addressed to his wife. (When I asked O'Casey if I was right in presuming so, he replied: "Yes, I think so.") The third section, "A Fall from an Irish Tree," has only one poem, "The Grand Oul' Dame Britannia," given chiefly to ridiculing Britain and that middling Irish patriot John Redmond. It was written in 1917 and included in Lady Gregory's *Kiltartan History Book*, where for some reason the author of the poem is not identified as O'Casey.

Of greater interest to us are the four short stories, rather unjustly described by St John Ervine as "a prolonged and terrifying scream that does no more than jar the ears of those who listen."[66] They have the pathos, the sympathy and the sharp observation that we find in the plays. The finest of them is "I Wanna Woman," a study of a young man's overwhelming desire to satisfy his sexual urge. Religious references are introduced through the picture of the Crucifixion hanging on the wall and the pealing of the church bells in the morning. O'Casey is not against sexual intercourse. What he disapproves of is sexual intercourse without love. In *Within the Gates* O'Casey disapproves of the Gardener's desire for Jannice, for in it there is no love; he approves of the Dreamer's passion for Jannice for it comes from love. For O'Casey, love alone sanctifies the sexual act. His God grants permission to young men and women to indulge in the sexual act "where love is the beginning, and love is the ending thereof."[67] Two other stories, "The Star-Jazzer" and "A Fall in a Gentle Wind," are studies of the wretchedness of tenement life. The former is a moving story of a woman who for a moment escapes from the gruesome actuality of her impoverished existence to jazz to the stars, and ends up in one corner of a bed, giving herself unwillingly to the sexual appetency of her husband. The other is a pathetic study of a highly sensitive girl, Mollser, who is wasted by tuberculosis.

[66] St John Ervine, *The Observer* (London), 11 Nov. 1934.
[67] "Gold and Silver Will not Do," *Windfalls*, p. 41.

Her world of dreams and her hope of recovery are shattered by the arrival of an ambulance to take her to "the Hospice for the Dying." In both these stories, as in O'Casey's plays in general, it is the women who suffer silently and bear sorrows courageously, while the men think only of themselves. "The Job" is the story of a pretty young girl who reluctantly agrees to go out on the coming Wednesday with the manager who has just given her a job. She returns home to prepare for a happy evening with her boy-friend, but she gets a telegram putting off the date till next Wednesday.

All these stories are tainted with despair, frustration and broken hopes. The reason for this may be that, as O'Casey said, three of them were written in an effort "to get rid of some of the bitterness that swept into me when the Abbey Theatre rejected *The Silver Tassie*."[68] O'Casey also included in *Windfalls* two one-act plays which are roaring fun from beginning to end.

Purple Dust was published in 1940 but it did not get its first performance in England till 1945, when it was staged by the Northern Company of the Old Vic at the Liverpool Playhouse. In England, performance was delayed since the play was looked upon as a travesty on the British at a time when they were fighting Hitler. James Agate denounced it as a worthless play, an attack on England when she was helpless and unable to reply.[69] Agate's criticism was not free from personal dislike of O'Casey, though a performance of the play might have offended many and would have brought financial loss to the producer. There are lines in it which in 1940 might have sounded a shade prophetic to Britain's enemies:

> Whether it is or no doesn't matter much, for in a generation or so the English Empire will be remembered as a half-forgotten nursery rhyme![70]

The possibility of a New York production in 1940 also fell through though Nathan hailed it as "a first-rate comedy";[71] a play "so full of reputable laughter that one would think it should find a producer overnight, even a producer among our

---

[68] *Windfalls*, p. vii.
[69] See *Sunset and Evening Star*, p. 149.
[70] *Purple Dust*, Act II, p. 74.
[71] See Clark & Freedley, *A History of Modern Drama*, p. 228.

peculiar lot."[72] The reason that prevented its performance was that London had just undergone the Blitz, and any play satirising the English would have strengthened the hands of the isolationists. The New York theatre world did not want to indulge in anti-British propaganda. Later the play ran for fourteen months in New York.

The play has a slight but unified plot. It concerns itself with two wealthy Englishmen, Basil Stoke and Cyril Poges (names taken from Stoke Poges, the village immortalised in Gray's "Elegy"), who acquire a tottering Tudor mansion in Clune na Geera in the west of Ireland, and settle down with their mistresses Souhaun and Avril to recapture the past and enjoy the pleasures of country life. They employ Irish workmen to repair the falling mansion and to bring back its early grace and splendour. But things go wrong from the start, and it is not long before they discover the impossibility of transplanting to a primitive countryside the comforts they were accustomed to in London. The task becomes all the more difficult, for English and Irish temperaments, outlooks and mannerisms clash until the whole house is in an uproar. In the end the flood rises and destroys their costly furniture. The two Irish girls get tired of their dull-witted Englishmen and are lured away by the charm and romantic approach of the foreman O'Killigain and the Second Workman. The curtains descend on the house engulfed in the flood waters, with Poges moaning: "My comfort's gone, and my house of pride is straining towards a fall. Would to God I were in England, now that winter's here!"[73]

By 1940 O'Casey had lived in England for nearly fourteen years. He had written plays about the Irish, and a play dealing wholly with the English. It was now left for him to write a play showing the characteristics of both these people; who, though geographically so close, are temperamentally so far apart. Shaw had done this in *John Bull's Other Island*, a play that had so absorbed O'Casey when he first read it that he did not put it down till the early hours of the morning.

There is much that is common to *John Bull's Other Island* and *Purple Dust*. Both plays are satirical comedies and both

[72] Quoted in Jules Koslow, *The Green and the Red*, p. 78.
[73] *Purple Dust*, Act III, p. 119.

dramatists attempt to contrast the peculiarities of the two races with which they are concerned. Shaw puts his finger on the pulse of both peoples, while O'Casey fails to see deep into the English character. This is the one serious flaw in his play. His Irishmen are living, full of imagination, displaying most of the characteristics of the Irish people; but his two Englishmen are nothing but pompous fools who lose their women to the liveliness and greater sexual potency of the Irish workers. There is no complexity in the Englishmen; they are puppets whose plight gets worse as the play proceeds to its weak climax: the flight of their mistresses with the workmen. Shaw on the other hand has infinite fun with Thomas Broadbent without reducing his stature or depriving him of our sympathy. Where O'Casey scores over Shaw is in his poetry, his imagery, the richness and beauty of his language. But these qualities in themselves cannot lift his play to the height of *John Bull's Other Island*.

O'Casey's purpose, like Shaw's, was to contrast the comic peculiarities of the two people and make fun of both of them. But in such an attempt a dramatist should not let his vision be blurred by prejudices or personal grievances. Shaw could penetrate into and faithfully observe the oddities of both the English and the Irish. In his Preface to Politicians he admitted that he liked "Englishmen much better than Irishmen."[74] This hybrid quality of being one and liking the other gives him an advantage over O'Casey in so far as objectivity is concerned: he can, with ease, be fair to both of them. But O'Casey cannot; he is too much of an Irishman to make a fair comparison between his own people and the English.

Let us take O'Casey's two Englishmen first, Cyril Poges and Basil Stoke. Poges is described as a man of sixty-five, inclined to be stout, broad-chested with a prominent belly, "a fussy manner, all business over little things; wants his own way at all times. . . ."[75] Stoke is pictured as a "long, thin man of thirty, with a rather gloomy face which he thinks betokens dignity, made gloomier still by believing that he is something of a philosopher."[76] Not only are both unpleasant to the eye but both are from the start presented as fools. How different

---

[74] G. B. Shaw, *John Bull's Other Island & Major Barbara*, p. x.
[75] *Purple Dust*, Act I, p. 6.   [76] *Ibid*.

they are from Shaw's Broadbent who goes to Ireland too on a different but equally stupid mission. Broadbent is drawn as a "robust, full-blooded, energetic man in the prime of his life, sometimes eager and credulous, sometimes shrewd and roguish, sometimes portentously solemn, sometimes jolly and impetuous, always buoyant and irresistible, mostly likeable, and enormously absurd in his most earnest moments."[77] Shaw scores over O'Casey from the very beginning. Broadbent is to provide amusement through being earnest but absurd; Poges and Stoke merely by being fools.

The whole play deals with the efforts of these two Englishmen to rebuild the manor house and enjoy the bliss of a quiet country life. That they are not going to have much of the peace they are seeking is hinted in the opening scene of the play in the conversation between the workmen, and it is not long before the two Englishmen see it for themselves: but they hold on to their purpose with that pugnacious tenacity with which the English held on to Ireland. Their confidence in themselves and their failure to see the trend of events are subtly hinted at at the close of the play, when O'Killigain and the Second Workman woo their mistresses before their eyes. Instead of turning the two workers out, they listen with contempt to what they consider to be idiosyncratic rubbish, till it is too late to mend matters and their mistresses run away.

Poge's talk of efficiency is an unworthy imitation of what Broadbent thinks of efficiency,[78] although the latter does not openly describe it as an English quality. Here is Poges speaking:

> I believe in efficiency! I demand efficiency from myself, from everyone. Do the thing thoroughly and do it well: that's English. The word given, and the word kept: that's English.[79]

In the same way what O'Killigain says of the English (a feeling, I think, most Irishmen share)—"a rascal, a thief, and a big-pulsed hypocrite"[80]—is said by Shaw in terms that do not appear brazenly vindictive. This is what Tim Haffigan

[77] G. B. Shaw, *John Bull's Other Island & Major Barbara*, Act I, p. 4.
[78] *Op. cit.*, Act IV, pp. 109, 112.
[79] *Purple Dust*, Act II, p. 67.
[80] *Op. cit.*, p. 72.

tells Broadbent when the latter asks him if he knows the English plan for handling estates:

> Bedad I do, sir. Take all you can out of Ireland and spend it in England: thats it.[81]

Shaw can laugh at the English and censure them without being churlish or cantankerous. O'Casey cannot, for where his country is concerned his judgment is often blurred.

O'Casey uses Poges to express a couple of his own opinions on Ireland and the Irish, but on the whole he leaves it for his Irish characters to reveal it through their words and deeds. Here is Poges's denunciation of the priests:

> Oh, these priests, these priests! Thick as weeds in this poor country. Opposed to every decent thought that happens not to have come from them. Ever on guard to keep the people from growing out of infancy.[82]

But the most accurate remark from Poges comes at the end of Act I when the maid-servant Cloyne asks what she must tell the Canon who is waiting outside to see him:

> Tell him I'll give him another cheque if he gets the telephone fixed for me before the night is out![83]

In one sentence O'Casey has summed up what he considers to be the potentialities, the power and the greed of the Irish Catholic clergy. Both Shaw's Broadbent and O'Casey's Poges realise the authority the Church wields in matters ecclesiastical, political and social; and both try to win her favour. For Broadbent the Church can secure him a seat in Parliament, for Poges it can fix up his telephone. And they never hesitate in being liberal with their gold to please its ministers.

Basil Stoke owes much of his present financial status and comfort to Poges, just as Larry Doyle owes it to Broadbent. But apart from this the two have nothing in common. Stoke is a complete ass who does not say a single sensible thing throughout the play. O'Casey has bestowed upon him an Oxford degree, in order to have fun at Oxford's expense.

---

[81] G. B. Shaw, *John Bull's Other Island & Major Barbara*, Act I, p. 8.
[82] *Purple Dust*, Act I, pp. 40-1.
[83] *Op. cit.*, p. 44.

Poges, who is equally ignorant, and who has failed to obtain an honorary degree from Oxford, turns angrily to him when a cow invades their parlour: "What's the advantage of your passing through Oxford if you can't face a bull with a gun in your hand? Be a man, man, and not a mouse."[84] After ridiculing Oxford education in several scenes in the play, O'Casey sums up his own impression of the University through O'Killigain: "The city of dissolute might!"[85]

With the Irish characters O'Casey is at home. He handles them with ease and effortlessly unfolds their salient characteristics. They are great characters in their own way, although they do not rise to the stature of Captain Boyle or Juno. Take Avril and Souhaun—a blot on Ireland's holy name! They, like most of O'Casey's heroines, are rooted to the earth. Avril is the mistress of Stoke and Souhaun of Poges, for pecuniary reasons only. After the two Englishmen have settled £500 a year on each, they do not take long to forsake the two buffoons to "abide with the men o' th' wide wathers."[86] No doubt the women have prostituted themselves for money, but O'Casey sets little store by mere chastity. To the average reader Avril's and Souhaun's flight with the workmen might seem inexpiable, but in O'Casey's sight this is a commendable step: to leave the mentally and imaginatively sick and go "where love is fierce an' fond an' fruitful."[87]

In depicting some of the important traits of the Irish, O'Casey has wisely laid special emphasis on the imaginative quality of his countrymen and their unbridled passion for the past. This should not be confused with the Englishmen's blind reverence for tradition as voiced by Poges. Tradition springs from a historical continuity and a steady growth which Ireland cannot boast. In some ways she still remains, what Thomas Moore said in 1824, a country "struggling, like Ixion, on her wheel of torture."[88] This to some extent accounts for the Irishman having a vivid picture of dramatic incidents even in the distant past, but only a vague idea of the continuity of his country's history. He manages to counteract the unhappiness of the present by calling to mind the legends of a

[84] *Purple Dust*, Act II, p. 57.   [85] *Op. cit.*, Act III, p. 103.
[86] *Op. cit.*, Act III, p. 105.   [87] *Op. cit.*, p. 106.
[88] Quoted in James Carty, *Ireland*, p. xxvi.

bygone age; such illusions afford him a natural escape and a sedative to despair. In *John Bull's Other Island* Larry Doyle makes a penetrating analysis of the Irishman's imagination:

> An Irishman's imagination never lets him alone, never convinces him, never satisfies him; but it makes him that he cant face reality nor deal with it nor handle it nor conquer it: he can only sneer at them that do, and . . . be "agreeable to strangers," like a good-for-nothing woman on the streets. . . . It's all dreaming, all imagination. He cant be religious. The inspired Churchman that teaches him the sanctity of life and the importance of conduct is sent away empty; while the poor village priest that gives him a miracle or a sentimental story of a saint, has cathedrals built for him out of the pennies of the poor. He cant be intelligently political: he dreams of what the Shan Van Vocht said in ninetyeight. If you want to interest him in Ireland youve got to call the unfortunate island Kathleen ni Hoolihan and pretend shes a little old woman. It saves thinking. It saves working. It saves everything except imagination, imagination, imagination; and imagination's such a torture that you cant bear it without whisky.[89]

O'Casey is not so explicit, but his characters fully bear out Shaw's diagnoses. Davoren playing the shadow of a gunman, Boyle recalling a fabled past and prophesying that he will serve his country in the future, Fluther boasting fidelity to the Shan Van Vocht, Peter Flynn dressed in his regalia maundering round the grave of Wolfe Tone: all are victims of an imagination that romanticises the past and the future but has no answer for the problems of the present. In *Purple Dust* all the Irish characters are dreamers; even O'Killigain who tells Poges that "I let the dead bury their dead," and "Life as it is, and will be, moves me more."[90] The most eloquent dreamer of the lot is the Second Workman who never misses an opportunity of extolling the glories of Ireland's past. Here he is rebuking Poges for calling him a fool:

> Hammerin' out handsome golden ornaments for flowin' cloak an' tidy tunic we were, while you were busy gatherin' dhried

---

[89] G. B. Shaw, *John Bull's Other Island & Major Barbara*, p. 18.
[90] *Purple Dust*, Act I, p. 21.

grass, an' dyin' it blue, to hide the consternation of your middle parts; decoratin' eminent books with glowin' colour an' audacious beauty were we, as O'Killigain himself will tell you, when you were still a hundhred score o' years away from even hearin' of the alphabet.[91]

A dramatist like O'Casey, writing about an imaginative people for whom the present has little meaning, easily acquires the licence to indulge in free and poetic fancy. Facts are brushed aside as prosaic and commonplace; reasoning is not sought for; a rioting imagination is driven home by a torrent of words which speak through sound and meaning alike. Even the playboy Christy Mahon's swelling account of how he "cleft his father with one blow to the breeches belt"[92] seems feeble beside what O'Casey's workmen have to say about the quality of the hens they wish to inflict on Poges. The scene is good enough to be quoted at length:

1st WORKMAN [*persuasively—towards Poges' paper*]: Listen, here, sir: if it's genuine poulthry you want, that lay with pride an' animation, an' not poor, insignificant fowls that set about th' business o' layin' like a member o' Doyle Eireann makin' his maiden speech, I have a sthrain o' pullets that'll give you eggs as if you were gettin' them be stream!

POGES [*angrily—glancing over the top of his paper*]: Go away, go away, man, and don't be driving me mad!

3rd WORKMAN [*towards Poges' paper*]: Oh, the lies that some can tell to gain their own ends! Sure, sir, everyone knows that his poor hins are harmless; only venturin' to lay when heavy thundher frightens them into a hasty sign o' life! But it's meself can give you what you want, with a few lively cocks thrown in, to help them on with the work of furnishing nourishment to the whole world.

POGES: Go away; when I want poultry, I'll get into touch with the experts in the Department of Agriculture.

1st WORKMAN [*horrified—partly to Poges and partly to Souhaun*]: Oh, listen to that, now! Didja hear that, ma'am? The Department of Agriculture, is it? Wisha, God help your innocence, sir. Sure, it's only a tiny time ago that the same Department sent down a special sthrong covey o' cocks to improve the

---

[91] *Purple Dust*, Act I, p. 35.
[92] J. M. Synge, *The Playboy of the Western World, Plays*, p. 228.

sthrain, an' only afther a short probation, didn't they give the
hins hysterics.

POGES: Hysterics? Good God!

3rd WORKMAN: Ay, an' hadn't the frightened farmers to
bring guns to bear on the cocks when they found their hins
scatthered over hill an' dale, lyin' on their backs with their
legs in the air, givin' their last gasp, an' glad to get outa the
world they knew so well! The few mighty ones who survived
were that stunned that there wasn't an egg in th' place for
years![93]

Here we have O'Casey's prose at its best: defiant, abundant,
rich, bursting with vitality. One cannot help admiring the
confidence with which he follows the lead of words; the noisy
rhetoric, the mighty exaggeration and incoherence that still
retain a crystal clarity: the exuberance and gusto before
which we find ourselves as "speechless as one is when assailed
by the eloquent expletives of a brilliant drunk or an imaginative
and irate woman."[94]

The irresponsibility of the Irish, their sense of humour,
their pride, their flattery of the English, the poetic brilliance of
their speech and their queer love-making, all in one way or the
other can be related to their heightened imagination. Both
Shaw and O'Casey have brought out these characteristics.
To take but one instance, when Broadbent arrives in Ross-
cullen he asks for the "finest hotel" about which the driver had
told him. To this Aunt Judy replies:

Arra would you mind what the like of him would tell you?
Sure he'd say hwatever was the least trouble to himself and the
pleasantest to you, thinkin you might give him a thruppenny
bit for himself or the like.[95]

Poges, who has bought a lawn-roller which is as high as he is
tall, obstinately insists in believing what the seller had told
him: "Once you got the knack of balancing it . . . you could
turn it with your little finger."[96] Next, when the quattrocento
desk gets stuck in the entrance Poges tells the workmen that
the driver of the furniture van had told him that it "would

[93] *Purple Dust*, Act I, pp. 32-3.
[94] Harold Clurman, *The Nation*, CLXXIX, 27 Nov. 1954.
[95] G. B. Shaw, *John Bull's Other Island & Major Barbara*, Act II, p. 41.
[96] *Purple Dust*, Act II, p. 78.

slide in without the slightest trouble."[97]　To this the First Workman retorts:

> Don't mind anything Larry Lunigan says, sir.　If your head was split he'd say it was only a scratch, to keep your heart up.[98]

Whether such similarities between *John Bull's Other Island* and *Purple Dust* are deliberate or accidental is immaterial.　What is important is that both the dramatists have their finger on the the pulse of the Irish, and the beat is the same.

The scenes in which O'Killigain and the Second Workman woo Avril and Souhaun bear some likeness to the scene in Act III of *The Playboy of the Western World* where Christy Mahon promises devotion to Pegeen Mike.　Phrases such as: "walkin' beside all the beauty that ever shone before the eyes o' man since Helen herself unbound her thresses to dance her wild an' willin' way through the sthreets o' Throy!"[99] or "a saint himself would shudder if he had to pass it on a dusky night, with only a sly chit of a moon in the sky to show the way"[1] have the ring of Synge's great masterpiece.　Again, Avril's admiration for O'Killigain's eloquence: "is there an Irishman goin' who hasn't a dint o' wondher in his talkin'?"[2] and Souhaun's for the Second Workman's "makin' gold embroidery out o' dancin' words"[3] may be compared with what Pegeen has to say to Christy:

> That'll be right fun, Christy Mahon, and any girl would walk her heart out before she'd meet a young man was your like for eloquence or talk at all. . . .

> And what is it I have, Christy Mahon, to make me fitting entertainment for the like of you, that has such poet's talking and such bravery of heart.[4]

Nathan must have failed to see the influence of *John Bull's Other Island* and *The Playboy of the Western World* on *Purple Dust*, for he called it "a completely original" farce-comedy.[5]　It is not strictly original in its conception and treatment, but rich and beautiful enough to be another feather in O'Casey's cap.

---

[97] *Purple Dust*, Act III, p. 96.
[98] *Ibid.*
[99] *Op. cit.*, Act I, p. 14.
[1] *Op. cit.*, p. 16.
[2] *Op. cit.*, p. 15.
[3] *Op. cit.*, Act III, p. 106.
[4] J. M. Synge, *The Playboy of the Western World, Plays*, Act III, p. 251.
[5] Quoted in Jules Koslow, *The Green and the Red*, p. 78.

The play is over-crowded with rough-and-tumble events. In this respect it stands in sharp contrast to Shaw's play which has only one knock-about scene: the accident resulting from Matthew Haffigan's pig jumping into Broadbent's lap while Broadbent is driving the animal to Haffigan's farm. Shaw introduces this scene to make a very accurate observation on both the English and the Irish. When Cornelius remarks (after Broadbent has made a fool of himself) that Broadbent would lose his candidature and be laughed out of the town, Larry Doyle unerringly replies:

> Oh no he wont: hes not an Irishman. He'll never know theyre laughing at him; and while theyre laughing he'll win the seat.[6]

O'Casey has no such observations to make when he brings the cow into the hall, lets the roller run away with Poges, or forces the quattrocento desk through the narrow entrance. The laughter he creates is through comic situations, and with him one farcical situation is as good as another. The reason why O'Casey is driven to knock-about is, as a reviewer said, "the inequality and unreality of the contest."[7] If his Englishmen were half as alive as his Irishmen, he would not have had the need to resort to such tricks.

O'Casey's chief spokesman in the play is the foreman, O'Killigain. He is a strange medley of a dreamer and a man of action. O'Casey's dreamers, as found in his later plays, are also men of action, rarely forsaking the present for the past or the reality for an illusion. In showing a *mélange* of two opposite qualities in the same person, O'Casey is throwing light on his own person. He is Irish enough to be given to dreaming, but at the same time intellectually aware enough not to brush aside the everyday realities. His dreamers are a compound of the two different qualities found to exist separately in his Abbey plays: the "reality" of the women and the "illusion" of the men. They are his ideal characters, harmoniously blending the two opposite qualities which in isolation remain insufficient, but when brought together create a perfect whole.

The Dreamer in *Within the Gates* is a dreamer in so far as he does no work, admires nature, and writes poems and songs.

[6] G. B. Shaw, *John Bull's Other Island & Major Barbara*, Act IV, p. 86.
[7] *The Times Literary Supplement*, 23 Nov. 1940.

On the other hand he is a practical man; more practical than
the Bishop, the Young Woman and the soap-box speakers
who fail to grasp their purpose in life. O'Killigain is a practical
man who can see the Englishmen's folly in venerating a dead
past and creating a halo of glory round a tumbling Tudor
mansion. But his practicality has in it a flavour of romantic
dreaming which gives him success with Avril. In the same
way the Second Workman is a dreamer who is practical
enough to elope with Souhaun. O'Casey first tried this
amalgamation of opposite qualities in the same person in
Within the Gates, and it is to be found in most of his later plays.

The purpose of the play is symbolised in the rise of the
river and the floods. The river is the river of time that over-
whelms a dead past to which it is futile and impossible to
return. This thought is expressed by O'Killigain to Poges:

> You have had your day, like every dog. Your Tudors have
> had their day, and they are gone; and th' little heap o'
> purple dust they left behind them will vanish away in th' flow
> of the river.[8]

The symbolism is open to more imaginative interpretations.
The river that floods the house and forces the rich Englishmen
to seek shelter on the roof may symbolise the rise of the common
man. It may also be taken to mean the end of British influence
in Ireland, or a warning to the Irish to look to the future and
not to venerate the past. But it is best not to stretch the
symbolic meaning too far.

[8] *Purple Dust*, Act III, p. 118.

VI

O'Casey and Communism

IT is necessary to understand O'Casey's political faith before proceeding to *The Star Turns Red* and the plays that follow it. In *Inishfallen Fare Thee Well* he claims to have been a Communist at the time he began his dramatic career in the Abbey Theatre. And yet there is nothing in his Abbey plays that would suggest that he even had Communist leanings then; on the other hand there is much in them from which one may conclude that he looked with suspicion upon Communists and Socialists alike. It is not until we come to *The Star Turns Red* that we find O'Casey concerned with Communism. The mere argument that he did not advocate his political faith in his early plays is no evidence that he was not a Communist at that time: but still one is left amazed at this singular omission, for so much of the man, his beliefs, his sympathies and his convictions are divulged in them. The problem that faces us is this: if O'Casey was a Communist in 1923 why did he not glorify Communism in his Abbey plays? Or is it that his outlook changed after 1940 and led him to present his political ideology in his creative work? This is by no means an easy question. Here, however, is O'Casey's answer to it in his letter to me dated 31 Mar. 1959:

> Communists have glorified themselves more effectively in the world than in fiction or plays. *Outlook* is always changing. I never lost my Communism, it merely changed by growing deeper and more certain within me—that was the one and only change.

O'Casey's statement that Communists have been more effective in the material, rather than the literary, world seems to constitute an admission that his "Red Plays" are not as good as his others. His statement that he never lost his Communism but that it only underwent a change and became "deeper" and "more certain" within him, answers our query. He was a Communist from the start of his dramatic career, but he was

not then sure if Communism was the only solution to the
world's evils. Also, in his early plays he was too busy telling
us about the problems facing Ireland in particular and mankind
in general, and not urgently concerned with their solutions.
It is after *Within the Gates* that he attempts to solve the enigma,
and the solution he offers is Communism: a Communism which
is strongly flavoured by his personality, proletarian background
and early disillusionment.

O'Casey insists that he is a Communist but not a Communist pamphleteer. Though he greatly admires the Russian
Revolution and all that it has brought to its people, he disapproves of always looking towards Russia for guidance. He
dissociates Communism from Marxism: "Communism isn't an
invention of Marx; it is a social growth, developing through
the ages, since man banded together to fight fear of the unknown, and destroy the danger from mammoth and tiger of
the sabre-tooth."[1] In saying so much he differs from the
average Communist to whom Russia, Marxism and Communism remain more or less inseparable. His attempt, and
perhaps a right one, to liberate Communism from the common
belief that it is a Marxist invention may be very much in his
own interest. Marxism refutes the existence of God and looks
upon religion (to quote Marx himself) as "the spirit of a
spiritless situation . . . the *opium* of the people. . . ."[2] With
such a contention O'Casey cannot wholly align himself; God
for him is as necessary as for Graham Greene or T. S. Eliot.
Therefore O'Casey prefers to call himself a Communist and
avoids the label Marxist, though it must be noted that it is
difficult to draw a clear line of demarcation between a Marxist
and a Communist, and that most Communists, like Marxists,
reject God. Stephen Spender calls O'Casey a "Christian
Socialist"[3] and there is much to be said in favour of this. There
is also some truth in Robert F. Aikman's analysis of O'Casey's
Communism:

> Mr. O'Casey is a Communist. A romantic Communist, of
> course. . . . What Mr. O'Casey wants is the brotherhood of

---

[1] *Rose and Crown*, p. 143.
[2] K. Marx and F. Engels, *On Religion* (Moscow, 1957), p. 42.
[3] S. Spender, *The New Statesman and Nation*, XIX, 16 Mar. 1940.

man, with music, dancing, wild humour, sexual ecstasy—and, oddly enough, the Protestant Church (he is himself a Protestant, a decisive fact for an Irishman). Students are familiar with this type of artistic Communist who wants nothing that Communism has ever in fact given . . . the artist who wants the world remade and accepts, through a merciful weakness in his capacity for political analysis, Communism's claim to be positively the only genuine instrument.[4]

O'Casey would surely object to being passed off as a "romantic Communist." He honestly believes that his Communism is in conformity with the general Party principles. This is not strictly so; his Communist heroes express many thoughts on which an average Party member would frown. The divergence is not due to his lack of understanding of Marxian Communism, but comes from his inability to accept the creed in all its rigidity. In his plays he often gives his own interpretation of Communism which, rather strangely, is Christian and pagan at the same time.

R. Crossman tells us that the intellectual who becomes a Communist, feels "the prickings of his Christian conscience far more acutely than many of his unreflective Church-going neighbours."[5] This is true of O'Casey, whose Communism reduced to its barest is nothing more than a deep concern for the poor and the neglected.[6] Intrinsically he is a Christian at heart who has turned Communist because Christianity has sat heedless in the midst of injustice and oppression while Communism, without acknowledging God, has moved forward to fulfil God's plan on earth. Like many other intellectuals he finds Communism to be the only gospel of deliverance whose possibilities are not yet fully explored, the one political religion that promises freedom from want and hunger in *this* world. Whether Communism will be able to fulfil its promise to its adherents is not within the scope of this book. What concerns us is whether O'Casey sincerely believes it will. The answer is "Yes," positively yes. O'Casey's certainty springs from this: that Communism appeals both to his intellect and to his Irish imagination, the imagination tying

[4] R. F. Aickman, *The Nineteenth Century and After*, cxxxix, Apr. 1946.
[5] Quoted in M. C. D'Arcy, *Communism and Christianity*, pp. 52-3.
[6] See my article in *The Illustrated Weekly of India*, 17 May 1959.

up the loose ends that the intellect fails to weave together.

The one serious issue that crops up is how Communism has affected him as a playwright of great gifts and endowments. That his political awakening has not been wholly to the good so far as his dramatic achievements are concerned can be seen, not by comparing his early plays with his later ones (for O'Casey claims to be an experimental dramatist) but from the later plays themselves. More often than not the best scenes in his later plays are those in which he forgets or deviates from Communist principles. Against the nature of his talents he makes his Communists all good and their opponents all bad. He also tries the difficult task of relating two different faiths that look upon each other with suspicion: Christianity and Communism. On the one hand he is eager to lead the starving masses to a religion of universal salvation that lays its entire emphasis upon life in this world; on the other hand he is unwilling to do away with God and other-worldliness as Communism demands. Though dramatically he very nearly succeeds, he wins few friends in either camp. The Communists feel that O'Casey is unnecessarily recreating a God that they have killed; the Christians think that he is siding with Communism and dragging an unwilling Christ along. Both are wrong, for Communism as O'Casey sees it is Christ's kingdom on earth.

Had O'Casey followed the advice of his favourite critic G. J. Nathan that "Art never follows a flag,"[7] or stuck to his own pledge that he would never try to write about heroes, he would have avoided such material as he employed in *The Star Turns Red*. Even Nathan, who had supported him through thick and thin, wrote: "The two worst influences on present-day playwrights are, very often, Strindberg and Communism. . . . And Communism, one fears, has now adversely affected Sean O'Casey as a dramatic artist."[8]

The play was first performed at the Unity Theatre on alternate nights from 14 Mar. 1940. It was more or less

---

[7] G. J. Nathan, *The World in Falseface*, p. 15.

[8] G. J. Nathan, *Encyclopaedia of the Theatre*, p. 287. For O'Casey's admiration of Strindberg see his letter to Robert Loraine as quoted in Elizabeth Sprigge, *The Strange Life of August Strindberg*, p. 229.

decried by the leading theatre critics. The play's faults were on the surface and were easily noticed, while its virtues failed to reveal themselves in the performance. Firstly, like *Purple Dust*, it was ill-timed: it came out during the period of the Nazi-Soviet pact and the Russo-Finnish War when respect for Russia had dropped low in England. Secondly, the beauty of O'Casey's prose and verse was lost on the lips of amateur actors who were unable to speak his glowing words.[9] A good performance might have made a difference, though it is doubtful if it would have substantially changed the opinions of the critics. It was not so much the play's weakness as its political contents that led to its denunciation.

The play should not be brushed aside as a Party pamphlet. O'Casey wrote to me: "There is no Communist *Dogma* in *The Star Turns Red*. It is, as Shaw saw—the spirit and prophecy of the Authorised Version of the English Bible."[10] This is partly true, and it can be argued that O'Casey is not propagating Communist ideology, though it is obvious where his political sympathies lie. The play is full of Communist trappings: use of the word "Comrade" by the workers, the sketch of Lenin hanging on the wall, Jack practising "The Internationale," the Red Star worn by Jack and Red Jim, the Red Flag, the workers consolidating in a movement to fight against the totalitarian régime consisting of the Saffron Shirts (Fascists), the established Church and the Christian Front, and much else.

O'Casey does not localise the Workers' Movement, for it is his prophecy that the Red Star will arise "the wide world over."[11] He does not give the name of the city where the action of the play takes place but just the time, which is "Tomorrow, or the next day."[12] Yet any reader can see for himself from the characterisation (the Lord Mayor is probably a caricature of a past Lord Mayor of Dublin, Alfie Byrne,[13] and Red Jim is obviously drawn from Jim Larkin) and the part the Church plays in political matters that the scene is Dublin. But O'Casey does not say so; on the other hand

[9] R. M. Fox, *Theatre Arts*, xxiv, Nov. 1940.
[10] Letter to me from O'Casey dated 31 Mar. 1959.
[11] *The Star Turns Red*, Act III, p. 327.
[12] *Op. cit.*, p. 240.
[13] James Brady McGuire, *Realism in Irish Drama*, p. 296.

the absence of Irish brogue hints that after all the play may not be set in Ireland. For two reasons O'Casey does not explicitly state that the scene of the play is Dublin. Firstly, he wants to give Communism a wider symbolic meaning: the coming of Communism is for him the coming of the promised kingdom of God on earth. It is immaterial where Communism shoots its first jet of flame, what is of significance is that it will envelop the whole earth. Secondly, O'Casey knew that to make Dublin the seat of the "New Faith" would be fantastic. The Irish in spite of their poverty and misery had from the beginning a profound distrust for Communist doctrines. What Engels wrote to Marx as early as 1869—

> Ireland still remains the *sacra insula*, whose aspirations must on no account be mixed up with the profane class struggles of the rest of the sinful world. Partially, this is certainly honest madness on the part of the people, but it is equally certain that it is partially also a calculated policy of the leaders in order to maintain their domination over the peasant—[14]

was still true in 1940. What was O'Casey to do? He was prophesying a millennium and wanted his beloved Dublin to have the first honours. And yet he knew that Dublin was the most unlikely scene possible as the centre for the spread of the faith. He solved the problem by vaguely suggesting that the scene is set in Dublin and dropping the matter there. The result is that one is left wondering: "Reason tells us that the only city in which it could happen is Dublin, and reminds us that it could not even happen there."[15]

The most noteworthy feature of the play is O'Casey's endeavour to relate Christianity and Communism, just as in *Within the Gates* he endeavoured to relate Christianity to sexual urges. O'Casey is by no means the only writer who has attempted to show a certain relationship between Christianity and Communism. Many have observed that among idealistic philosophies and mystical religions Christianity and Communism have much in common. Paul Tillich thinks that though Marxist philosophy is atheistical in conscious intention

---

[14] *Marx Engels Selected Correspondence*, pp. 278-9. For Communism and Ireland, see Ch. III of Nicolas Mansergh, *Ireland in the Age of Reform and Revolution*.
[15] Ashley Dukes, *Theatre Arts*, XXIV, Jun. 1940.

still it is religious in essence.[16]   John Macmurray in his brilliant
study *Creative Society* writes that "It is only the negations and
limitations of Communistic theory which are anti-Christian."[17]
Dean Hewlett Johnson in his *Christians and Communism*, William
Hordern in *Christianity, Communism and History*, D. F. Buxton in
The Challenge of Bolshevism, Alexander Miller in *The Christian
Significance of Karl Marx* and Charles C. West in *Communism
and the Theologians* have all attempted to show where Christianity
and Communism meet and where they differ.[18]   O'Casey,
perhaps, is the only great living dramatist who in a dramatic
work has shown the close affinity between these two most
potent faiths in the modern world.

From the start O'Casey has tried to knit Christianity and
Communism together.   The action of the play takes place on
a Christmas Eve and the "Red Star" is surely the Star of
Bethlehem that leaves its "silver shine" of the kings for the
"red" of the people.   The Star is also symbolic of the rise of the
common man, of Christ's prophecy that the hungry shall be
filled with good things.   It shines throughout the play; in the
first three acts near the church steeple, in the fourth act next
to the foundry chimney.   It turns red suddenly in the final
act when the "Internationale" is heard and the workers
advance.   The symbolism introduced through the star is very
neatly done and is more effective than that of the rising river in
Purple Dust.   The star does not merely symbolise the workers'
aspirations;   it implies the acquiescence of Christianity (the
star being the Star of Bethlehem) to the revolutionary triumph
of the Communists.

Several passages spoken by the Communist characters
show that they are Communists and Christians at one and the
same time.   Julia, when she sees the dead body of her father
whose shooting was approved by the Purple Priest says:

> And the priests that sanctioned your shooting shall fall and
> shall be dust and shall be priests no longer!   [*She glances at the*

---

[16] See M. C. D'Arcy, *Communism and Christianity*, p. 77.

[17] J. Macmurray, *Creative Society*, p. 149.

[18] A few other books treating Communism and Christianity are: *Christian Faith
and Communist Faith*, ed. D. M. Mackinnon, London 1953; N. Berdyaev: *The
Realm of Spirit and the Realm of Caesar*, London 1952; C. W. Lowry: *Communism
and Christ*, London 1954.

the crucifix]. Against you, dear one, we have no grudge; but those of your ministers who sit like gobbling cormorants in the market-place shall fall and shall be dust, and shall be priests no longer.[19]

This is what Red Jim says when the Brown Priest of the People entreats him to obey the orders of the Church:

If the heritage of heaven be the heritage here of shame and rags and the dead puzzle of poverty, then we turn our backs on it! If your God stands for one child to be born in a hovel and another in a palace, then we declare against him. If your God declares that one child shall be clad in silks and another in sores, then we declare against him. If your God declares that it takes a sack of sovereigns to keep one child and a handful of pence to keep another, then we declare against him. If your God declares that one child shall dwell in the glory of knowledge and another shall die in the poverty of ignorance, then we declare against him: once and for all and for ever we declare *against your God* [italics mine], who hath filled the wealthy with good things and hath sent the poor empty away![20]

These passages disprove the old notion that O'Casey is anti-religious or anti-Catholic. O'Casey himself told me: "I am not anti-Catholic. I only attack some of their practices which I think to be wrong."[21] Julia has no grievance against Christ but against the ministers. Red Jim is to declare against God only if God is responsible for the sufferings of the poor. But this is a big "if," made bigger still because we know that the true God cannot be held responsible. It is God as portrayed by the corrupt Churches who sends the poor empty away.

The most significant words in the play, which not only show what O'Casey means by the true Church but which also link the Church with Communism, are said by Julia when the workers march in to claim her father's body: "The People's Church has come to claim him now!"[22] Note that it is not the people with whom Michael lived and for whom he died that take his body, it is the People's Church: a Church that

---

[19] *The Star Turns Red*, Act III, p. 315.
[20] *Op. cit.*, pp. 324-5.
[21] My interview with O'Casey on 6 Apr. 1959.
[22] *The Star Turns Red*, Act III, p. 323.

automatically comes into existence when the workers unite to fulfil God's promise on earth. This is the true Church, in contrast to the official Church which excels in Christian burial when one is dead, never in Christian treatment while one is alive. O'Casey has indeed woven God and Communism very successfully together and served the cause of the workers well. He has deviated from Communist doctrine in laying a strong emphasis on God, but he has stuck to the Party line in stressing the needs of this world. What is important is human happiness here and now, not hereafter; and if the Christian Church is out to serve God, let it first serve His children here.

There is one little scene which disturbs this line of argument. At the end of Act I when Michael is shot by Kian and is dying, the Brown Priest of the People comes to bless him but is gently set aside. This is the very opposite of what takes place in *Within the Gates*, where the dying Young Woman craves for and finally secures the Bishop's blessing. Why does O'Casey in this play make Michael wave the Brown Priest aside? These may be the reasons:

(1) If Michael had sought the blessing of the priest some critics might have blamed O'Casey for repeating himself. He had already been attacked by Horace Shipp in *The English Review* in 1926 for copying *Juno and the Paycock* too closely in *The Plough and the Stars*.

(2) The Brown Priest has not yet openly sided with the people. He is, in spite of his sympathy for the poor, still a member of the corrupt ecclesiastical hierarchy of which the Purple Priest is the head. Thus Michael is right in refusing his blessing.

(3) His body is reserved to be claimed by the People's Church: the Church in which he believed and for which he gave his life. He needs no blessings or forgiveness from the official Church. The cause for which he died sanctifies him.

Some Communists may not approve of O'Casey's enthusiasm for God and religion in *The Star Turns Red*. They may even view the conception of a "People's Church" as an abstract idea, a weak compromise, a serpent's egg which when hatched will grow dangerous. However, our concern is with the reasons why O'Casey steeps his play in religion. Firstly, it is because of O'Casey's own religious nature. His parents were good Christians and he himself as a young man came under the influence of the rector of his parish. Secondly, and perhaps more decisively, he knew from personal experience that religion has a strong hold on the people and that Communism could never become a world order unless it embodied a religious faith within itself. Once the material wants of the masses are satisfied the need of the soul would arise. Communism must satisfy this need too. It may oust a corrupt Church but that is not enough; it must replace it, for religion is essential to the world. O'Casey's solution is that once the false God of the existing Church is displaced, the true God of the people must take its place. And Communists have nothing to fear, but march hand in hand with God, for is not Communism the promised kingdom? In saying so much O'Casey has done a splendid service to Communism, if only all Communists would see it.

What is anti-Christian about *The Star Turns Red* is its bloodshed and hysteria. William York Tindall described it as a play whose "revolutionary violence makes English fellow-travelling seem pale."[23] The play more than justifies O'Casey's assertion: "I am not a pacifist: I believe in fighting for my rights."[24] The statement stands in sharp contrast to the pacifism found in his earlier plays: the contention then was that even a single life lost is too high a price for political gains. It is clear that O'Casey had now discarded his pacifism for a militant attitude, which justifies the sacrifice of human life for the achievement of political ends. Note the conversation between Red Jim and the Red Guard:

> RED GUARD [*at buzzer*]: Commandant Jack reports that he is hard pressed.
> RED JIM: Tell him to hold out till the last!
> RED GUARD [*at buzzer*]: Captain reports, too, that half of his men are down and he can't hold out much longer.
> RED JIM: Tell him to hold out till they're all down![25]

Of course O'Casey attaches a religious significance to the political cause, but the methods he advocates frankly clash with the fundamental teachings of Christ. The lines quoted above

[23] W. Y. Tindall, *Forces in Modern British Drama: 1885-1946*, p. 87.
[24] My interview with O'Casey on 6 Apr. 1959.
[25] *The Star Turns Red*, Act IV, p. 349.

will surely please Party members. It may even please O'Casey (since Communism also appeals to him imaginatively) if the action of the play takes place nowhere but on a theatre stage. But many of us are likely to look upon it with horror if these are the only means offered as a step towards a better society.

Like most Party writers O'Casey makes his Communists all good and their opponents all bad. The result is that there is no conflict (except a little in the Brown Priest, and even less in Kian) in the minds of his characters. This is done with a purpose, for the characters exist only as symbols to expound a morality. From the Party angle the mixing of good and evil could be injurious. It might blunt the sharp edge of the play as propaganda and the message might easily be lost in the haze of dramatic conflict. Therefore Red Jim, Jack and Julia are shown as brave, noble and virtuous. The Fascists, the Purple Priest and the Mayor are figured as self-seeking rascals who must be exterminated at any cost. They must not be shown to have a grain of nobility, for who knows if their little goodness might not eventually conquer their wickedness, or if the workers might not tolerate their masters further in the hope that in the end they might be reformed? In short a conflict between good and evil in the same character might confuse the mind of the workers (surely O'Casey does not think much of the intelligence of his comrades!) and so it is best to keep the virtuous and the wicked apart.

This segregation of men into water-tight compartments is partly responsible for the huge number of characters in the play, all of whom O'Casey handles most skilfully. For example, there would have been no necessity to introduce the Brown Priest had O'Casey made his Purple Priest a little virtuous. But since he is wholly corrupt and evil another priest has to be brought in to show that all priests are not irrevocably bad. In *Within the Gates* one priest suffices, for virtue and vice—as in life—exist in the same person, and the triumph of the good over the evil in the character of the Bishop in no way hinders O'Casey's moral purpose. But in *The Star Turns Red* there is not only a "moral purpose" but also a "moral plan"; a line of action that O'Casey wishes to recommend. This is the tragedy of the play. It is a matter for regret that O'Casey should go against his innate dramatic genius and dedicate his

N

talents to a cause that may best be left in the hands of the politicians. But before we chide him let us not forget that he is knowingly immolating his art for what he considers to be a universal need. This sacrifice arises from the magnanimity of his character, for greatly as he values great art, he loves something more—the welfare of his brethren.

Though O'Casey has done his best to make his Communists wholesome, their words and deeds are often such that they bring little glory to Communism. Ashley Dukes records how a party member caustically spoke of the Star "blushing a modest pink."[26] The behaviour of the big brawny drunkard Brannigan must be embarrassing to the comrades, so also must be the corruption shown in the Union Committee: the envy which makes the Committee members side with the Purple Priest against Red Jim. This is taken from real life, for such corruption did exist in Jim Larkin's movement in 1913. O'Casey wrote to me:

> Yes, the reactionary leaders who sold Larkin (and labor) were those boyos shown in *Red Star*. Some of them are still there. They hated me as much as they hated Jim. They have now a million pounds tucked away in the bowels of the Bank of Ireland. Jim died worth ten pounds, counting all his possessions. They are all snug and comfortable, even very well off: the difference? It is there.[27]

The abusive language and epithets used by the comrades for those with whom they disagree are unpleasant and make one feel that it is a guttersnipe movement. Here are a few of the phrases used by O'Casey's Communists:

Jack to Lord Mayor: "So I do, you hopabout little bugger!"[28]

Brannigan to the Committee member Brallain, after spitting in his eye: "You envy-stippled titivated toad!"[29]

Second Workman to Lord Mayor: "It's time the workers began putting their bums into soft places, isn't it?"[30]

[26] Ashley Dukes, *Theatre Arts*, XXIV, Jun. 1940.
[27] Letter dated 5 Jul. 1959.
[28] *The Star Turns Red*, Act I, p. 269.
[29] *Op. cit.*, Act II, p. 287.
[30] *Op. cit.*, Act IV, p. 331.

Even Julia behaves in a most unbecoming manner with her fiancé's father, the Old Man. She calls him a "withered stick,"[31] one whose eyes are always in search of trim-looking lasses. Perhaps all this is not as offensive as I infer, for to a Communist the only relationship that matters is that of a comrade. O'Casey makes this clear in the conversation between Jack and his mother:

> OLD WOMAN: Jack, Jack, he is your brother.
> JACK: I have brothers everywhere, Mother; but I have none in this house.
> OLD WOMAN: He is my son; you are my son: therefore you are his brother.
> JACK: He is dead; I see him not, I hear him not, I touch him not—he is dead.[32]

Compared with O'Casey's other plays, *The Star Turns Red* fails to leave a lasting impression on us. The lack of dramatic conflict, the puppet characterisation, the revolutionary violence of the whole thing prove too much for an audience which demands the highest wherever O'Casey is concerned. This does not mean that the play is bad: there are several splendid scenes which taken in isolation can be compared to the best in his earlier plays. The argument that goes on between the Old Man and his wife is full of O'Casey's broad humour. So is the scene in Act IV where the "Catholic flag-wagger," Joybell, and the Old Man take upon themselves the job of decorating the Lord Mayor's house. But the scene that deserves special notice is in Act III where the crowd, consisting of a few well-dressed people but mostly of wretched-looking, miserable beings, comes in to pay its respects to the dead body of Michael. The crowd here may be compared to the "Down-and-Outs" in *Within the Gates*, who stand for the negation of life. O'Casey does not blame the Church alone for doling out to the poor hunger, poverty, wretchedness and misery, flavoured with a colourful dream of heaven; he blames the poor for being taken in by the deception, for silently forbearing and even siding with those very forces which are responsible for their misery. He censures them for going against that section of themselves that have dedicated their lives to their own release. Note

---

[31] *The Star Turns Red*, Act I, p. 265.   [32] *Op. cit.*, p. 249.

how the crowd sides with the Church that is responsible for their ills:

> HUNCHBACK: A world to gain! Ay, and, at the same time, lose the dignity and loveliness that priests say poverty gives the poor.
>
> OLD WOMAN: They haven't got these things themselves, and they want to snap them from us.
>
> MAN WITH CRUTCH: What greater can we be than what the holy Purple Priest said we were, and he preaching on the twenty-seventh Sunday after Pentecost, during the holy communion of Reparation?
>
> WOMAN WITH BABY: Kings and priests unto God, Who has called us out of darkness into His marvellous light!
>
> BLIND MAN: "In the doze and drab of life", says he, "we are as pearls quietly aglow with a great beauty."
>
> YOUNG MAN WITH COUGH: Could the Communists say more than that—the bowseys!
>
> HUNCHBACK [*proudly*]: The Purple Priest patted me on the head, saying, "You're all the more beautiful in the sight of God because of the hump on your back."
>
> BLIND MAN: Look at that now!
>
> WOMAN WITH BABY: Could the Communists say more than that—the bastards![33]

Behind the biting humour one can see O'Casey's honest indignation. If the Church is powerful it is because society is weak. The Church has been comfortably enthroned, not merely by its own ingenuity but also by the envy, self-deception and thoughtlessness in the rank and file of society. The Church can be deposed only if society is aware of its folly. The play is but one step towards this awareness.

With *Red Roses for Me* (published in 1943) O'Casey once again returned to the agitated Dublin of his youth which he had forsaken since his exile. His deep concern for the Irish, coupled with the memories that must have been roused while he was writing the second and third volumes of his autobiography, may have induced him to dramatise himself with the famous Irish Transport Workers' strike as a background. It is not surprising that as a Communist writer he chose the strike— one in which he had played his part—rather than the purely

---

[33] *The Star Turns Red*, Act III, pp. 313-4.

nationalistic rising of 1916 which he thought to be "a terrible mistake."[34]

The play has a slight plot. It revolves round the aspirations and love of a doomed idealist named Ayamonn Breydon, a young Protestant in love with a Catholic girl, Sheila Moorneen. There are many things in which Ayamonn is interested, but most of all he wants to stand and fight by the side of his comrades for a shilling-a-week increase in their wages. Ayamonn, like Jack in *The Star Turns Red*, is killed in the fight, but while in *The Star Turns Red* the ultimate victory of the proletariat was shown, there is no such victory here. The main plot, however, occupies only a small part of the play. Of greater interest are the humorous incidents skilfully woven into the plot such as the one in which a Protestant, a Catholic and an atheist discuss their beliefs while sheltering from bullets behind tables and chairs. Equally charming is the tale of the Protestant Brennan stealing the statue of the Blessed Virgin and giving it a wash and a coat of paint and then returning it to its niche, an event which is hailed as a miracle by his Catholic neighbours.

The play, like *The Shadow of a Gunman*, is highly autobiographical. The setting of the first two acts—"The front one of two rather dilapidated rooms in a poor working-class locality"[35]—surely derives from the O'Casey apartment at 18 Abercorn Road in north Dublin. The description of the room with its one-wick oil-lamp, the horsehair sofa, the large basket used by actors, the row of secondhand books, the geranium, musk and fuchsia plants growing in biscuit tins which Mrs Breydon (who is drawn from his mother) tends, all these are to be found in his autobiographies. The third act is set on a bridge over the River Liffey, and the fourth in the Church of St Burnupus, which is really the Church of St Barnabas, very near to the place where O'Casey lived with his mother till her death.

Ayamonn Breydon is modelled on the young Sean O'Casey as the old Sean O'Casey now dreams of him. In sketching the character, O'Casey has drawn heavily on past memories and his boyhood likes and dislikes. To point a few instances,

---

[34] Lady Gregory's *Journals*, ed. L. Robinson, p. 260.
[35] *Red Roses For Me*, Act I, p. 127.

his love for painting is given prominence: on the wall of
Ayamonn's room hangs a coloured reproduction of Constable's
"Cornfield," and "a childlike brightly-coloured pastel of what
is meant to be a copy of one of Fra Angelico's angels blowing a
curved and golden trumpet."[36] Few know that O'Casey's
first interest was painting, not playwriting. If he unfortunately
failed to "throw a whole world in colour on a canvas"[37] he later
did succeed in throwing a world of colour into his plays in a
manner never attempted before. Mr Tom Sutton, an old
friend of O'Casey's, told me that O'Casey as a young man
was very good at sketching and would go about drawing in
chalk on walls and doors.[38] This, as well as his love for painting, is brought out in Ayamonn's conversation with Roory
O'Balacaun:

> ROORY: What kid was it sketched th' angel on th' wall?
> AYAMONN: Oh, I did that. I'd give anything to be a
>   painter.
> ROORY: What, like Oul' Brennan o' th' Moor?
> AYAMONN: No, no; like Angelico or Constable.
> ROORY [*indifferently*]: Never heard of them.
> AYAMONN [*musingly*]: To throw a whole world in colour on a
>   canvas though it be but a man's fine face, a woman's shape
>   asthride of a cushioned couch, or a three bordered house on
>   a hill, done with a glory; even delaying God, busy forgin'
>   a new world, to stay awhile an' look upon their loveli-
>   ness.[39]

Nor is Shakespeare forgotten. The play opens with Ayamonn
declaiming lines from *The Third Part of King Henry the Sixth*,
Act v, Sc. vi; Shakespeare is freely quoted throughout the
play and the play ends in a Shakespearian manner with the
corpse of Ayamonn borne onto the stage. Ayamonn's interests
in "Sketchin', readin', makin' songs, an' learnin' Shakespeare"[40]
are really O'Casey's interests. The way in which Ayamonn
saves sixpences to buy himself a reproduction of Constable
reminds us how young Johnny O'Casey saved pennies to buy
himself books. The account of Ayamonn's early schooling

---

[36] *Red Roses For Me*, Act I, p. 127.   [37] *Op. cit.*, p. 157.
[38] My interview with Mr Tom Sutton in Dublin on 14 Jun. 1958.
[39] *Red Roses For Me*, Act I, p. 157.
[40] *Op. cit.*, p. 132.

bears a close resemblance to O'Casey's own; and O'Casey through Ayamonn thanks his mother for it:

> AYAMONN: It's I who know that well: when it was dark, you always carried the sun in your hand for me; when you suffered me to starve rather than thrive towards death in an Institution, you gave me life to play with as a richer child is given a coloured ball.[41]

These are but a few of the many instances where O'Casey has turned to his early life in portraying the character of Ayamonn. But Ayamonn also sums up the later O'Casey in so far as he embodies those social, religious and political views that recur in plays written after the nineteen-twenties.

Ayamonn's mother, Mrs Breydon, is plainly a picture of O'Casey's own mother. Mrs Breydon possesses all the salient characteristics of Susan O'Casey except her gay laugh: she is brave, courageous and kind, always seeing to others' comfort at the cost of her own. Like Mrs O'Casey she is ignorant and superstitious, but has plenty of sound common sense that mildly rebukes Ayamonn's idealism. Like all O'Casey heroines she is rooted to the earth, but not so stolidly as to lose sight of the stars. Between Mrs Breydon and Ayamonn there is that same deep attachment that existed between O'Casey and his mother.

Sheila Moorneen is drawn from the Catholic girl Maura, who is still alive and lives in Dublin.[42] O'Casey lays too heavy an emphasis on Sheila's narrow religious belief. Her love for Ayamonn and her desire to keep him safe from all harm do not ennoble her, for she is shown as essentially selfish and incapable of appreciating the grandeur of the cause for which he fights. In spite of Ayamonn's claim that "Fair she is, and her little ear's open to hear all that I thry to say,"[43] she does not come any closer to him. On the other hand what he tells his mother: "I am drifting away from you, Mother, a dim shape now, in a gold canoe, dipping over a far horizon"[44] can more rightly be applied to Sheila. Note the conversation

[41] *Red Roses For Me*, Act I, p. 135.

[42] One of Maura's friends told me that she and Maura went to see the play when it was performed in Dublin, and that Maura burst into tears, saying O'Casey had portrayed her unkindly.

[43] *Red Roses For Me*, Act I, p. 134.

[44] *Op. cit.*, p. 135.

between the two—how close Sheila is to the earth, how near Ayamonn is to the stars:

> SHEILA [*rising from the chair—vehemently*]:   I'll listen no more; I'll go.   You want to make me a spark in a mere illusion. I'll go!
>
> AYAMONN: Rather a spark from the althar of God, me girl; a spark that flames on a new path for a bubbling moment of life, or burns a song into the heart of a poet.
>
> SHEILA: I came here as a last chance to talk things quiet with you, but you won't let me; so I'll go.   [*As he seizes her in his arm*] Let me go!   [*Pleadingly*] Please, Ayamonn, let me go!
>
> AYAMONN: I tell you it is a gay sight for God to see joy shine for a moment on the faces of His much-troubled children.[45]

The Rector, the Reverend E. Clinton, is modelled both on the Reverend Harry Fletcher who had won O'Casey back to the faith of his baptism, and the Reverend E. M. Griffin who was O'Casey's friend and benefactor.   Like Harry Fletcher, Clinton in the play is attacked by the extreme Protestant element in the Church for encouraging what they consider to be Popish practices.   Like Mr Griffin, Clinton has a hasty temper, cannot stand fools, and has a sensitivity which prevents him from looking at the results of poverty.   Roory O'Balacaun is drawn from an old friend of O'Casey's, a tram conductor and a zealous Irelander.   The discussion over Ruskin between Ayamonn and Roory at the end of the first act is to be found almost word for word in *Pictures in the Hallway*.   The old landlord, Brennan o' the Moor, is based on an old man O'Casey knew in Totnes.[46]   Dowzard and Foster are obviously caricatures of the Orangemen who made a nuisance of themselves to the Reverend Harry Fletcher.

From our angle of study this play is of special interest. Once again we find O'Casey wrestling with the problems that he had dealt with in his Abbey plays.   We also see him expressing his views on some of the problems raised in his later plays. Here, as in his Abbey plays, O'Casey is vehemently concerned with portraying the destitution and suffering of the poor. Ayamonn is struggling hard to save a few shillings to buy a Constable reproduction; little Ursula is trying in vain to save a few pennies to buy a new robe for the statue of the Blessed

---

[45] *Red Roses For Me*, Act I, p. 143.   [46] See Foreword, p. xv.

Virgin. There is the same lack of privacy. Ayamonn, like Donal Davoren in *The Shadow of a Gunman,* is constantly interrupted by his neighbours while he is studying Shakespeare or discussing matters with Sheila. The old problem of a woman caught in a pandemonium of political struggle recurs. Sheila, like Nora in *The Plough and the Stars,* pleads in vain to keep Ayamonn away from the fight, offering him the blessings of family life. Like Nora, she is brushed aside. Her chances of success are from the start far more remote in the face of Ayamonn's idealism than those of Nora in the face of her husband's personal ambition and vanity. Yet Sheila has our sympathy till the final act when, perhaps out of sheer loneliness, she momentarily toys with the proposal of Inspector Finglas. This is the cruellest moment in the play, and Maura may well have shed tears over it.

O'Casey gives this twist for a definite reason. In *The Plough and the Stars* he was busy stating a problem and not giving a solution for it. As he saw things then, even half a loaf was better than no bread. Thus his sympathies were with Nora, for she was the innocent victim of a fight that would bring her nothing, but would take away the little that she had. But by the time he came to *Red Roses for Me* his views had changed. He had discarded his earlier pacifism for the belief that one must fight for one's rights. In such a fight a few Ayamonns must die so that the many may live. And as Sheila stands in the way of this fight for the common good, he has not the same sympathy for her as he had for Nora. She is made small so that Ayamonn may look big. Just as he sacrifices Ayamonn for the sake of the "Cause," so does he sacrifice Sheila in an attempt to add to the stature of Ayamonn.

This departure is due to a positive development in O'Casey's outlook. The cynicism of his early plays has been replaced in his later ones by a vision of hope for the future. Take Ayamonn's last words: ". . . this day's but a day's work done, an' it'll be begun again tomorrow."[47] Not only do these words hold forth a promise but they are prophetic, for the struggle was renewed again in 1916, though in a different shape. But these words could have been said of the Easter Rising as well, which, in spite of its immediate failure,

[47] *Red Roses For Me,* Act IV, p. 221.

eventually brought freedom. Yet O'Casey used no such words in *The Plough and the Stars*. Why? Simply because he saw no "vision of hope" then.

Red Roses for Me has also much in common with some of his later plays. Ayamonn, again, is a combination of the dreamer and the man of action. Like the Dreamer in *Within the Gates* and Jack in *The Star Turns Red*, he is engaged in a struggle against the corruption of modern life. As in the previous play, we have the workers fighting the capitalists, religious tolerance pitted against religious intolerance, and schism among the workers which makes their task all the more difficult. The "down-and-outs," the living dead, figure again but they are no longer voluble or offending. Note O'Casey's description of them:

> The three women come a little way into the room; the men stand around the door. All their faces are stiff and mask-like, holding tight an expression of dumb resignation; and are traversed with seams of poverty and a hard life.[48]

Symbolism is neatly introduced, no longer by means of stage technique like the war memorial in *Within the Gates* or the red star in *The Star Turns Red*. Nor does it come upon us unexpectedly like the rising river in *Purple Dust*. Ayamonn dies not for what the single shilling is worth but because he sees "the shilling in th' shape of a new world."[49] The shilling is, to use his own words, "our Shechinah, showing us God's light is near; showing us the way in which our feet must go; a sun-ray on our face; the first step taken in the march of a thousand miles."[50]

Though it is a Communist play it is not, strictly speaking, what Richard Findlater calls it: "in essence another Communist morality play."[51] The strike merely forms the background material, as did the political events in his Abbey plays; nowhere does it become the plot itself. So far it is a positive advance on *The Star Turns Red* where the workers' struggle against the capitalists was set in the foreground, and where the dramatist forsook the artist's impartiality to speak

[48] *Red Roses For Me*, Act I, p. 136.
[49] *Op. cit.*, Act IV, p. 225.
[50] *Op. cit.*, p. 211.
[51] Richard Findlater, *The Unholy Trade*, p. 179.

from the political platform. Moreover, a better result has been achieved by the elimination of the hysteria and violence of phraseology which abound in his previous plays. There are no Fascists, no Purple Priests to curse with bell, book and candle; there are no Jacks and Red Jims forever attacking the Church and the state. The only representative of the ruling class in this play is the Inspector, and he too has a lot of good in him. He advises the Rector to warn Ayamonn to keep away from the meeting, and himself tells Ayamonn before the trouble begins: "Bear back, my boy, when you see the horsemen charging!"[52] Later, when Ayamonn is shot dead, he confesses to Sheila:

> Oughtn't you to go from this gloom, Sheila? Believe me, I did my best. I thought the charge would send them flying, but they wouldn't budge; wouldn't budge, till the soldiers fired, and he was hit. Believe me I did my best. I tried to force my horse between them and him.[53]

O'Casey has portrayed the workers' opponents sympathetically —but not because his opinion about them has changed; he attacks them as trenchantly as he did in his previous play, but now with a different method. Instead of showing them as horrible brutes and making his Communists rant at them, he keeps them off the stage but shows the effect of their system on the masses. In Act III he introduces the Rector dressed "in immaculate black," and the Inspector in a blue uniform "slashed with silver epaulettes on the shoulders," among the abject misery of the poor. The mere contrast speaks, and leaves a more haunting effect on the mind than anything said in *The Star Turns Red*. By a similar technique O'Casey brings the play to an unforgettable ending. Instead of getting a Red Jim to sing a splendid eulogy on Ayamonn's corpse, he has the bier borne into the church where Mrs Breydon receives the dead body of her son. The words exchanged between the mother and the priest are simple but more soul-stirring than anything of their kind O'Casey has written:

> RECTOR [*arranging a shawl round Mrs. Breydon's shoulders*]:
> There; that's better! My wife insists you stay the night with us, so there's no getting out of it.

---

[52] *Red Roses For Me*, Act IV, p. 213.   [53] *Op. cit.*, p. 225.

MRS. BREYDON: She's kind. [*She pauses to look at the rowan tree.*] There's th' three he loved, bare, or dhrenched with blossom. Like himself, for fine things grew thick in his nature: an' lather come the berries, th' red berries, like the blood that flowed today out of his white body. [*Suddenly— turning to face the church.*] Is it puttin' out th' lights he is?
RECTOR: Yes, before he goes home for the night.
MRS. BREYDON: Isn't it a sad thing for him to be lyin' lonesome in th' cheerless darkness of th' livelong night!
RECTOR [*going to the porch and calling out*]: Sam, leave the lights on tonight.
    [*The church, which had dimmed, lights up again.*][54]

The play should have ended here. But then we would have lost another touching scene where Brennan bribes the verger to sing a little song "as a finisher-off to a last farewell."[55] Placing a coin in the verger's hand he begs him to "leave th' door open so's th' sound'll have a fair chance to go in to him,"[56] and sings:

> A sober black shawl hides her body entirely,
> Touch'd be th' sun an' th' salt spray of th' sea;
> But down in th' darkness a slim hand, so lovely,
> Carries a rich bunch of red roses for me![57]

I am sure it is scenes such as these, few though they be, that justify the remark that "in [O'Casey's] temperament there is a drive towards cosmic grandeur and a persistent village homeliness."[58]

In *The Star Turns Red* O'Casey had shown the official Catholic Church siding with the Fascists against the workers; in this play we have the Protestant Church siding with the workers against the capitalists. This change does not imply that O'Casey favours the one Church against the other. In the religious and atheistical discussions in the play, comparable to those in *Within the Gates*, he takes no part but plays one faction against the other, handing insults right and left in a riot of loving fun. Here are the Catholic Roory and the Protestant Brennan arguing what St Patrick was:

BRENNAN: Looksee, if I believed in the ministhration of Saints on' Angels, I'd say thut th' good Protestant

---

[54] *Red Roses For Me,* Act IV, p. 227.   [55] *Ibid.*
[56] *Op. cit.*, p. 228.   [57] *Ibid.*
[58] Harold Clurman, *The Nation*, CLXXXII, 14 Jan. 1956.

St. Puthrick was at the hud of what fell out at Durry, Aughrim, on' th' Boyne.

ROORY [*stunned with the thought of St. Patrick as a Protestant*]: Protestant St. Pathrick? Is me hearin' sound, or what? What name did you mention?

BRENNAN: I said St. Puthrick—th' evangelical founder of our thrue Church.

ROORY: Is it dhreamin' I am? Is somethin' happenin' to me, or is it happenin' to you? Oh, man, it's mixin' mirth with madness you are at thinkin' St. Pathrick ever looped his neck in an orange sash, or tapped out a tune on a Protestant dhrum!

BRENNAN [*contemptuously*]: I refuse to argue with a one who's no' a broad-minded mon. Abuse is no equivalent for lugic— so I say God save th' King, an' tae hull with th' Pope!

ROORY [*indignantly*]: You damned bigot—to hell with th' King, an' God save th' Pope![59]

Equally amusing is the scene where the atheist Mullcanny, called "Th' New Broom" by the neighbours because he is out to sweep the idea of God out of the minds of men, rallies his arguments to convince Roory and Brennan that man originates from the monkey. Ayamonn (*i.e.* O'Casey) keeps aloof but offers protection to Mullcanny against the physical violence from Protestants and Catholics alike: "I'll stand by any honest man seekin' th' truth, though his way isn't my way."[60] Note the words: "his way is not my way." What then is his way? It is the way of tolerance and freedom, of allowing each man to question "all things, ay, life itself."[61] His God is not the God of sorrow and suffering, for these are evils that man has brought upon himself by his superstition, lack of imagination, and bigoted conception of religion. The true God is the God of love, forgiveness, sexual ecstasy; a God demanding not prayer and penitence but song, music and dance; a God delighting "to see joy shine for a moment on the faces of His much-troubled children."[62] It is the God that appears recurrently in all of O'Casey's later plays; it is the God in whom the dramatist firmly believes.

In *Red Roses for Me* we find O'Casey, almost for the first time, out to ridicule superstition. He does this with a good

[59] *Red Roses For Me*, Act II, p. 167. [60] *Op. cit.*, p. 165.
[61] *Op. cit.*, p. 169. [62] *Op. cit.*, Act I, p. 143.

deal of sympathy and good humour. He takes no sides but
laughs at Catholics and Protestants alike, not even sparing
Mrs Breydon, in whom can be traced some of his own mother's
superstitions. If the scales weigh a little heavily against his
Catholics, it is simply because they are on the whole more
superstitious than his Protestants. Superstition is bad enough
even for the uninventive mind, but when it happens to coincide
with the turgescent imagination of the Irish the results are
fantastic. See how Ayamonn's Catholic neighbours describe
their vision of the statue of the Blessed Virgin returning to her
worshippers, after Brennan has returned it to its niche:

> EEADA [*coming forward a little*]: She came back to Her poor
> again, in raiment rich. She came back; of Her own accord.
> She came to abide with Her people.
> DYMPNA: From her window, little Ursula looked, and saw
> Her come in; in th' moonlight, along the street She came,
> stately. Blinded be the coloured light that shone around
> about Her, the child fell back, in a swoon she fell full on the
> floor beneath her.
> 1st MAN: My eyes caught a glimpse of Her too, glidin' back
> to where She came from. Regal an' proud She was, an'
> wondrous, so that me eyes failed; me knees thrembled an'
> bent low, an' me heart whispered a silent prayer to itself as
> th' vision passed me by, an' I fancied I saw a smile on Her
> holy face.[63]

Once again we have Irish fancy at its peak, quite out of touch
with any concrete reality. In *Purple Dust* imagination ran
wild, but in *Red Roses for Me* there is an advance, in that the
characters now see what they imagine. What is strange is that
Ayamonn, instead of censuring them for their reverie, goes to
the other extreme of silencing Mullcanny who enjoys mocking
at things that are sacred. Here we have O'Casey employing a
new technique: not to allow the central character to expose
the follies of others, but to let the bubble of stupidity emerge to
the surface and burst by itself.

The finest thing in the play is the third act, where, to
quote Audrey Williamson, "O'Casey's genius takes a transient
fire," and in which "Each word hangs like a jewel in an

---

[63] *Red Roses For Me*, Act II, p. 177.

Ethiop's ear."[64] Like the second act of *The Plough and the Stars* it can stand by itself and be taken out of context, but greatly to the disadvantage of the play as a whole. Its purpose is, like that of the second act of *The Silver Tassie*, to give a wider significance to what may otherwise appear to be an individual or a group problem. Expressionism is used but not till the middle of Act III. This delay helps us to become familiar with the characters so that they do not lose their separate identity. On the whole the effect is created not so much by words spoken, as by stage technique and setting. To appreciate it fully one must imagine an ideal performance: the tall gaunt houses; the brown parapets; the sickening, cursing crowd surging with a new life as Ayamonn unfolds to them a vision of the city's hidden splendour. The gloomy, grey skies give way to the bright and lovely colours of the setting sun and everything for a moment is transformed.[65] A flute-player plays a joyous tune and Finnoola, forgetting her sorrows, swings out into a hectic dance. Ayamonn dances out to meet her while the people around clap their hands to the tap of the dancers' feet. The scene deserves comparison with the poem "A Piper," by Seumas O'Sullivan:

> A Piper in the street today,
> Set up, and tuned, and started to play,
> And away, away, away on the tide
> Of his music we started; on every side
> Doors and windows were opened wide,
> And men left down their work and came,
> And women with petticoats coloured like flame,
> And little bare feet that were blue with cold,
> Went dancing back to the age of gold,
> And all the world went gay, went gay,
> For half an hour in the street today.[66]

What is important is that the scene is factual. What O'Casey has described on the Liffey one can see in any part of Dublin: the grey skies suddenly caressed with lovely colours, the

---

[64] Audrey Williamson, *Theatre of Two Decades*, p. 189.

[65] Raymond Williams writes that in "*Red Roses For Me* the keypoint for analysis is O'Casey's handling of colour." See R. Williams, *Drama from Ibsen to Eliot*, pp. 173-4.

[66] Seumas O'Sullivan, *Dublin Poems*, p. 6.

misery of the people transformed into joy as little feet tap to a
popular tune. And in most cases it lasts just as long as it does
in this act. The grey skies reappear, the music ceases, the
joys fly; only the vision lingers on.

I have described the second act of *The Plough and the Stars*
as a one-act vignette of the period. The third act of *Red Roses
for Me* is a vignette of Ireland as it was in 1913, and of Ireland
as it is today. This is because O'Casey is showing those salient
characteristics of the Irish people which have remained
unchanged through its centuries of political and social history.
The misery and torture of the present is counteracted by a
romantic interpretation of the past. The stories "of Finn Mac
Cool of th' golden hair, Goll Mac Morna of th' big blows,
Caoilte of th' flyin' feet, an' Oscar of th' invincible spear"[67]
provide an antidote to despair. This romantic dreaming was
initially inspired by the hopeless discontent of the Irish against
English rule, and nourished on the faith that Ireland's "Golden
Age" would return after independence was won. For one
reason or another the much cherished independence did not
fulfil all that its adherents had hoped for. Even today the
average Irishman makes up for his present plight by recalling
to his mind the heroism of the past. The ageless quality of
their dreams still continues; their sorrows are occasionally
lightened by a song or a dance, their indeterminate future
glows under the sound of the marching feet of revolutionaries.

Red Roses For Me had its first performance in London at the
Embassy Theatre, on 26 Feb. 1946. It was well received by
the critics, James Redfern describing it as "an undoubtedly
successful and moving play."[68] One may judge of its success
from a letter which Sir Bronson Albery (Managing Director
of Wyndham Theatres Ltd) wrote to Cyril Cusack when the
latter refused an invitation to produce *The Bishop's Bonfire*
at the theatre:

> I am not sure that you are wise to refuse the invitation from the
> Embassy Theatre. I produced *Red Roses for Me* there and we
> had a snow storm for the first night. The notices were good,
> but, even before that, the advance was excellent, and, in

[67] *Red Roses For Me*, Act III, p. 192.
[68] J. Redfern, *Spectator*, CLXXVI, 8 Mar. 1946.

spite of the continuance of the snow storm, we beat all records up to that time at the Embassy Theatre. *Red Roses for Me* successively went to the Lyric, Hammersmith, the New Theatre and Wyndham's Theatre.[69]

The play had its Broadway performance in 1955, the first new full-length play of O'Casey to reach New York since *Within the Gates* some twenty years earlier. Its reception was on the whole mixed: *The New York Times* described it as "a beautiful play," while *The Daily Mirror* doubted if it "would have better than a limited appeal."[70]

The play has been praised highly for the beauty of its language. Splendid passages so abound that it is difficult to pick and choose. Therefore I have taken the easier task of quoting some opinions. *The Times* critic says:

> Mr. O'Casey writes with superb Elizabethan energy, using the language of the English Bible, the language of the Dublin Streets, and the language of the Irish poets to comic or to tragic ends, swinging it to a rhythm which is all his own.[71]

Harold Clurman writes:

> O'Casey's poetry at best is, for all its musical clangor and reaching for the moon, a helter-skelter, tatter-demalion, bubbling poetry in which the characters are usually unaware of poetic intent. They speak in alliteration and in chaotic effusiveness with the natural vigor and pleasure of a street boy's slang. Great phrases come pouring out of O'Casey's people as if an overturned garbage pail revealed gems as well as refuse—and little distinction were made between one and the other.[72]

And this is what Alan Dent has to say:

> And not since Synge have we heard such floods of rapturous words about love, and hunger and thirst, and martyrdom, and religion, and poverty, and of the rights of man, and of Cathleen ni Houlihan. . . . It is a feast of beautiful lush language. It is mad, grave, funny, rhapsodical. It is the work of an undeniable and quite unbridled genius[73]

---

[69] Letter dated 29 Mar. 1955. In Mr Cusack's possession.
[70] Quoted in *The Times* (London), 30 Dec. 1955.
[71] *The Times* (London), 27 Feb. 1946.
[72] Harold Clurman, *The Nation*, CLXXXII, 14 Jan. 1956.
[73] Alan Dent, *Nocturnes and Rhapsodies*, pp. 100-01.

Even in the midst of such praise it is hard to ignore Sewell Stokes's objection that it is difficult to surrender to the high-flown rhetoric that O'Casey puts in the mouth of his humblest characters.[74]　The criticism is more true than harsh. Shakespearian as O'Casey's language is, his characters are not, so that one often feels the lack of harmony between the speaker and the spoken words.

The few faults in the play have not escaped notice.　O'Casey was blamed, with some reason, for over-extending the last act and for introducing new characters at this late stage.[75]　Allan Lewis regrets that there is so much religion and politics in the play that we do not get more than a peep at the lovers.[76]　Theophilus Lewis, amidst a lot of unfair criticism, observes the one serious flaw in the play, the lack of an "head-on conflict of virtue with the powers of darkness."[77]　Not only is this conflict absent in Ayamonn, but so also is the tussle between the call of duty and the call of love.　His ears are too full of the sound of marching feet to hear Sheila's entreaties. Ayamonn's idealism reduces Sheila to a secondary character without actually enhancing his own stature.　He is rather too perfect to be of much dramatic interest.　He fights the easier fight against the enemies of the "Faith"; the hard fight between the flesh and the soul, it seems, O'Casey fought and won for him off the stage.

Whatever be the faults in the play, and they are more than I have touched upon, it still ranks with the finest in our present-day theatre.　If it lacks some of the dramatic intensity of his Abbey plays, this is more than compensated for by the richness of its language, music, songs and dances, all of which O'Casey uses most skilfully to advance his theme.　For those critics who feel that O'Casey's dramatic gifts declined after his exile, this play is a serious challenge.

[74] Sewell Stokes, *Theatre Arts*, xxx, Jun. 1946.
[75] Henry Hewes, *Saturday Review*, xxxix, 14 Jan. 1956.
[76] Allan Lewis, *The Nation*, clxxxi, 24 Dec. 1955.
[77] Theophilus Lewis, *America*, xciv, 21 Jan. 1956.

VII

The Exile Plays : II

OAK LEAVES AND LAVENDER was published in 1946. Its alternative title, "A Warld on Wallpaper," is ironically derived from Yeats's letter to O'Casey on *The Silver Tassie*, where he says that "the whole history of the world must be reduced to wallpaper in front of which the characters must pose and speak."[1] O'Casey is obviously sneering at Yeats's dramatic theory, for in this play, more than in *The Silver Tassie*, war is the leading motif rather than the background. The play had its first, and perhaps only, professional performance at the Lyric Theatre, Hammersmith, opening on 14 May 1947, when, to use J. C. Trewin's words, it was "murdered . . . in a timid, blurred production that did no kind of justice to O'Casey."[2] No doubt an imaginative and gifted producer could make a success of this play, but I am doubtful whether it could rank beside his better-known works.

The play has a Prelude. In a dimly-lit room of an old manor house the ghosts of its previous inhabitants appear. They dance stiffly to the music of a minuet played on a piano, and speak in a level tone without any inflexions. They complain of being tired and neglected; they express the fear that England's freedom may be lost as power now rests with the masses. The shadows prepare to go forth and fight for England when the Young Son of Time reminds them that "Time has brought a change." The voice of the Lavender Seller (O'Casey uses an old Cornish legend that the smell of lavender pervades an old house when evil overtakes it) is heard and the dancers fade out of sight. They reappear at the end of the play to dance again their graceful minuet. The return of the shadowy figures is a clever invention, for it imposes on the play a unity which it would otherwise lack.

[1] W. B. Yeats, *The Irish Statesmen*, x, 9 Jun. 1928.
[2] J. C. Tewin, *The Theatre Since 1900*, p. 289.

The Prelude is the most original item. Not all of it is good—the Third Gentleman Dancer uses highly rhetorical words:

> It is dark to us; but Goldsmith, Berkeley, Boyle, Addison Hone, Swift and Sheridan still bear flaming torches through the streets of life.[3]

And the Young Son of Time makes the most commonplace comments in the most profound manner. He reminds the spirits that they belong to the past; surely they need no ghost to tell them that! O'Casey has used him to link the Prelude with the main action of the play. Had the first act followed the Dancers alone, there would have been a gap between the Prelude of the past and the first act set in the present. Through the Young Son of Time O'Casey has made a feeble attempt to bridge this gap and to bring in a sense of continuity. But in spite of such weaknesses the Prelude is a piece of craftsmanship. A solemn atmosphere is created by the dim light, soft music, low voices, and the rustling of dresses as the ghostly figures dance. The Lavender Song is neatly introduced. Its presence in the Prelude forebodes a calamity, not on the manor house alone as it does later in the play, but on England. In *Oak Leaves and Lavender* O'Casey moves from the universal to the particular and then back again to the universal, the process being the opposite of what he tried in *The Silver Tassie* and *Red Roses for Me*. Here England's struggle is symbolised in the Prelude and realised in the play.

The story is set during the Battle of Britain in a large room of a manor house belonging to Dame Hatherleigh. Feelim, the Irish butler, suffers and expresses the atmosphere of wartime activity created by the Home Guards, policemen, farmers, land girls, crowds seeking shelter, etc., who continuously invade the room with one foolish protest or another. Amid all this confusion, Drishogue, Feelim's son, and Edgar, Dame Hatherleigh's son, have a riotous time with their girls, Monica and Jennie. Drishogue and Edgar have just got their wings and are spending their last few days of leave before reporting for active service. Their leave is cut short by a sudden order to return to their squadron. They leave for the front and the

---

[3] *Oak Leaves and Lavender*, Prelude, p. 9.

smell of lavender, which was noticeable from the beginning, becomes more insistent. Both the boys are shot down by the enemy. Jennie dies in her attempt to save Edgar from the burning wreck of his plane, while Monica, carrying Drishogue's child in her womb, turns to Feelim for protection: "My dad won't, so you must stand by me now."[4] Feelim's orthodoxy is shocked but he accepts the responsibility. Dame Hatherleigh, standing in the midst of the Dancers, who have reappeared, expresses the usual O'Casey optimism: "We must all go soon. Our end makes but a beginning for others."[5] The play ends with the Dancers singing in chorus, "The lavender shall bloom again,"[6] which means that the good and the beautiful in life shall continue to flower.

A few incidents and discussions are fastened to the plot which have little bearing on the main action. Numerous characters are introduced, some of them serving no specific purpose and giving the play a disorganised appearance. But one cannot complain much: O'Casey introduces disorder to show the chaos that was created during the War. When men and women from different walks of life, with different outlooks and faiths assemble, even though to fight against a common enemy, harmony is impossible. If a dramatist wishes to show such an anomaly in life he has no choice but to introduce anarchy to the stage. O'Casey had done this in *Within the Gates* and very successfully too. But there he had imposed on the minor conflicts an artistic serenity and a settled design which we do not find here. Also, in *Within the Gates* the inconsequential characters and their trifling arguments were a vital part of the play as they summed up life in its different moods. But in this play there are characters which are palpably dragged in for no other purpose than to give the dramatist a chance to express his beliefs. A notable example is Mrs Deeda Tutting (she figures as Mrs Creda Stern in *Sunset and Evening Star*), whose sympathy for Fascism provides an opportunity for O'Casey's chief spokesman, Drishogue, to praise Russia. O'Casey doesn't play fair either; he does all he can to make the woman seem unattractive: "She is a tall, gaunt, plain-faced woman of forty or so . . . rather untidy,

---

[4] *Oak Leaves and Lavender*, Act III, p. 107. [5] *Op. cit.*, p. 110.
[6] *Op. cit.*, p. 111.

with wisps hanging down her neck and over her ears."[7] He gives her the worst of possible arguments to mouth in her denunciation of Russia: "Their rifles are soft-tube toys; the wings of their warplanes fall off in a sturdy wind . . ."[8] so that Drishogue has no difficulty in silencing her, even with such highfalutin Irishisms as, "Woe unto any nation making war on the Soviet Union! She will slash open the snout, and tear out the guts of any power crossing her borders!"[9] It may be noted that O'Casey rarely takes sides in religious discussions, but he always does so in political discussions when the Communist ideology is involved.

Mr Constant and Pobjoy are of greater consequence to the play than Mrs Deeda Tutting. Constant, who uses his wife's pregnancy—it occurred as soon as the raids began!—as an excuse to fly to safety, is not a character of the first importance, but he represents those who evaded their duty towards England in her hour of trial. Pobjoy, the conscientious objector, is an interesting character. Like Constant he is a coward, but unlike Constant he is self-opinionated and clever. To avoid risks he has dubbed himself a "conscientious objector," and does not give a farthing what the others think of him. Knowing what he wants, and the easiest way to get it, he does not waste his time making excuses, but cuts short Feelim's splendid arguments with sharp and pert replies. In the end he turns the tables on Feelim by saying; "Get your own rats to go into the fight, and then you'll have a surer right to lecture us."[10] The characters present, who were all along siding with Feelim, now turn against him, and in the confusion that is created Pobjoy manages to slip away. Feelim, his racial pride aroused, meets the challenge and at some length points out that there never was a war where the "Irish Green" was not seen. Feelim is, of course, expressing the dramatist's sentiments when he recounts the battles all over the world in which Irish regiments have fought. In this lively scene the dramatist does not commit

---

[7] *Oak Leaves and Lavender*, Act I, pp. 46-7. Cp. Horace Gregory, "Playwright on a Soapbox," *The Saturday Review*, 20 Nov. 1954.

[8] *Oak Leaves and Lavender*, Act I, p. 51.

[9] *Ibid.*

[10] *Op. cit.*, Act III, p. 96. O'Casey gives a good chronicle of the wars in which the Irish have fought in *They Go—The Irish*, ed. Leslie Daiken, pp. 7-25.

the error of openly championing the Irish against the English as he had done in *Purple Dust.*

Feelim O'Morrigun, who is "as cunning as a fox," is the only character worth remembering. The confusion he faces and the bickerings among other characters that he tries to settle with the tetchy wisdom of a tenth-rate schoolmaster are splendidly amusing. A reviewer described him as "a comic philosopher fit to talk on equal terms with Fluther and the 'Paycock'."[11] No doubt Feelim has some of Fluther's gusto and exuberance; there is never a dull moment when he has something to say, and fortunately he has a lot to say. Nothing is outside his jurisdiction and there is not a thing in which he does not meddle. Even in the argument between Drishogue and Mrs Tutting on the merits of Communism and Fascism, of which he knows nothing, he has something to edge in. It is his presence that somewhat redeems this scene which otherwise would be boring.

Feelim has all the Irish peculiarities except a fondness for drink. He is religious, superstitious and gifted with an imagination that encourages him to see all that he fears or suspects. He also has the typical Irish shrewdness, pride and sense of superiority which prevent him from taking the English too seriously. When Constable Dillery chides him for breaking the black-out regulations, he says:

> Fuss an' fury. God must ha' had a rare laugh when He made a serious Englishman.[12]

Feelim's genius remains purely comic until calamity overtakes the house. His plaintive cry on hearing of Edgar's death contains the finest lines in the play, comparable to the prayer of Juno when her son is shot for being a traitor:

> From the hurt of th' burnin', from the lost alliance of loved ones here on earth, from th' blackened dust of a vanished life, give the vision of perpetual light in th' peace of eternal rest, O God of th' many kindnesses, and th' darin' deeds of mercy![13]

Courageously he receives the news of his son's death: "God knows I'll miss you, Drishogue!"[14] But the great moment of

---

[11] *The Times Literary Supplement,* 11 May 1946.
[12] *Oak Leaves and Lavender,* Act I, p. 21.
[13] *Op. cit.,* Act III, pp. 90-1.
[14] *Op. cit.,* p. 105.

his trial comes when Monica informs him that "There's more to come; a living spark from himself that will soon be a buoyant symbol of our Drishogue who is gone![15] His puritan outlook is shocked but he accepts the challenge, even as he regretfully shakes his head in sorrow: "Oh! Which is worse—th' burden of th' dead who are with us now; or that of the living still to come!"[16] In creating the character of Feelim at the age of sixty-six, O'Casey, with a wave of his creative wand, dismisses the contentions of numerous critics who keep asserting that in his later plays there are no characters worthy to stand besides Boyle, Joxer or Fluther Good.

Unfortunately there are no other characters in the play that interest us even moderately. Drishogue is the usual O'Casey hero, irksome by now as we have met his kind in almost all of O'Casey's exile plays. There is not even the semblance of a conflict in his mind. He is brave, honest, noble, imaginative: but these qualities alone do not make a dramatic hero. Edgar, who shares some of Drishogue's qualities, is more matter-of-fact and a little unscrupulous. For him there is only one life, the one that exists in the present; there is only one joy, the one that is readily available. He is attached to Jennie not because of his love for her, but to while away the sheer humdrum of non-active life. Note the conversation between Drishogue and Edgar:

> DRISHOGUE: Don't you ever get tired of walking or lying with Jennie?
> EDGAR: Often; but with her the tiredness is always restful. She's grand for the time being.
> DRISHOGUE: But you don't value her enough to want to spend a lifetime with her?
> EDGAR: Well, hardly; in the cool of the evening, in the deep dusk of the night, she is lovely; but I shouldn't care to have to welcome her the first thing in the morning.[17]

Edgar is on the stage for a few minutes only. His presence and comments give Drishogue an opportunity to display his idealism, which is clearly O'Casey's own. We hardly get a glimpse of Edgar and Jennie together; their relationship with

---

[15] *Oak Leaves and Lavender*, Act III, p. 107.   [16] *Op. cit.*, p. 108.
[17] *Op. cit.*, Act I, p. 26.

one another is conveyed to us through what the other characters say. We do not get very many opportunities of seeing Drishogue and Monica together either. Had O'Casey trimmed down some of the political and idealistic discussions and concentrated more on the love story, the play might have been better. Once again, as in *The Star Turns Red* and *Red Roses for Me*, O'Casey commits the error of allowing man's external activities to overshadow his study of domestic life.

Not much can be said of the female characters in this play. Mrs Watchit, the Dame's housekeeper, is a fidgety old woman. Her "'Usband says" this and "'Usband says" that begin by telling on the nerves of Feelim and eventually grate on the nerves of the audience. Dame Hatherleigh is self-sacrificing, brave, understanding and steadfast. She suffers the most: she loses her husband and son in the War and sees her house converted into a factory. To what purpose O'Casey substitutes her for the Young Son of Time is not clear. It may be because the Young Son of Time has outlived his usefulness of bridging the past with the present, and is now not necessary. Dame Hatherleigh, put in his place, symbolises the ruin of a generation—war having swallowed the young and the brave and left behind fastidious old men and crazy old women. Jennie and Monica are like most of O'Casey's heroines except that they are sexually more alive. Both go to the extent of yielding themselves physically to their lovers and providing them with the maximum of pleasure during their last few days of leave. Jennie perishes in her attempt (rather an improbable one) to rescue Edgar from his burning aircraft—her death mocking Edgar's selfish love. Monica, worn out with sorrow, comforts herself with the thought of the new Drishogue that is to be born. When Feelim describes it as wrong, she replies: "It was right and proper of him, for I wanted a pledge of all he meant to me; and I got it; and I'm glad."[18]

The characters throw light on O'Casey's beliefs and convictions, though much of what we learn through them is no longer new to us. O'Casey supported Britain in her fight against the Nazis, not because he himself believed in the English political system, but because Britain was fighting against the tyranny of Fascism to defend her cultural and

[18] *Oak Leaves and Lavender*, Act III, p. 107.

scientific heritage. He clarifies his stand in the conversation that takes place between Drishogue and Monica:

MONICA [*clinging to him*]: . . . I sometimes wish you hadn't ventured into danger for the love of England!

DRISHOGUE [*starting away from her—with startled indignation*]: Love of England! Good God, woman, I have no love for England!

MONICA [*startled too*]: But aren't you fighting for her?

DRISHOGUE [*passionately*]: No, I'm not! I'm fighting for the people. I'm fighting against the stormy pillagers who blackened the time-old walls of Guernica, and tore them down . . .[19]

Drishogue's alliance with England is symbolic of Russia's temporary alliance with the Western Powers. It is also symbolic of the temporary reconciliation between people of different classes and different political faiths in order to fight against a common enemy. Men and women differ, argue, swear at each other but still work bravely together to win the War. O'Casey gives unstinting praise to the English for their courage and fortitude. A. E. Wilson writes that if he made anything of the play, "it was a paean of praise and a tribute to those who withstood the ordeal during the Battle of Britain."[20]

Among other things Drishogue expresses O'Casey's love of the earth, not bartering away the gifts of this world for some forlorn hope of life after death. This is what he tells Monica when she assures him that death cannot mean the loss of life:

Perhaps not; I only know it means the loss of many lovely things: the moving patterns of flying birds; the stroll through crowded streets, crudely strewn about, that the moon regenerates into silvered haunts of meditative men; the musical wile of waves racing towards us, or slowly bidding us farewell; the wild flowers tossing themselves on to the field and into the hedgerow; the sober ecstasy, or jewelled laugh, of children playing; the river's rowdy rush or graceful gliding into sea or lake; the sun asthride the hills, or rainfall teeming down aslant behind them; a charming girl, shy, but ready with her finest favours—oh, these are dear and lovely things to lose![21]

---

[19] *Oak Leaves and Lavender*, Act II, p. 61.
[20] A. E. Wilson, *Post-War Theatre*, p. 103.
[21] *Oak Leaves and Lavender*, Act II, pp. 58-9.

O'Casey's views on sex remain more or less the same as in his previous plays. Through Drishogue's affair with Monica (only his Communist heroes appear to have a satisfactory sexual relationship) he seems to say that love alone justifies the sexual act; that no sense of guilt or shame should follow it; and that sexual intercourse performed in honest love means marriage. The Church ceremony, or the State's consent, is of secondary importance.

When one speaks of "sexual ecstasy" in O'Casey's plays it should not be confused with mere pleasure-making or debauchery. Sexual intercourse entails a moral responsibility which his heroes are willing to shoulder. The crux of the matter is that few of them live long enough to prove their mettle.

In *Red Roses for Me* O'Casey made his first drive towards ridiculing superstition; this he continues mildly in *Oak Leaves and Lavender*. Dame Hatherleigh procures an image of an angel for her son's protection, and we are not surprised that Drishogue looks upon it with condescension. From Drishogue's talk we infer that he is not superstitious, and yet we find him at one moment telling Edgar that he could swear that he "heard last night the timid music of a frightened minuet."[22] How do we solve this contradiction in Drishogue? And solve it we must, for it is through Drishogue that O'Casey speaks. To arrive at an answer we must understand that O'Casey uses the legend of the lavender, not to mock at superstition, but to prophesy what is to come. Fun is made of superstition, not through the characters' belief in the old legend but through Dame Hatherleigh's faith in the image of an angel that she has bought for her son. To ridicule superstition, the first need is that it must prove to be false. When it turns out true, as in the Abbey plays, it is not truly ridiculed.

The Cornish legend, apart from its use as a prophecy, is used, like the Young Son of Time, to link the present with the past. When Edgar says that "the past is gone for ever," Drishogue replies: "No, Edgar, you're wrong: the past has woven us into what we are."[23] In *Purple Dust* O'Casey had pointed out that it is impossible to recreate the past, and that

[22] *Oak Leaves and Lavender*, Act I, p. 26.
[23] *Ibid.*

one must live in the present. In *Oak Leaves and Lavender* he
says that though we live in the present, the past in some
mysterious way has its influence on us. When we put these
two views together we come to the conclusion that though we
cannot recapture the past, we cannot escape from it either.
In the play the past is used as an oracle that forebodes the
danger facing the present.

The play has been harshly criticised, and often without
much justification. Vivian Mercier described it as "embarras-
singly bad,"[24] and Richard Findlater wrote that it reveals "most
clearly [O'Casey's] weaknesses."[25] The play has serious faults,
but much of the hostility against it is due to the failure of the
critics to visualise what the dramatist is trying to get at. The
full significance of the Young Son of Time, Dame Hatherleigh's
presence among the Dancers at the end of the play, "Germany
Calling"—a reminder of Lord Haw Haw's Berlin broadcasts
during the War—and much else, remain partly obscure and
open to conjecture. Besides, symbolism is too freely strewn over
the pages of the play and the majority of the characters are
symbolic (I say this in defiance of Mr Findlater's observation
that none of the characters have any symbolic reality).[26] To
point a case, Mr Constant stands for all those who thought
only of their personal safety during England's hour of trial.
His dress is significant: the long, heavy overcoat hiding most of
his blue shirt, grey coat and yellow trousers. The overcoat
symbolises the all-over fear that hides his perplexed inner
motives. A reader who disregards O'Casey's instructions, or
a producer who replaces Mr Constant's overcoat by a dinner-
jacket, has no reason to grumble except at his own uninventive-
ness. O'Casey does not attire his characters in haphazard
colours merely to relieve the drabness of contemporary clothes;
they are often there to reveal some aspect of the character in
question. This was also to be found in his early plays. In
The Plough and the Stars, Peter Flynn's gorgeous dress and ostrich
plume go with his character. Just as the ostrich thinks it is
evading its enemy by screwing its head into a hole in the sand,
in the same way Peter Flynn evades the immediate danger by

[24] V. Mercier, *Commonweal*, LXIV, 13 Jul. 1956.
[25] R. Findlater, *The Unholy Trade*, p. 181.
[26] *Ibid.*

maundering around the grave of some old patriot. To understand O'Casey's later plays fully, it is necessary to pay attention
to the setting, stage directions and descriptions, all of which are
carefully set out in the published text of the plays.

With *Cock-a-doodle Dandy* (1949) O'Casey returned to
what he describes as his "first principle of a phantasy."[27] It
will be remembered that he had written two in the early days
of his career as a dramatist: *The Robe of Rosheen*, which was
published in a Republican weekly, and *Cathleen Listens In*, which
failed at the Abbey Theatre in 1923. After this O'Casey told
Holloway that he would write no more fantasies, although he
liked the form.[28] It was in fact twenty-six years after *Cathleen
Listens In* that *Cock-a-doodle Dandy* appeared, and it soon became
his favourite play. A favourite only, for O'Casey considers
his most powerful play to be *The Plough and the Stars*—an opinion
which most critics share.

The play opens with Michael Marthraun, a small farmer,
warning Sailor Mahon, now the owner of a fleet of lorries, of
the evil and sinister things happening in Nyadnanave after
Loreleen (the former's daughter by his first wife) has returned
from England. The topic of their discussion changes and the
two start chaffering over the additional charges that Sailor
Mahon demands for carrying each load of turf from the bog to
the village. Shaanar—a hedge preacher—comes in to direct
their thoughts back to the most unseemly things happening
in the unfortunate town. Soon an indomitable cock invades
Michael's house, spreading devastation wherever it goes. Cups
and saucers fly out of the window, the chairs collapse under
the haggling old men and the whiskey changes colour. The
bird flies about the house, clawing the holy pictures and
pecking at Michael's tall hat. Father Domineer, Michael, a
Police Sergeant and One-Eyed Larry fight a fantastic battle
against the mettlesome Cock. At first the Cock definitely gets
the better of its opponents. It batters the priest, raises a wind
that whips off the pants of the policeman, rocks the house as
if in an earthquake and finally blows down the proud Irish
flag. It kidnaps Father Domineer, who is rescued and carried
safely home on the back of a goose. He soon returns to the

---

[27] Letter to me from O'Casey dated 20 Apr. 1958.
[28] J. Holloway, MS. 1881, Sep.-Dec. 1923, p. 696.

scene of the battle and summons his flock to stand firm against "th' onward rush of paganism."[29] Just then Loreleen is dragged in by two Rough Fellows in a tumbled and dishevelled state. She had been discovered making love to Sailor Mahon who had promised her £5 so that she could go back to England. Father Domineer rebukes her for living a life of joy that has caused such strange things to happen in Ireland, and banishes her to England. Lorna, Michael's second wife, accompanies her stepdaughter into exile, saying: "we go not towards an evil, but leave an evil behind us!"[30] The Messenger, and Marion, a maid employed in the household, follow Loreleen and Lorna. Michael, left alone, buries his head in his arms.

To the neat structure of the plot O'Casey has fastened two incidents which he fails to integrate into the play. The first is that of the parish priest accidently striking a lorry-driver dead. Vivian Mercier writes that "Such an incident did occur in Ireland some years ago—like a true Irish Protestant, I have the clipping filed away—but O'Casey totally fails to integrate it into his play."[31] This is true. O'Casey has brought into the play an incident which he knew to have occurred, just to have a lunge at the Catholic clergy. That he failed to fuse it into the plot is regrettable since the story has enough dramatic verve to be of interest if rightly handled. The second incident is the direct result of O'Casey's disbelief in miracles. Julia, Michael's sister-in-law, goes to Lourdes for a cure, but she returns unhealed and renounces her faith in miracles. That the incident has little to do with the main theme is not so annoying as the inconsistency of the whole episode when it is fastened to the play. From the setting, the main story and the haggling of the two misers over the price to be paid for moving the turf it would appear that the action of the play take place in a single day. How then, we may ask, is it possible for a sick woman to leave a remote rural town in southern Ireland for Lourdes in the morning and return the same evening?

The fantasy in the play mingles freely with the realism. O'Casey has mixed the two to bring home his purpose. He had learnt from past experience (the failure of *Cathleen Listens*

---

[29] *Cock-a-doodle Dandy*, Sc. III, p. 211.
[30] *Op. cit.*, p. 217.
[31] V. Mercier, *Commonweal*, LXIV, 13 Jul. 1956.

In) that the dramatist's motive may remain clouded to the audience unless the fantasy is relieved by streaks of factual incidents. Much in the play is taken from real life. O'Casey says:

> In spite of the fanciful nature of the play, almost all the incidents are factual—the priest that struck the blow; the rough fellows manhandling the young, gay girl; the bitter opposition to any sign of the strange ways of a man with a maid; the old, menacing fool, full of false piety, going round inflicting fear of evil things on all who listen to him; and, above all through the piety, through the fear, the never-ending quest for money.[32]

However it is of first importance to scrutinise the fanciful and the supernatural in the play and to apprehend its symbolic significance.

"The cock is," writes O'Casey, "the joyful active spirit of life as it weaves a way through the Irish scene. . . ."[33] But it is something more than this: It is the symbol of the ardent sexual ecstasy that O'Casey advocates in his gospel to the young. The cock has been frequently used as a symbol of sexual fertility, more so since the decline of the goose, which also had a similar significance. Professor Allardyce Nicoll quotes a writer on physiognomy who describes the cock as a bird which is "insatiably libidinous."[34] D. H. Lawrence's use of the cock in *The Man Who Died* is primarily symbolic of male fertility. O'Casey's use of the cock is also symbolic of this fertility as well as what he terms the "active spirit of life." It stands for joy, courage, love, sexual ecstasy and vibrant living. To the bigoted, superstition-soaked, middle-aged philistines of a provincial town it is a demon cock (in some folk-lore the cock was supposed to have been created in opposition to demons and wizards)[35] creating havoc, but to minds that are clean and fearless it is a friendly bird. For Loreleen, who lives to wrench joy out of life, the Cock holds no terror, for it is "a symbol of her spirit and vivacity."[36] There is a close relationship between them. The Cock crows lustily

---

[32] O'Casey, *The New York Times* (international edn.), 10 Nov. 1958.
[33] *Ibid.*
[34] A. Nicoll, *Masks, Mimes and Miracles*, p. 32.
[35] See Alexander Haggerty Krappe's *The Science of Folk-lore*.
[36] Letter to me from O'Casey dated 31 Oct. 1959.

when Loreleen first appears in Scene I. The Bellman announces that the Cock is coming in the shape of a woman in Scene II, just before Loreleen enters. In the third scene the priest and his puritanical crew seize the young girl in their attempt to collar the Cock, and are satisfied. The play ends with Father Domineer's victory: not in banishing the Cock, for it is the inextinguishable spirit of joy, but in banishing Loreleen who had given a practical shape to what the Cock symbolised. This is what the priest tells the girl's father:

> Be of good cheer, Michael; th' demon is conquered—you can live peacefully an' happy in your own home now.[37]

Loreleen and the Cock appear alternately on the stage but never together. This is because essentially the two are indivisible; one is the body, the other the spirit. Each represents the other.

The Messenger, who has spent a month in jail for kissing Marion in public, has no fear of the Cock either, for he, like Loreleen, believes in living completely. Lorna's and Marion's position is not very clear at the start. Their initial fear of the Cock shows that they waver between the ascetic teachings of the priest and the vivacious spirit in themselves. But as the play proceeds they begin to live in obedience to the dictates of their innermost feelings, and the fear of the Cock vanishes. Sailor Mahon, though he longs to live a fuller life, has not the grit in him to defy the priest. He suffers from the mischief of the Cock in the first two scenes, but wisely decamps in the third scene to "ruffle" Loreleen, while a raging wind ruffles his companions as they battle against the bird. Shaanar, the "Latin-lustrous oul' cod,"[38] fights the bird from a distance with his Latin exorcism, which does not flutter a feather. But the chief antagonist to the spirit of gaiety is the priest, and among his blind followers are Michael, the Sergeant, One-Eyed Larry and the Bellman. They are the people who face the full fury of the Cock and the weird happenings its presence brings about. The gale that blows in Scene III and shakes the house has no effect on the women but it terrifies the men. Moreover, the horrors which their petrified minds imagined in fact take place: they see horns on women's heads when they fear it, the

---

[37] *Cock-a-doodle Dandy*, Sc. III, p. 217.   [38] *Op. cit.*, Sc. I, p. 148.

chairs collapse just when Michael and Mahon think they can no longer sit serene, and so forth. To the imagination seething with furtive desires and fears the Cock is a demon, but for all who are joyous and gay it is the very breath of life. What is the very devil itself for the priest is for Marion a "saucy bird" giving "an hilarious time,"[39] for which she will "have a wreath of roses"[40] to hang round its neck. As the devotees of puritanism march to fight the bird, Marion asks:

> MARION: D'ye think they'll get him? Th' place'll lose its brightness if th' Cock's killed.
>
> LORNA: How can they desthroy a thing they say themselves is *not of this world?*[41] [Italics mine].

To which world does the Cock belong? It belongs to the indestructible world of the human heart, to the world of the healthy human spirit rejoicing in the pleasures that God has given. It cannot be conquered but it can be banished by the philistines, as Loreleen's exile signifies.

Not much can be said about the characters in the play. The most captivating is Sailor Mahon. He is drawn from a man O'Casey met in New York.[42] A man of the wide waters with "a touch of the sea-breeze in his way of talking and his way of walking,"[43] he is "free with whales an' dolphins an' octopususas"[44] but refuses to squander his energy controlling land-fowls. Like Joxer he has a vocabulary peculiarly his own:

> I seen you meself throtting afther her from starboard to port, from poop to quarther-deck, hoistin' before her th' fancy of ribbon an' lace, silver-buckled shoes, an' a silk dhress for Sunday.[45]

> Young lass, may you go through healin' wathers, an' come back a clipper, with ne'er a spar, a sail, or a rope asthray![46]

> Are you goin' to tell me that th' skipper aloft an' his hierarchilogical crew are concerned about th' Mayor, the Messenger Marion, me, an' you as much as they are about them who've been promoted to th' quarter-deck o' th' world's fame?[47]

---

[39] *Cock-a-doodle Dandy*, Sc. I, p. 145. [40] *Op. cit.*, Sc. II, p. 162.
[41] *Op. cit.*, Sc. III, p. 190. [42] *The Green Crow*, p. 233.
[43] *Cock-a-doodle Dandy*, Sc. I, p. 122. [44] *Op. cit.*, p. 140.
[45] *Op. cit.*, p. 126. [46] *Op. cit.*, p. 154.
[47] *Op. cit.*, Sc. II, p. 157.

Aw, God, no! Me sails of love are reefed at last, an' I lie quiet, restin' in a lonely harbour now.[48]

He is as inseparable a companion to Michael as Joxer was to Boyle. If he is unable to get the extra two shillings, he at least manages to get a free drink and a good time with Loreleen. And that is something in Nyadnanave!

O'Casey's sympathies, as in most of his previous plays, are with his women characters. We have the Messenger, one from a long line of O'Casey's spokesmen such as the Dreamer, O'Killigain, Ayamonn and so on, but he carries little symbolic meaning; he is a man of few words, more of a spectator than a character. He sits on the wall playing the accordion and only at crucial moments does he speak or interfere to set wrong aright. Taken as a body the women in the play are brave, youthful and kindly, fighting against the narrow prejudices of man-made morality to give love and life its rightful place.

The play is important since it shows a certain development in O'Casey's attitude towards Ireland and the Catholic Church. In plays such as *Purple Dust* and *Red Roses for Me* O'Casey had attacked some of the evils in Ireland, but he had taken care to show the good and had held forth a hope for the future. But in *Cock-a-doodle Dandy* he seems to have lost faith in Ireland completely. The Messenger, quite unlike the heroes of his previous plays, has little to say, for what is there left to be said when the Church and the state have decided to hound joy out of life. For those who wish to lead a fuller life the only hope lies in flight, rather than a fight. "Is it any wondher that th' girls are fleein' in their tens of thousands from this bewildhered land?"[49] says Loreleen when she is pelted with stones. The exponents of joy leave Ireland, first Loreleen and Lorna, then Marion and the Messenger. Where to? asks Michael. "To a place where life resembles life more than it does here,"[50] answers the Messenger. O'Casey may be seeing in the escape of these characters the story of his own exile. He too had fled from a land that seemed to have closed round him. But whether he really believes that life in present-day Ireland is as bad as

[48] *Cock-a-doodle Dandy*, Sc. III, p. 194.   [49] *Ibid.*
[50] *Op. cit.*, p. 220.

he features it is difficult to say. When I spoke to him of the lust for life in Ireland, he leaned back on the sofa and sadly shook his head. "That Ireland is gone," he said. "That Ireland is gone."[51]

O'Casey's attitude towards Ireland emanates from his fear of the power the Church wields in matters of state and in the life of the individual. He disapproves of the ascendancy of the clergy over their flock and unrelentingly holds them responsible for the poverty and misery in the land. Shaw nurtured a similar opinion, as can be seen from his *Preface for Politicians*:[52] but in O'Casey's words, "he devoted a tremendous lot of energy to a hell of a lot of things besides the 'mocking of the Christian faith'."[53] O'Casey devotes the greater part of his energy to ridiculing the clergy (hardly ever the main tenets of religion), for he, unlike Shaw, is a writer mainly concerned with Ireland, and no writer can possibly ignore the religious set-up if he attempts to give a comprehensive picture of Ireland. Even when a play has an extra-territorial significance he cannot break away from his country, for, as he admits:

> Like Joyce, it is only through an Irish scene that my imagination can weave a way, within the Irish shadows or out in the Irish sunshine, if it is to have a full or, at least a fair, chance to play.[54]

One notices in O'Casey's plays that the more he ages and mellows, the more he sings of joy and ecstasy and the keener is the edge of his attack against the clergy. The gradual hardening of the dramatist's attitude can be seen by studying the plays, as we have done, in the order in which they have appeared since his exile, the satire reaching its climax in *Cock-a-doodle Dandy* and *The Bishop's Bonfire*. In *The Star Turns Red* he had shown the Church and the state as two distinct organisations coming together to fight against their common enemy—the poor who had assembled under the "Red" banner. In *Cock-a-doodle Dandy* the state and the Church have merged into one, forming what has often been referred to as the

---

[51] See my article in *The Irish Times*, 25 Jul. 1959.
[52] "The Revolt Against the Priest," in *Preface for Politicians*.
[53] O'Casey's letter to Cyril Cusack dated 25 May 1956. In Mr Cusack's possession.
[54] O'Casey, *The New York Times* (international edn.), 10 Nov. 1958.

Church-state in Ireland. The Sergeant and the Bellman, like the rest, take their orders from the priest. The state as a secular power does not exist. The Irish Tricolour fluttering in the breeze is a mockery under present conditions and it is no accident that a sudden gale blows it down. The fall of the flag symbolises the fall of the secular power in Ireland; it also symbolises the end of the human freedom for which the Irish had fought for so many centuries. Ireland once again becomes a subject-nation, the tyranny of English rule being replaced by that of the Church.

To the vast majority of Catholics throughout the world the priest, the Church and the Roman Catholic faith are one. Thus any attack on the first two is taken as an attack on their religion. O'Casey's bringing in the names of some of their Saints and coining a few more is obnoxious to them as blasphemy, though "Kissalass, Velethighs, Reedabuck, Dance-solong . . . Anticlericus, Secularius an' Odeonius,"[55] may be amusing to a playgoer who can see that O'Casey has spent his maximum energy in railing at the priest and the killjoys. These figures, says *The Times* critic, are "drawn with ferocious exaggeration and are difficult to take seriously even in an allegory."[56] The two inorganic incidents, the priest killing the lorry-driver and Julia returning unhealed from Lourdes, are a further proof that O'Casey is even willing to go out of his way to sneer at what is sacred to Catholics. No wonder that there were boycotts and protests and the police had to be sent for when the play was performed at the Playhouse Theatre in Toronto in October 1958. A woman in the audience gasped "Oh my God!" when the priest accidentally killed the driver; and a man shouted, "You're a liar!" when Julia returned and renounced her faith in miracles.[57]

The play was performed at the Edinburgh International Festival in 1959. After its short run there it was taken to the Royal Court Theatre, London, where it ran for a month from 17 Sep. The immediate reaction of the theatre critics varied Mention might however be made of the opinion of two persons

---

[55] *Cock-a-doodle Dandy*, Sc. III, pp. 198-9.

[56] *The Times* (London), 19 Sep. 1959.

[57] *The Irish Times*, 7 Oct. 1958. For protests, boycotts, etc. see: *Evening Herald* (Dublin), 2 Oct. 1958 and 7 Oct. 1958; *Irish Press*, 7 Oct. 1958; *Dublin Evening Mail*, 2 Oct. 1958.

who were directly connected with its production: John Bassett, Assistant to the Artistic Director of the Edinburgh International Festival, and George Devine, Artistic Director of the Royal Court Theatre, London. John Bassett wrote:

> The production in Edinburgh excited great interest, most of the reviewers regarding it as by no means one of Sean O'Casey's best plays, but certainly one of his most interesting ones. The combination of the fanciful theme of the cock allied to the question of the power of the church aroused great controversy.[58]

And George Devine wrote:

> My opinion on the play's reception at the Royal Court Theatre is that, in fact, it has a limited audience appeal. It is difficult to gauge such matters here and we are dependant upon press reaction and the press as a whole is out of touch with the real things in the theatre.
>
> However, I think O'Casey suffers as a man who has written, in fact, three masterpieces in his early years and although what he writes now is infinitely more exciting than anything else you can see, his later works suffer inevitably by comparison. One must add to that, the fact that the play can only really be played by absolutely top Irish artists such as played his original plays, and these persons are just not available, if they exist at all.
>
> One must attribute some of the lack of direction to the limitations of the performers.[59]

The lack of really good Irish actors and actresses outside Ireland is the one serious problem that O'Casey's plays have to face. In Ireland, where there are the right sort of artists, his later plays are avoided because of his attitude towards the Church. Thus O'Casey has become almost a playwright without a theatre.

The fact that O'Casey has marked this out as his favourite play has probably led some critics to overrate it. Henry Hewes calls it a "wonderful piece."[60] John Gassner describes it as "the most entrancing and incisive of his non-realistic plays,"[61] and one that has "more dramatic sinew and vitality

---

[58] Letter dated 18 Sep. 1959, in my possession.
[59] Letter dated 7 Oct. 1959, in my possession.
[60] H. Hewes, *Saturday Review*, xxxviii, 19 Nov. 1955.
[61] J. Gassner, *Masters of the Drama*, p. 728.

than anything written by him since *The Plough and the Stars* a quarter of a century ago."[62]   This is perhaps an exaggerated paean, though the play does make a strong appeal because of its fanciful theme, its rare, rich prose, its exuberant humour and the undying sympathy behind all its ferociousness.   One can laugh or weep over his characters but cannot loathe them. Even the priest, for all his obduracy, is far from abominable. He faces the demon Cock with the zeal of a Crusader.   Harassed, battered and torn, he returns again and again to the scene of the battle to the infinite delight of the audience.   In the end he shows kindness in following Loreleen a part of the way "to prevent anyone from harming her."[63]   This humanity, underlying the violence of his characters, is peculiarly O'Casey's own.

The Bishop's Bonfire centres round the visit of Bill Mullarkey —once a wild lad with a patch on the seat of his trousers, now a Bishop—to his home town of Ballyoonagh.   The little town prepares itself to receive the Bishop (he never appears in the play) and to seek his blessing so that it can reach a little nearer to heaven.   Count Reiligan, who is also a Councillor and the richest man in the district, and Canon Burren, the Parish Priest, busy themselves to give the Bishop an enthusiastic welcome accompanied by a bonfire in which "piles of bad books an' evil pictures on top of it are to go away in flames."[64] Masons and workmen are employed to redecorate and refurnish Reiligan's house for the Bishop's stay.   His two daughters, Keelin, a lively, uninhibited girl, and Foorawn, who has taken a vow of perpetual chastity, are also busy helping the workmen.   To the main theme of the visit are allied a number of sub-plots.   There is the love affair between Manus Moanroe, Reiligan's employee, and Foorawn, frustrated because of Foorawn's vow.   There is the love affair between Daniel Clooncoohy, a workman, and Keelin, equally frustrated because of class distinctions.   As the play proceeds and the preparations to receive the Bishop near completion, the romantic hopes of Keelin and Daniel are smothered by the Canon and the Councillor.   Manus, anxious to leave Ballyoonagh but having no money, invades Reiligan's drawing-room

[62] J. Gassner, *Theatre Arts*, xxxv, Jun. 1951.
[63] *Cock-a-doodle Dandy*, Sc. III, p. 217.
[64] *The Bishop's Bonfire*, Act I, p. 29.

to steal a bundle of notes. Foorawn appears on the scene and threatens to send for the police. Manus shoots her. Dying, she acknowledges her love for Manus, and writes a note confessing suicide. The play ends with two of Reiligan's employees, the Codger and the Prodical, hurrying off with a bottle of whiskey to "keep the night aglow by a tait-a-tait talk about the woes an' wonders of the world."[65]

This is but a superficial outline of the play. A careful study will show that many of the incidents are closely copied from O'Casey's earlier plays. To point to a few instances, the confusion and the mess the workers make while setting the house right may be compared with what happens in *Purple Dust*. The methods used by Reiligan and Canon Burren to persuade their employees to work hard are the same as those used by the Mayor in the final act of *The Star Turns Red*. The blast from the buccina of Saint Tremolo has close symbolic links with the crow of the Cock in *Cock-a-doodle Dandy*. Also the problem of exile, and of the Church and the state coming together to hound joy out of life, is the same as in his previous play. The last scene of *The Bishop's Bonfire* can be favourably compared with the last scene in *Juno and the Paycock*. Like Boyle and Joxer, the Codger and the Prodical, unmindful of the tragedy that has overtaken the house, retire for a night of maudlin drunkenness.

Some of the characters, too, are modelled on the heroes of his earlier plays. There is Dick Carranaun, known as the Prodical, whose promises to abstain from drink, like those of Fluther Good, are equalled only by his knack of breaking them. Just as Fluther loves using the words "derogatory" and "vice versa," the Prodical has a peculiar fondness for phrases such as "ipso factos," "sub rosa," and "primae facie." Richard Rankin, the mason, and Father Boheroe, a curate, have their counterparts respectively in Joybell and the Brown Priest in *The Star Turns Red*. The killjoys, Count Reiligan and Canon Burren, and the vivacious, joysome Keelin are similar to many of O'Casey's characters in his later plays. But there is one character, Codger Sleehaun, who is entirely a fresh creation and has no prototype in any of O'Casey's plays.

"In the Codger we have a beautiful creation," wrote the

---

[65] *The Bishop's Bonfire*, Act III, p. 120.

producer, Cyril Cusack, on reading the play for the first time,[66] and there and then decided that he would play the old man's part if he got a chance.[67] O'Casey, who is particularly fond of the Codger, wrote to Cusack: "The Codger is one who queuing up for the Judgment might forget the solemnity of it, and break into a song, and maybe, none of God's Spirits would shout out Silence."[68] A tough old rhymer of eighty-four, not only does he carry his age defiantly, but he also carries the weight of the play, which would sag considerably without him. Employed to look after the hay, he discovers a keg of alcohol and soon makes for the congenial company of Manus, Daniel and the Prodical. Emerging from the revelry with eyes "half-lit with diluted gin," he goes to show his "butties" his physical prowess—which results in his falling headlong with a sack of cement on the new carpet laid out for the Bishop. Having added to the already heavy work of the household he goes off for a second round of drinks. On his return he gets involved in a heated argument over prospective Red aggression in Ireland. This he follows up with a dance. His gaiety even infects the melancholic Foorawn who joins him in the goose-step, but the ever-watchful St Tremolo puts an end to it with a wailing blast from his buccina (the Codger initially does not hear the blast; its effect, like that of the Cock in *Cock-a-doodle Dandy*, is felt chiefly by those who are given to fear and suspicion). The Codger's presence, though invaluable to the onlookers, is a positive hindrance to the preparation to welcome the Bishop, and Count Reiligan gives him the sack. Though he takes his dismissal stoically this is the saddest moment in the play, sadder than Daniel's betrayal of Keelin or Foorawn's death at the hands of her lover. O'Casey must have known that the Codger would by now have endeared himself to the audience and that his removal from the stage might ruin the play. For this reason, I think, he twice brings the Codger back: first to return the farm implements, and then to steal a bottle of whiskey that the Prodical, in one of his numerous vows "never for ever to drink again," had given to the Canon to be presented to St Tremolo.

[66] First impression notes. In Mr Cusack's possession.
[67] My interview with Mr Cusack on 31 Jul. 1958.
[68] Letter dated 15 Jan. 1955. In Mr Cusack's possession.

Though the play has some remarkable scenes there are a few that are tiresome. The first act as a whole is masterly and I can understand Gerard Fay believing, after seeing it, that this might turn out to be O'Casey's best play.[69] That it failed to do so was because of the sag in the second and the third acts. The first act has some of the boozy low melody of *Juno and the Paycock*. There is the Prodical, a "God-fearin' mortal whose one failin' is an occasional drink,"[70] tearing at the prayer-mumbling Rankin but unable to squeeze a reply from him. There is the amusing quarrel between the two masons over bricks:

> PRODICAL [*indignantly—as Rankin is bedding it*]: You're a nice christian cut-throat, denyin' a buttie a few bricks! . . . [*He snatches the brick back angrily and starts to set it in his own part of the wall.*] Good catholic an' all as you call yourself, you're not goin' to be let bounce yourself into an authority you've no legal or christian right to! I'll not be bounced.
>
> RANKIN [*indignantly*]: It's you's a bouncer, but I'm not goin' to stand you bouncin' away the bricks I carried over for meself! I'll not be bounced either!
> [*Prodical has tapped the brick home with the tip of the handle of his trowel, and now goes to take another brick from those beside Rankin; but Rankin pushes him away so that he has to jump down from the scaffolding. Rankin then takes the brick Prodical has set, and starts to bed it in his own part of the wall.*]
>
> PRODICAL [*angrily getting back on to the scaffold and sending Rankin off it with an angry push*]: Mind who you're pushin'! You're exhibitin' a nice kind of catholic conduct.
>
> RANKIN [*getting back on to the scaffold*]: I am what I am, but you'll not lord it over me. It's my brick—I carried it.
>
> PRODICAL: It's not your brick an' it's not my brick; it's nobody's brick; if it's anybody's brick, it's God's brick.[71]

Better still is the scene in which the Codger comes in with a keg of gin. The Prodical can keep his promise to abstain no longer.

> RANKIN [*persuasively*]: Be careful, man. Look the other way, Prodical. Have a little spiritual spunk, an' act as if the gin-keg wasn't there.

---

[69] Gerald Fay, *The Abbey Theatre*, pp. 146-7.
[70] *The Bishop's Bonfire*, Act I, p. 3.
[71] *Op. cit.*, pp. 7-8.

PRODICAL [*firmly*]: It is there, isn't it? I didn't call the keg
into being, did I? I haven't the power to conjure the keg
into bodiless existence, have I? I can't work miracles,
can I? Your likes or dislikes isn't goin' to control the progress
of the world. The keg's here now, an' can't be avoided, can
it? We'll have to suffer it, like it, or dislike it. . . .

[*The Prodical goes to take a drink.*]

RANKIN [*firmly—turning to shout after the Prodical*]: My angel's
tellin' me to urge you to listen to your own angel's warning!
PRODICAL [*shouting back from where he stands at the tree*]: I'm not
goin' to have your angel interferin' with my angel! A keg
here, or a keg there, is no proper positive subject for an angel
to bother about.[72]

Equally charming is the last scene of the act where the Codger,
the Prodical and Daniel return drunk from behind the ash tree.
The Prodical, who has no opinions, demands a wider world
"where a man can roar his real opinions out";[73] Daniel, who
has done scant work, says: "I'm in a mood for work no
longer,"[74] and the Codger, after talking about the lark's song,
ends up with one of his own.

The second act belies the high expectations held out by the
first. The lengthy argument between the characters about a
Russian invasion of Ireland has nothing to do with the plot and
is not very amusing. The whole episode is adapted by O'Casey
from his article "Jeep be Jeepers!," first published in *The New
Statesman and Nation* of 18 Jul. 1953, and later incorporated in
Sunset and Evening Star. Lieutenant Reiligan is brought into the
play as a military man to start the ball rolling, and once this
scene comes to an end we hear no more of him. This is the sort
of weakness that arises when a play lacks a strong plot. A
number of loose incidents and futile arguments have to be
fastened on to give the play an appropriate length and the
dramatist enough scope to express himself. A play may
succeed in spite of a weak plot if the incidents are immensely
amusing and the scenes well handled. But it is dangerous for
a dramatist to have a weak plot to work on. It was not for
nothing that Aristotle described plot as the soul of the drama.

---

[72] *The Bishop's Bonfire*, Act I, pp. 17-19.　　　[73] *Op. cit.*, p. 44.
[74] *Ibid.*

Even if Aristotle were wrong, one might still say that O'Casey is too abjectly dependent on stray incidents.

O'Casey makes amends for this weak scene by following it up with an interesting one: the arrival of the Porter who complains of the blast St Tremolo blew every time he thought of a drink or a comic line from a song. This scene is followed by Reiligan and the Canon stifling the love affair between Daniel and Keelin. Keelin, broken-hearted, turns to Father Boheroe for comfort as a cold wind sweeps through the suddenly-darkened room.

> KEELIN [*frightened*]: What is it? What was it, Father?
> FATHER BOHEROE: It was, my child, a long, sad sigh from God.[75]

It is a moving scene and a good climax to the second act. One anxiously awaits what is to follow.

O'Casey's hatred of hypocrisy, a violent resentment against the killing of all joy and the waste of youth, brings the play to a shocking conclusion in Act III. Keelin is left desolate, the Codger is sacked and Manus Moanroe decamps with the Count's bundle of notes after killing Foorawn. The killing of Foorawn is the one serious flaw in the play and comes very near to spoiling it. The *News Chronicle* described it as "pointless, violent and ugly."[76] Jack White, writing in the *Spectator* said that the tragic impact of the scene is no greater than Punch's killing of Judy.[77] *Punch*'s attack was the most scathing of all. After describing it as "preposterous melodrama," it goes on:

> A little startling, but no more; one was fascinated that as she slithered to the ground she contrived to write so long a letter, confessing suicide, that it must have been in shorthand.[78]

In the published version of the play the letter is not long, but it was so, according to Cyril Cusack, in the typescript from which the play was produced in Dublin.[79]

[75] *The Bishop's Bonfire*, Act II, p. 81.
[76] Quoted in *Evening Herald* (Dublin), 1 Mar. 1955.
[77] J. White, *Spectator*, 4 Mar. 1955.
[78] *Punch*, 9 Mar. 1955.
[79] Letter to me from Mr C. Cusack dated 14 Dec. 1959.

O'Casey publicly defended the killing of Foorawn. He told a London journalist:

> The whole play is symbolical. . . . The critics say that I spoilt the last act with melodrama. But the shooting is symbolical.
> Besides I am still interested in melodrama. I don't see why there shouldn't be a bit of it.[80]

But to Cyril Cusack he admitted the play's weakness:

> I daresay the play ends on "a weak hand", and I know that is, naturally, an actor's bane; but I shouldn't worry too much. *Major Barbara, John Bull's Other Island*, end on weak hands, too. It isn't a happy ending; and, possibly, may be a mistaken one. I'm not sure; but it can't be altered in Dublin. If you like, I'll think of a possible alternative for London; though a change wouldn't appeal to me; but I might think of something which would give a longer space between the death and the fall of the curtain. . . . Look for perfection, but don't be too unhappy if you don't find it. Take me, do you think that I am satisfied with the play as I've written it? By God, I'm not! But it was the best I could do in the mood of the moment, and to that extent I am satisfied—and it is a great extent. . . . Remember that Tyrone [Tyrone Guthrie directed the play's performance in Dublin] is a "alien" in production to Dublin, and there will be jealousy against him; but if an Angel did the Production of an O'Casey play, and another had leaned over me shoulder when writing it, it would still be a wretched work to the Irish Professional critics.[81]

I may add that neither O'Casey nor Cusack foresaw the criticism the melodramatic end would invite, and that both were taken aback by the sudden attack. In fact Cusack told me that he thought the shooting of Foorawn right.

What is the play about? What is the dramatist trying to drive at? O'Casey, in his introduction to the play's programme gave a hint as to the play's purpose:

> Well, here's another plume of smoke which I hope may have a little flame in it to light up life for a moment or two; to make us think again of some of the problems Ireland has to

---

[80] Quoted in *Evening Herald* (Dublin), 5 Mar. 1955.
[81] Letter dated 10 Mar. 1955. In Mr Cusack's possession.

face in the midst of the sound from the singer's song and the politician's shout.[82]

It was not till the play had had a run of two weeks and aroused heavy criticism that O'Casey spoke his mind frankly to the critic of *Time*:

> *The Bishop's Bonfire* . . . is a play about the ferocious chastity of the Irish, a lament for the condition of Ireland, which is an apathetic country now, losing all her energy, enthusiasm and resolution.[83]

But better than the dramatist himself did the critic of *The Times* sum up the author's purpose:

> It represents with a judicious mixture of naturalism and symbolism his own very individual vision of a modern Ireland in which priests and men of property and other agents of established institutions are leagued against the free mind of man seeking to fill it with a superstitious dread of life and a distrust of happiness. Youth, according to this vision is the chief victim of the conspiracy and youth, Mr. O'Casey suggests, too often lacks the courage of its natural convictions and fails to insist on its birthright.[84]

Of course, this has been the aim behind most of O'Casey's later plays. Having had very little happiness in his youth, he has made the cause of young lads and lasses his own, and tries to see that they get from life the joys that were denied to him. And as he looks upon the Church and the Church-state in Ireland as the chief antagonists of the spirit of joy, he attacks them with every dramatic weapon at his command. *The Bishop's Bonfire*, like his previous plays, is violently anti-clerical but not anti-religious. Robert B. Considine, columnist for the International News Service, New York, wrongly calls the play "interestingly blasphemous."[85]   O'Casey does not blaspheme. He has given the Saints fictitious names, so that his mockery of them may not hurt the feelings of those who have reverence for saints.

O'Casey's chief target in the play is the Canon. He makes

---

[82] See the programme to the play produced by Caps Publicity, Dublin.
[83] *Time*, 14 Mar. 1955.
[84] *The Times* (London), 1 Mar. 1955.
[85] Quoted in *The Standard* (Dublin), 8 Apr. 1955.

the priest, says Cecil Wilson, "such an unctuous villain . . . that the play positively cries out for trouble."[86]   O'Casey does this from no personal malice but to stress his point.   He follows that school of painters who distort and exaggerate those features they wish to underline.   So we have the Christian priest, Canon Burren, exercising his authority with un-Christian severity.   And there is his curate, Father Boheroe, who apparently speaks for the author.   The humility and liberalism of the curate are brought into contrast with the haughtiness and puritanism of his superior.   It is doubtful whether the Church of Rome could tolerate a dissenting pastor like the curate; it is even more doubtful that a man like the Canon could rise to such eminence and power.   But these are not the issues with which O'Casey is concerned. His aim is to drive home his purpose and he will not allow realism to bully him.   He has drawn his Canon louder and larger than life simply in order to emphasise those features he wishes to ridicule.

Though O'Casey's tirade is directed against those institutions that are opposed to the spirit of joy, he does not forget to blame the victims for not insisting on what is theirs by right. Daniel is upbraided for giving up Keelin under Reiligan's threat, and Foorawn is rebuked for holding to a foolish vow against her natural inclinations.   Rankin is jeered at for his continual praying.   Reiligan speaks for O'Casey when he tells Rankin: "You prayer-gasper, if you prayed less, you'd see more!"[87]   O'Casey is not against praying as such, but against excessive formal prayer.   In a comment on the Chinese invasion of Tibet he said:

> It was near time to send the landlords of Tibet and the hordes of useless, idle monks packing.   6000 monasteries in a little land!   These monks can go on praying as long as they like when a useful day's work is done; but they must do something more than pray for their suppers.[88]

A very similar thought is expressed by Father Boheroe to Rankin:

Too   much   formal   prayer,   Rankin,   sometimes   makes   a

---

[86] Cecil Wilson, *Daily Mail*, 1 Mar, 1955.
[87] *The Bishop's Bonfire*, Act I, p. 32.
[88] Letter to me from O'Casey dated 5 Jul. 1959.

soul conceited; and merriment may be a way of worship![89]

Though O'Casey does not object to prayer he believes that God can be served better through service to man. Father Boheroe tells Foorawn about the Prodical:

> He has helped to build hospitals where the sick shelter, homes where we live, churches even where we worship; he serves God as a mason better than I do in my priesthood, or you in your chastity.[90]

But service to God does not imply that man must forgo the pleasures of this world. God is more readily accessible through joy than through suffering. Father Boheroe tells Daniel, who is apologising for having kissed Keelin:

> No need to be penitent, Danny; a man in a woman's arms may indeed be close to God.[91]

When the Canon objects to the Codger's songs, Father Boheroe tells him:

> I wish I could put into my prayers the spirit he puts into his songs. I'm afraid, Monsignor, God listens more eagerly to the songs of the Codger than He does to our prayers.[92]

O'Casey does not believe in saints or their intercession. He looks upon the Catholic faith in saints as a superstition for which the Church is responsible. In a letter to Cyril Cusack he wrote:

> About Foorawn crossing herself before the statue, I'd very much rather she didn't. Let us look upon the statue as unblessed, for they are but fantasies, and as such, need no gesture. The whole idea (from my point) is a cry against the habit of using the Saints by believers to do work for them that they can damn well do for themselves.[93]

People appealing to saints for help instead of working their own way out infuriate O'Casey. Yet, in the play, he delivers

---

[89] *The Bishop's Bonfire*, Act I, p. 26.
[90] *Op. cit.*, Act III, p. 113.
[91] *Op. cit.*, Act II, p. 75.
[92] *Op. cit.*, Act III, pp. 105-6.
[93] Letter dated 14 Feb. 1955. In Mr Cusack's possession.

his castigation with a gentle good humour so as not to hurt the
sentiments of the believers. This is what Father Boheroe tells
Foorawn when she complains that he has failed to help her:

> Here in the room, Foorawn, you have two saints, and neither
> the one here [*he indicates St. Tremolo*], nor that one there [*he
> indicates St. Casabianca*], opened a gob, or blew the Bookineeno,
> to say a word, or give a sign of help. When we have problems,
> Foorawn, ourselves are the saints to solve them. Our weakness
> —and our strength.[94]

Certainly O'Casey is expressing his own views through Father
Boheroe. His own hard struggle must have swum before his
eyes as he wrote these lines: the misery, the poverty and the
privations he suffered in his youth; the heroic effort with which
he saved sixpences to buy himself books even as he starved;
the robust determination with which he fought against every
obstacle that came in his way, to survive and become a great
dramatist. No saints came forward to help him. But, of
course, some Catholics might say, he is a Protestant!

The play's première at the Gaiety Theatre, Dublin, led to
an unanticipated controversy among the critics and the public.
O'Casey, while advising Cyril Cusack not to bother about what
the Irish critics said,[95] himself entered the fray and attacked
them—"bum critics" as he calls them—in interviews with
correspondents, and through letters to the papers. The whole
story of the reaction of the English and the Irish critics to the
play and of O'Casey's reaction to their criticism is amusingly
told by the dramatist himself in *The Green Crow*. But let us
first see how the play reached the Dublin stage.

Cyril Cusack having heard that O'Casey had completed a
new play, wrote to him asking to see it. O'Casey replied on
30 Apr. 1954, that the play was about to be typed, and con-
cluded: "I still, foolishly enough, hesitate to give permission
for a new play in Dublin till the Abbey has had time to notice
it, and has passed it by with eyes shut, or eyes open, but her
nose in the air."[96] Cusack repeated his request to see the
play, and as the Abbey Theatre showed no interest,[97] O'Casey

[94] *The Bishop's Bonfire*, Act III, p. 114.
[95] Letter to Cusack dated 10 Mar. 1955. In Mr Cusack's possession.
[96] Letter in Mr Cusack's possession.
[97] O'Casey's letter to Cusack dated 12 Aug. 1954. In Mr Cusack's possession.

sent it over for a week.[98] Cyril Cusack read the play and wrote to O'Casey on 9 Sep.:

> I think *The Bishop's Bonfire* is a grand play. Maureen [Cusack's wife] also is enthusiastic, and I believe our individual reactions are fairly individual. . . . I can't refrain from saying that I feel Dublin needs this play. As Maureen says, it is exciting, and furthermore, that it should be salutary. It may seem impertinence for me to say so, but I must add that, as it impresses me, it has great dramatic value and would be particularly valuable to Irish theatre to-day; the modern craftsmanship is, of course, a delight; the characterisation immense; the language glorious; humour abounding; and finally and over all it tells most movingly a tale of national tragedy.[99]

After giving vent to such profusion of praise, at which even O'Casey's greatest admirers—the Cornish critic J. C. Trewin and the American critic G. J. Nathan—might blush, Cusack went on to make a few reservations. O'Casey, naturally happy, wrote back in his modest way that there might be weaknesses in the play of which at the moment he was not aware, and that "If it be three-quarter as good as you both think it to be, I shall be well pleased."[1]

Cusack, having secured O'Casey's permission to produce the play in Dublin, sent it on to Tyrone Guthrie. Guthrie wrote: "The more I read the play the more I am impressed by its quality."[2] All this was going on behind the scenes when the *Manchester Guardian* "blew the bookineeno" on 29 Dec. 1954:

> The Irish actor Cyril Cusack has taken the Gate Theatre [*sic*] in Dublin for three weeks in February to put on a new play by Sean O'Casey. . . . A most distinguished director, Tyrone Guthrie, has been invited to produce the play and has accepted.

Soon a tremor ran through Dublin. Cyril Cusack had expected criticism and was not shaken when it came. To test his ground he had already sent the play to a Catholic prelate in

---

[98] O'Casey's letter to Cusack dated 1 Sep. 1954.
[99] Copy of letter in Mr Cusack's possession.
[1] Letter dated 11 Sep. 1954. In Mr Cusack's possession.
[2] Letter of 29 Dec. 1954. In Mr Cusack's possession.

London for his opinion. His letter and Cusack's reply give two points of view which—whether they are right or wrong—we cannot ignore.

The prelate wrote to Cyril Cusack:

> I have read *The Bishop's Bonfire* and set down what I think—though I am afraid it isn't going to please you. Yet you would not have me dissimulate, I feel sure.
>
> My immediate reaction is one of regret that you have decided to put it on. Of course it is good theatre; anything of Sean O'Casey would be that. But the bitterness that runs through all his plays and his scorn of the Church and of religious practice vitiate his art. . . . I know there are ecclesiastics rather like the Canon, and prominent Catholics like the Count; there may even be priests like the curate; and all of them are distasteful and deserve to be pilloried. But are all Parish Priests as blind as the Canon (to put it no worse) or as ignorant as the curate? Are all "good" laymen as unChristian as the Count, all "good" women as hypocritical as Foorawn? Is it only drunkards and ne'er-do-wells that have the vision of the truth? Is all prayer to be sneered at and the intercession of the Saints a thing for mockery?
>
> I hate hypocrisy, as I know you do. I gladly see it exposed, as I know you do. But in this play there is not a hint of the existence of anything else in the Church or in Catholic life. There is complete ignoring of the revelation of the Incarnation, of which we were speaking, of the glory of the body/soul unity it manifests, of the inspiring examples of the same which we see every day in priests, nuns and lay-people alike. Even if this play were a true reflection of Irish village life (which even I know from my own experience it is not), it would fail lamentably as a work of art in its complete disregard of the truth there should be in Catholic life. As a farce it might be let go, if it were not so clearly a tragedy.
>
> Knowing you as I do, knowing something at least of your own Catholic life, of your integrity, of your understanding of your religion, I should be sorry to see your own great artistry applied to the presentation of this product of a desperately unhappy and cankered soul.[3]

Cyril Cusack replied:

> I am committed to presenting the play, having agreed to

---

[3] Letter dated 4 Jan. 1955. In Mr Cusack's possession.

do so. . . . I recognize that it intends bitter criticism of a state of things in Ireland and that its viewpoint comprehends only one unhappy aspect of the country which the playwright from a too distant pinnacle perhaps sees as a whole view rather than as a single facet. We have only to refer to the rapid emigration of our younger people from these shores and the consequent denudation of the rural areas; and, moreover, the loss of faith amongst a certain percentage of these emigrants under the weight of materialism as they meet up with it in whatever shape and in countries not necessarily Communistic. That frustration occurs amongst our youth cannot be denied. That there are those who would jail the spirit of our youth as well as the body, that also cannot be denied. And it is not solely an economic problem.

If O'Casey sees such an evil should he not—though he might be digging with the wrong foot, as we say in Ireland—express his detestation of it? . . . But are there not, in this O'Casey play, characters containing something of nobility and a desire for what is good? So I see the "Codger" and "Father Boheroe". So I see in others amongst the dramatis personae, only that that desire is misdirected. And does not this indicate a nobility of purpose in the author? . . .

Another motive I had in mind in my decision to present this play was that it should rather be produced in Ireland out of whose—shall we say—evil genius it springs where it might be considered and passed through the sieve of Catholic—universal not parochial—thought; this rather than it should receive possibly an irresponsible and less authentic rendering abroad where it might be sponsored by some who might be indifferent or even inimical to the Catholic ideal. . . .

On my visit with Maureen to Sean O'Casey recently I formed the impression of an idealist—however misdirected his idealism may be, which history indicates to be a dangerous thing—whose one obsession was Ireland. If he is a tormented soul may not this be an encouraging sign? May he not hate what he believes to be evil? I sometimes think that O'Casey's egomania—which, may I add, is better vented than sequestered, left lurking in the secret places of the soul—comes from an identification of himself with Ireland. I had the impression that he was possessed with the thought of Ireland and that his passion was a strange compound of love and hate.[4]

Cusack had not asked for an answer to his letter, and got

[4] Letter dated 5 Jan. 1955. Copy in Mr Cusack's possession.

none. He had taken the plunge and there was no turning back. He proceeded with rehearsals and asked O'Casey's permission to make a few cuts here and there. This O'Casey allowed. Cusack also wanted O'Casey's son Breon—a painter —to do the designs for the scenes of the play. Breon did the designs but Tyrone Guthrie found them unsuitable. Cusack and Guthrie did not altogether see eye to eye about the manner in which the play was to be presented.

The curtain went up on *The Bishop's Bonfire* on 28 Feb. 1955. According to one paper, "A queue which began forming outside the entrance to the gallery had stretched over two hundred yards down South King Street into South William Street by 7 o'clock."[5] Plain-clothes policemen, in disguised radio cars, patrolled outside the theatre, while some were scattered among the crowd so as to avoid the sort of riot that took place over *The Plough and the Stars* in 1926. It was quite an occasion, this first night. The play had received immense publicity and had brought the largest assembly of foreign dramatic critics ever to come to Dublin. The theatre was packed to the doors, all tickets were sold and some members of the Diplomatic Corps could not find a seat. In the dress circle Mrs O'Casey and her daughter, Shivaun, sat tense with excitement.

The play went off in comparative silence. Even those who had come to protest against O'Casey's anti-clericalism had a thin time of it. But at the end a storm of angry boos and catcalls broke out from among a section of the audience. Mr Cusack came on the stage and spoke:

> Thank you for coming and for holding your heretical hisses until the end—those of you who are heretical. I am very, very proud of having this opportunity of bringing Sean O'Casey back to Dublin, because this is where he belongs. . . . Mr O'Casey is a playwright of deeply religious feelings.[6]

The Press reaction was mixed. On the whole the English and American critics praised it. The critic of the *Daily Mail* said: "Sean O'Casey exploded a stick of dramatic dynamite. . . . It is an ugly play beautifully told."[7] The *Daily Express* said

---

[5] *Irish Independent*, 1 Mar. 1955.   [6] *Ibid.*
[7] C. Wilson, *Daily Mail*, 1 Mar. 1955.

that "It is written in language of piercing beauty."[8] The critic of the *Manchester Guardian* said: "It succeeds beyond the hopes of its enemies. It fails a little more than O'Casey's friends would wish it."[9] And *The Atlantic Monthly* after calling it "a bitter and very nearly hopeless play," hailed O'Casey for conveying the grim view without sacrificing the play's comic eloquence as "an amazing achievement."[10] On the other hand the majority of the Irish papers condemned it. *The Leader* described it as "A very poor play indeed."[11] The *Irish Tatler and Sketch* commented that "the excitement was chiefly outside the theatre,"[12] and the critic of the *Evening Herald* wrote: "In fairness to himself as a creative writer, Sean O'Casey should return to Ireland without delay. At present he is completely out of touch with modern Irish life and thought."[13]

O'Casey, who enjoys a fight even more than Yeats did, was delighted by the fire that he had lit in Dublin. It provided him with an opportunity to have a smack at the critics and to voice his opinions. Here are a couple of his remarks on the Irish critics:

> I am so used to them now that anything nice from them would get me down. . . .[14]

> I am tired of listening to critics. . . . Did you ever see the critics agreeing on anything? . . . Anyway, if you want to comment on what the critics say you would be commenting all your life.[15]

O'Casey defended his play brilliantly against the charges that the play was not factual, that he was out of touch with life in Ireland, that the priests were no longer a power in the land. All this can be seen in *The Green Crow*. Though he had been

---

[8] John Barber, *Daily Express*, 1 Mar. 1955.

[9] Gerard Fay, *Manchester Guardian*, 2 Mar. 1955.

[10] P. L. Adams, *The Atlantic Monthly*, CIVC, Oct. 1955.

[11] *The Leader*, 12 Mar. 1955.

[12] *Irish Tatler and Sketch*, Apr. 1955.

[13] *Evening Herald*, 1 Mar. 1955. Because of the very hostile attitude of the Irish papers in general, and *The Standard* in particular, a mild reaction set in in O'Casey's favour. To trace its development see the following Irish papers: *The Standard*, 25 Feb., 4 Mar. and 25 Mar. 1955; *Irish Press*, 8 Mar. 1955; *Evening Herald*, 8 Mar. and 15 Mar. 1955.

[14] *The Irish Times*, 23 Mar. 1955.

[15] *Evening Press* (Dublin), 1 Mar. 1955.

in exile for nearly thirty years he still had his finger on the Irish pulse. This was because of the deep interest he had always maintained in Ireland. Through newspapers and occasional visitors he had kept a note of all that was going on in his country. And then there is the reason that he himself gives:

> I know the mind of Ireland because I am within it; I know the heart of Ireland because I am one of its corners; I know the five senses of Ireland because I am within them and they within me; they bid me look, and when I look, I see; they bid me listen, and when I listen, I hear.[16]

The more O'Casey cornered the Dubliners, the more aggressive they became. Abusive letters were sent to him. Writing to Cusack he says:

> I got a number of letters warning me of the Judgment; that I am on the margin of the grave; others calling attention to "immodest dress", another saying I should be in Grangegorman [a mental asylum in north Dublin] and quite a lot of ones that thunder, but few have an identity.[17]

On the other hand Cyril Cusack wasn't very happy about the way the Irish Press was reacting. He thought that all this might be bad for business. Mrs Cusack invited O'Casey to Dublin, hoping that his presence would give the play fresh publicity. But O'Casey wrote back:

> My presence would bring you but one more hand-clap, me own; and what use would that be? Probably, not even one more, for I could hardly clap my own play; and, if I clapped the acting, they'd all say O'Casey was clapping himself.[18]

The play, however, needed no fresh publicity. O'Casey's enemies had unwittingly done the job. It had been put on initially for three weeks, but since it continued to draw large crowds it was played for five weeks—a record run, according to Mr Cusack, for an Irish straight play at the Gaiety Theatre.[19]

Cyril Cusack was anxious to take the play on tour to England and America after its Dublin run. The Embassy and

---

16 *The Green Crow*, pp. 137-8.
17 Letter dated 28 Mar. 1955. In Mr Cusack's possession.
18 Letter dated 11 Mar. 1955. In Mr Cusack's possession.
19 My interview with Mr Cusack on 31 Jul. 1958.

the Wimbledon Theatres in London were offered to him but he thought it "below dignity" to produce the play at a suburban theatre, while the West End theatres made no offers. The Broadway theatres made no offers either. Therefore the plans to take it abroad were dropped.

One may ask what was achieved by performing *The Bishop's Bonfire* in Dublin? As O'Casey puts it to Cusack:

> After all, you have done a tremendous achievement in Dublin; and, however things may go, you have really lighted a big theatrical bonfire in Dublin that will be long remembered; and that is far more than something; even in spite of the critics, who, like the old prophets of Baal, poured water over it to prevent its burning.[20]

And to a friend a couple of months later:

> Don't worry about *The Bishop's Bonfire*. After all, a good many seemed to have warmed their hands at it, once the Irish critics burned their arses, so that something was attempted and something was done by its flame and its spark.[21]

According to Cusack the play's performance brought some liberalism into Irish life. If this is so, O'Casey's great reforming zeal had at last borne fruit.

In 1958 the Dublin Tostal Council proposed to hold an International Theatre Festival during An Tostal, and requested O'Casey to send in a new play. This theatre festival, which had been inaugurated the previous year, had on its programme the works of three notable Irish writers: O'Casey's *The Drums of Father Ned*, Joyce's *Ulysses* (dramatised by Alan McClelland and titled *Bloomsday*), and three mime plays of Samuel Beckett. Not too surprisingly for those who are aware of the power which the Catholic Church wields in Ireland, none of these plays was performed. The theatre festival, which was to have opened on 11 May, was first postponed and later abandoned for the year. The controversy which led to this washout is not only as interesting as the O'Casey play itself, but equally it exposes the order that O'Casey is attacking. It further dismisses the accusation of

[20] Letter dated 19 Mar. 1955. In Mr Cusack's possession.
[21] Letter dated 12 May 1955. In Mr John Beary's possession.

O'Casey's discreditors that most of the playwright's fears and grievances exist only in his imagination and nowhere else.

> But this that I am gaun to tell . . .
> Is just as true's the Deil's in hell
>   Or Dublin city. . . .

O'Casey had sent his play to the Council of An Tostal in early September 1957, and they had written to him saying that they liked it immensely.[22] But, on 10 Jan. 1958, *The Irish Times* announced:

> For the past week, there has been some doubt whether these two plays would be part of the festival programme. Last week the Council became aware that the Most Rev Dr McQuaid, Archbishop of Dublin, did not approve of their inclusion in the programme. As a result of their inclusion, this year's Tostal will not be marked by an official Mass.

By turning down the Committee's request for a Votive Mass and withdrawing permission for the customary Low Mass, the Archbishop had very plainly indicated his disapproval of the plays which, incidentally, he had not even read. The Council, all the same, declared to the Press that it would abide by its original decision.

Under pressure from a section of the public which lined up with the Archbishop against "plays of doubtful morality,"[23] the Council's decision to go ahead with the staging of *The Drums of Father Ned* and *Bloomsday* began to weaken. On 24 Jan. O'Casey received a letter, signed by the directors of a theatre to whom he had not sent the play, asking him to give the producer "the necessary authority to make such alterations as he requires," and affirming that "its structural state made the play unproduceable. . . ."[24] This was soon followed by a letter from the Council itself to the same effect. O'Casey immediately surmised that here was an untidy way of getting rid of him: by asking him for a concession that no dramatist

---

[22] O'Casey's letter to *The Irish Times*, dated 5 Mar. 1958.

[23] The Dublin Council of Irish Unions stood solidly behind the Archbishop and played no small part in making the Tostal Council abandon its ambitious scheme. See *The Irish Times* and *Irish Independent* of 12 Feb. 1963.

[24] See O'Casey's letter in *Enquiry* (Nottingham), 1 Jun. 1958. Also as quoted by Robert Hogan in *The New Republic*, cxxxviii, 19 May 1958.

of repute would permit. He reacted sharply by announcing in *The Irish Times* of 12 Feb. that he was withdrawing his play "for very cogent reasons"; the Council simultaneously announced that it was dropping the play because the producer was not allowed to make "structural alterations."

Three days later, on 15 Feb., the Council of An Tostal announced through *The Irish Times* that it had decided to drop *Bloomsday* as well. It went on to clarify that it was acting under the pressure of "public controversy" and that it had found nothing "offensive" in the Joyce play. This statement, however, did nothing to pacify its author, Alan McClelland, who told the *Sunday Press* reporter:

> They got from me the rights of the Dublin premiere. By leading me to give them the rights, they kept me out of the market for a considerable time and kept me away from potential bidders. I shall have to examine the matter on these grounds. . . . In my opinion their action is a scurrilous treatment of me and my works. I think their action stinking.[25]

Some days later Samuel Beckett, who had been following the vicissitudes of the O'Casey and Joyce plays, withdrew his own plays as a mark of protest against the attitude of the Council of An Tostal.

There is no doubt that the Council of An Tostal seriously wanted to stage *The Drums of Father Ned*; that, like Cyril Cusack three years earlier, they may even have had hopes of rehabilitating O'Casey in the Dublin to which he belonged. But they had not the courage to stand up for their convictions, far less to accept a defeat. When the Archbishop signified his disapproval of their choice of plays only two courses were open to them. The first was to go ahead with the performances. This, of course, would not have been easy; in Dublin city, to alienate the Archbishop would be the height of rashness. The second and more sensible way out would have been to accept the fact that they could not proceed with the staging of the plays, and to inform the dramatists concerned accordingly. Instead, the Council embarked on a hunt for excuses. It began by asking O'Casey for permission to make "structural

[25] *Sunday Press* (Dublin), 16 Feb. 1958.

alterations" in his play, without telling him what was really wrong with it. No wonder O'Casey lost his temper.

The Council of An Tostal made itself a laughing-stock before the world: not so much for dropping the plays as for its burlesque handling of the whole affair. Open-minded critics sympathised with O'Casey. In *The Times Literary Supplement*, Robert Hogan said:

> The Tostal Council seems engaged in parody as well as farce. The Council first desires to tidy up the play's structure. Although there might be some doubt about the Council's competence to rewrite a play of Ireland's greatest living dramatist, there can be no doubt of the Council's presumption. The Council next avers that production of the play will hurt the author's prestige. I would suggest that a prestige that can weather *The Star Turns Red* can weather anything, and I would further suggest that the author's prestige is not the concern of the Council.[26]

But public sympathy is no substitute for personal revenge; and O'Casey, bent on punishing the Dubliners, announced in late July that he had withdrawn permission to produce his plays from the Abbey as well as from the other theatres in Dublin:

> If Dublin isn't allowed to see my new play, I am withdrawing my old plays as well. . . . As an Irish citizen . . . I claim the right not to be shut down in my native country and my native city.[27]

This came as a shock to the theatre-goers of Dublin. That the public should be punished for what was no fault of theirs was sad. O'Casey's action epitomises the tragic theme of his earlier plays: the innocent and the weak paying the maximum price for a war or a revolution for which they are not responsible. In this feud between O'Casey and the Council of An Tostal the victims again were the innocent—the audiences who delight in his plays.

The Drums of Father Ned (published in 1960) comfortably lives up to what O'Casey said about it, "I don't say it is a good

---

[26] *The Times Literary Supplement*, 21 Mar. 1958.
[27] *The Sunday Press* (Dublin), 27 Jul. 1958.

play. It is fun from beginning to end."[28] It is the sort of fun at which we have laughed before, and we laugh again for lack of anything better. More even than in *The Bishop's Bonfire*, O'Casey has faithfully copied scenes and incidents from his earlier plays. To single out a few: the theme of this play is the preparation for the Tostal; the theme of *The Bishop's Bonfire* was the preparation to receive the Bishop. In both plays the priest in the title role does not appear; in both plays there is the burning of books the clergy consider harmful. Skerighan's affair with Bernadette is a weak copy of John Jo Mulligan's with Angela in *Bedtime Story*; the retorts exchanged between McGilligan and Skerighan in defence of their respective religions smack of the discussion between Brennan and Roory in *Red Roses for Me*. And there is the chanting which reminds one of the chants of the Down and Outs in *Within the Gates*.

Apart from such familiar material, there is also another of O'Casey's assaults on the priests and the rich, both out to exploit the working man. There is the fight of the young for sex, freedom and a fuller life. Lastly, there is O'Casey's prose, rich as in his earlier plays, but not as effective. We find it a little stiff and laboured in places, at times overdone.

The play opens with a "Prerumble," a flashback set in the Ireland of the nineteen-twenties. As the town of Doonavale shoots into flames, a party of Black and Tans amuse themselves by plaguing two bigoted Irishmen, Binnington and McGilligan, whose hate for each other surpasses their hate for their British oppressors. And it is precisely because of the trenchant hate they nurse that their lives are spared, for the British officer rightly surmises "that these two rats will do more harm to Ireland living than they'll ever do to Ireland dead."[29]

This observation—enunciating the principle of "*divide et impera*"—is borne out in the play. Having prospered materially in Independent Ireland, but mentally as dwarfed as ever, Binnington and McGilligan become Mayor and Deputy Mayor of Doonavale. Though unable to bear the sight of each other, they come together to sell "Red" timber, for

[28] See *The Irish Times*, 15 Feb. 1958.
[29] *The Drums of Father Ned*, "Prerumble," p. 10.

"business is business." In enriching themselves, they have the assistance of the honest but obstinate parish priest Father Fillifogue, who tries to impress upon the labourers that working for their greedy but Church-supporting bosses is the same as "workin' for God." Against them and their way of life are their children Michael Binnington and Nora McGilligan. Contrary to their parents' wishes, the two young people stand for the Dail, and the sound of the beat of Father Ned's drums symbolically proclaims the ultimate victory of the dramatist's values. Father Fillifogue's reluctance to meet the challenge is significant: if the old priest is to be vanquished, it is not because he is downright wrong, but because there is little fight left in him. This sudden softening towards the end is the result of O'Casey's ingrained respect for the clergy in general. Regardless of the harm that his priests do, he never presents them as villains.

In one respect *The Drums of Father Ned* shows a positive advance over previous plays: in its blatant advocacy of youthful sexuality. The distance O'Casey has covered since he wrote his first play *The Shadow of a Gunman*, where all that the hero is able to manage is a quick kiss, may be gauged from what Michael and Nora tell their parents:

> BINNINGTON [*to Michael—violently*]: When this damned Tosthal's over, you'll see no more of that girl there!
> McGILLIGAN [*to Nora—violently*]: Ay, an' you'll see no more of that fella there!
> MICHAEL [*laughingly*]: A bit late now to give th' ordher.
> BINNINGTON [*angrily*]: How's it too late?
> NORA: Well, we studied at the same College.
> MICHAEL: An' lived in the same flat.
> NORA: An' slept in th' same bed o' Sundays.[30]

Note what Nora says. It is the first time O'Casey speaks so plainly, though he has often approved of sexual relationship among his characters. That Nora should say this, rather than Michael, as one would expect if such a thing is to be said at all, is telling. For O'Casey the sexual act is tantamount to courage, and his women (who are brave and earthy) are given the first right to express it. Nora goes out of her way to

---

[30] *The Drums of Father Ned*, Act 3, p. 99.

mention that they sleep together on Sundays. Why, of all days, Sundays—the Sabbath day? Simply because for O'Casey the sexual act, when emanating from love, is something pure and holy—a ritual, a prayer—and he sees no better occasion for it than God's chosen day.

Earlier in the play O'Casey expresses a thought which also is new to us. When Michael tells Nora, "All the stars of heaven are close to me when you are near," she replies: "For a brief while, my Michael. The purple tint of love must fade, and its passion becomes a whisper from a night that's gone. May our love pass quietly into companionship, for that is the one consummation of united life."[31]

Charmingly though it is expressed, the thought is out of key with the speaker's character. An unmarried girl, full of youth and sex, talking of love slowly passing into companionship sounds a little strange. The thought, however, has to be expressed, for it is something O'Casey has discovered for himself from a long and happy married life. Apart from Nora and Michael, in whom such concern for the future at the most sounds premature, there is no one else in the play to mouth it. O'Casey's elderly and married people are generally opinionated and selfish, and therefore he has to turn to the young and those in love—though they may not be the right persons, either.

I have already said elsewhere in this book that O'Casey does not allow realism to browbeat him. All this is, perhaps, another slap at realism.

[31] *The Drums of Father Ned*, Act 3, p. 83.

VIII

The One-Act Plays

U P to 1960 O'Casey had had five one-act plays published. Of these *The End of the Beginning* and *A Pound on Demand* first appeared in *Windfalls* (1934). The former appears to be the more popular of the two. George Jean Nathan wrote that it "would prove to be as hilarious a one-acter as our theatre has ever seen."[1] St John Ervine, who was by no means an indulgent critic of O'Casey, described it as "the most gorgeously funny one-act play I have read in my life."[2] The play was first performed at the Théâtre de L'Œuvre, Paris, in May 1939, and later at the Q Theatre, London, in October of the same year.

The story, a slight one, deals with Darry Berrill and his wife Lizzie, who exchange jobs for a few hours, Lizzie going out to mow the meadows, while Darry remains behind to do the housework. No sooner has Lizzie gone than Darry is joined by his friend Barry Derrill, whose near-sightedness is such that "he can't see the sky, unless the moon's shining in it!"[3] The two friends, after some exercises and a song, hasten to finish the housework before Lizzie returns. The obstinate Darry and the near-sighted Barry fumble about the house, spoiling or breaking everything they touch. They tie the heifer that is grazing outside to a chair in the house, the rope being brought down the chimney. The heifer wanders, and Darry is pulled up the chimney as he holds on to the rope fastened to the chair. Lizzie, returning after mowing the meadow, takes the rope off the heifer. Darry falls down the chimney, exhausted and sooty, but as pig-headed as ever:

DARRY [*to Lizzie*]: Now you see the result of havin' your own way! Why the hell didn't you hold on to the rope when you

---

[1] G. J. Nathan, *The Entertainment of a Nation*, p. 176.
[2] St John Ervine, *The Observer* (London), 11 Nov. 1934.
[3] *The End of the Beginning*, p. 268.

took it off the heifer, so that I wouldn't come down with a
bump?

LIZZIE: How'd I know you were hangin' on the other end?

DARRY [*indignantly*]: You didn't know—my God, woman,
can you do nothin' right![4]

The End of the Beginning may be more popular but *A Pound
on Demand* is the better play. In *The End of the Beginning*, a playgoer, though for a moment he may be convulsed with laughter,
cannot get over the feeling that the extravaganza on the stage is
purely farcical, and that such absurdity cannot happen even
in the most absurd situations. But when a dramatist chooses
for his hero a man "in a state of maudlin drunkenness,"[5] and
takes him into a sub-post office where little work is being
transacted, no demand is made on our credulity. A couple of
pints gives the character freedom to act as he wants; moreover,
it gives the dramatist licence to break the character's skull if he
so wishes. O'Casey's genius is on the whole comic and he is
always at home with his drunkards.

Jerry, a workman, drags Sammy, his drunken mate, into a
sub-post office. Sammy has a Savings Bank account and Jerry
wants him to withdraw a pound. The girl in charge of the
post office treats them with suspicion but hands over the
necessary form for signature. Sammy is far too drunk to sign
his name, but fit enough to get involved in a quarrel with a
woman writing an important letter to Tarraringapatam. When
Jerry does manage to get Sammy's signature, the girl at the
counter refuses to give the pound, for the signature on the form
does not tally with that in the bank book. A policeman appears
on the scene and throws the two rascals out. They disappear,
giving their ultimatum: "That's the last penny of our money
the Government'll ever get from us!"[6]

Both these plays are pure entertainment. They are the only
plays that have nothing to do with O'Casey's purpose, message
or convictions. There is no irony, no bitterness, not a thread
of tragedy in their comic structure. The laughter is free,
sportive and jaunty, got by putting his ludicrous but earnest
characters in the most farcical situations. O'Casey's humour is

---

[4] *The End of the Beginning*, p. 291.   [5] *A Pound on Demand*, p. 295.
[6] *Op. cit.*, p. 314.

generally broad and carefree, just as Shaw's humour is fine-edged and subtle.   The former would take any risk to exploit a situation, the latter would go all out to exploit national or professional characteristics.

O'Casey's other one-act plays are *A Time to Go, Bedtime Story* and *Hall of Healing,* all three published in 1951. *A Time to Go* is a morality comedy having two types of character, the good and the bad.   The good consists of Kelly from the Isle of Mananaun, who has bought a cow and is troubled with the thought that he has paid too little for it, and Widda Machree, who has sold the cow to Kelly and is haunted by the feeling that she has charged too much for it.   The bad are Michael Flagonson and his wife, who own a tavern, Bull Farrell, who is the proprietor of a general store, and Conroy, who owns a hundred and fifty acres.   These two sets of characters are contrasted with one another.   Kelly and Widda Machree are denounced as insane and dangerous to the public peace by their antagonists and are arrested by the Civic Guards.   But by the power of magic they free themselves and disappear.

The play is overcrowded: there are as many as thirteen characters.   Three, A Young Man, A Young Woman and Barney O'Hay, are brought in to show the meanness and unscrupulousness of Michael Flagonson and Bull Farrell. One character would have been sufficient for the purpose, though we could have done without all three of them.   Flagonson and Farrell sum themselves up well in their conversation, and Widda Machree's denunciation of the two is enough to remove any doubts that we might still have.   Another weakness in the play is that O'Casey struggles with too many major themes at the same time and comes to grips with none.   He touches on the problem of the poor, of Irish emigration, of the Church and its priests, human justice, etc.   Any one of them would have been sufficient for a full-length play, let alone a one-act sketch, but O'Casey scatters his energy in trying to squeeze in more than he can handle.

But faults such as these sink to insignificance before O'Casey's virtues.   Though some of the characters are superfluous, they are still handled skilfully.   Their entry, their position on the stage and their departure accord to a studied pattern as exquisite as *Within the Gates.*   Songs, music, colour, dance and speech interlace with each other and move forward to advance his theme. The moral of the play—the need for unselfishness—cuts its way through the numerous sub-themes and makes its presence unmistakably felt.

Bedtime Story is a satire directed against those morally frightened young men who crave for sexual intercourse, but are continually haunted by a futile sense of sin. John Jo Mulligan gets a pretty young girl, Angela Nightingale, to his flat on the pretext of reading Yeats's poems to her. But before he has got as far as "I will arise and go now, and go to Innisfree," he is tempted into "sin" by what he describes as "the dance that uplifted your skirt out of the way of your movements and juggled a vision of spiritual desolation into a mirage of palpitating enjoyments."[7] Having got what he had sought for, he hurries to get Angela out of the flat before his friend Daniel Halibut returns from a dance, and before Miss Mossie, the landlady, wakes up. He succeeds, but not before she has swindled him of £28, his best coat, an umbrella and a ring. He runs out to recover his belongings from her. His sudden disappearance and the disorderly state of his room convince Miss Mossie and Halibut that Mulligan has become mentally deranged. When he returns he is politely received by Miss Mossie who has in the meantime summoned a doctor, a nurse and a policeman. Mulligan, on being confronted by the lot who have come to help him, sinks into his chair in a dead faint.

The play is entertaining both as reading and as theatre. It is not as derogatory to the Catholic Church as may appear from a superficial study. In Mulligan there is the tussle between the flesh and the spirit; the flesh wins, for he never was one with the faith he professed. As Angela tells him: "You took care to leave your saints out on the doorstep; ay, and shut the door in their faces, too."[8] The continuous appeal that Mulligan makes to the Blessed Saints and angels to save him from public scandal after his sexual venture may shock some orthodox minds. Jack Carlton, M.B.E., a former Festival Gardens Entertainments Manager, described the performance of the play at the Unity Theatre as "blasphemous, salacious

---

[7] *Bedtime Story*, p. 237.
[8] *Op. cit.*, p. 236.

R

and unsavoury." On hearing this O'Casey said: "The God-damned fellow is a God-damned fool."[9]

For me, *Hall of Healing* is easily the best among O'Casey's one-act plays. The scene is a waiting-room of a Parish Dispensary in Dublin on a winter's day. The few patients are bullied by Aloysius, the fussy caretaker, as they wait for the doctor. The doctor's arrival does not make things easier for them, for he is even fussier and more inconsiderate. But all the same there is a stir now, though it be no more than patients being hurried in and out of the surgery. Red Muffler, who is among the first to have come to the dispensary, is the last to receive attention. As he persuades the doctor to come and see his sick daughter, his wife comes to inform him that the child is dead. On hearing this Red Muffler tells the doctor: "You might have safely said you'd come, an' kept hope danglin' still in front of us that healin' still was here, an' common goodness."[10]

We know that as a child O'Casey regularly attended St Mark's Ophthalmic Hospital, an account of which he has given in *I Knock at the Door*. The narrative there concludes with words that leave no doubt of how close he was to hospitals:

> Then a nurse heavily bandaged his eyes, and his mother led him forth from the hospital, having finished his first day with an Institution that was to know him so well in the future that the doors nearly opened of their own accord when they saw him coming.[11]

The heartlessness of some doctors, the despicable conditions and the rigid rules of the dispensaries pained and angered him. The worst of these was the insistence on the part of the medical authorities that no medicines could be dispensed to the poor unless they brought empty bottles with them. On one occasion O'Casey himself went in search of a bottle for an old woman who had not complied with the regulation. Perhaps such a state of things no longer exists in Dublin though it is discomfiting to read O'Casey's letter to *The Irish Times*, saying: "Little did I think, when I wrote *Hall of Healing*, that the conditions of fifty years ago in the dispensaries of the poor would be the same today."[12] However, one thing is certain, that this play is

[9] *Daily Worker*, 20 Feb. 1954.   [10] *Hall of Healing*, p. 271.
[11] *I Knock at the Door*, p. 36.   [12] *The Irish Times*, 28 Dec. 1951.

based on facts, and that while writing it O'Casey has drawn
on his reminiscences.

Hall of Healing can hardly be said to have a plot. The
dialogue rambles, the climax—the death of Red Muffler's
daughter—is weak, and Aloysius and the doctor are caricatured
with undue severity. And yet I have called this the best of
O'Casey's one-act plays. This is because there is a wealth of
characterisation, so rich, so manifold, so individual that one is
left dazzled. O'Casey cannot portray the rich, the ruling
classes or the well-to-do. But when he sets out to draw the
poor, the down-trodden or the outcast—and should they be his
own countrymen—he shows a compassion and understanding
that are astonishing. Fame, a happy family life, the fulfilment of
the daily needs and comforts, have not been able to dwarf
the "homeric social angers" that he feels for the poor. He is
one with them; they claim every ounce of his love, his
humanity and his tenderness.

Most of the characters are, to use a phrase of Eric Bentley's,
"a gallery of charming children."[13] Each is a symbol and yet
is strictly an individual, with peculiarities of his own. The
old woman is the most lovable of the lot. An incurable
chronic case—she wants her back which has been bent by age
straightened—she spends her Monday mornings at the dispensary, for "you can never tell with God."[14] She keeps going
a perpetual stream of conversation, edging in, not a word, but
a whole history. She defends the old doctor—now dead—for
his humanitarian approach, offers a gleam of hope to every
suffering patient, and also quaint medical advice as she
awaits her turn. Her remarks are gloriously funny:

> BLACK MUFFLER [*holding the bottle at arm's length*]: Oh, a lovely
> yella, this time; th' last was blue.
> YOUNG WOMAN: Mine was red, so it was.
> OLD WOMAN: Show us. [*He hands her the bottle and she holds it
> out at arm's length.*] . . . Be th' look of it, son, that should
> do you a power o' good. This fella thinks more o' bottles than
> th' other fella did—I'll say that of him![15]

Where do we find colour better infused into the theme than we

---

[13] Eric Bentley, *What is Theatre?*, p. 111.   [14] *Hall of Healing*, p. 241.
[15] *Op. cit.*, pp. 261-2.

have here?   And which of us has not felt, at one time or
another, the "power o' good" a flashy-coloured medicine could
do?

Slightly less interesting than the Old Woman is Black
Muffler. His faith in the bottle is absolute: "Bottles there was,
bottles there is, bottles there must be!"[16] He naively relates the
fright the old doctor once gave him by telling him that health
cannot be drunk out of a bottle—surely "th' poor man wasn't
a docthor at all!"[17] Jentree too believes in the bottle—"I
dunno how life could be lived without some kinda bottles"[18]—
but in those containing porter. He is one whose nerves are
ruined from excessive drinking. The doctor has ordered him to
swallow half a gallon of water a day to nullify the effects of
alcohol. A sound treatment, but there is a snag in it which
the Old Woman points out to Aloysius (and to which Jentree
wholeheartedly agrees): "If th' poor man has to negify th'
wine with wather, and then has to negify the wather with wine,
sure th' poor man'll burst himself thryin' to find a solution
for his ailment."[19]

No less captivating is Green Muffler who is made to spend
his last penny procuring three bottles for medicine. Imagine
his indignation when the Apothecary shoves his bottles aside
and hands him a tiny box of pills.

> GREEN MUFFLER [*to the patients—who keep a tense silence*]: Did
> yous see what's after happenin'? Did yous or did yous not?
> Yous all saw me entherin' burdened with bottles, be strict
> orders forced to spend me last penny to get them. An' when
> I present them, as sthrictly ordered be a certain person,
> I'm shouted at to take them away, an' even th' use of one
> was denied me. [*He extends his hand with the tiny pill-box on
> its palm.*] Looka what I got; just looka what I got! [*He comes
> into the centre of the room.*] I'm not dhreamin', mind you.
> This isn't fairyland either. Yous all seen what happened.
> After all me huntin' after bottles, looka what's been handed
> out! . . . Yous all heard what a certain person said to me.
> You must have three bottles, he says, one for a mixture, one
> for a liniment, he says, an' one for a draught. Three, mind
> you. Yous all sung a song about the necessity for bottles.

---

[16] *Hall of Healing*, p. 254.   [17] *Op. cit.*, p. 251.
[18] *Ibid.*   [19] *Op. cit.*, p. 260.

An' what was the outcome? Yous all seen it yourselves.
Yous all seen the bottles scattered about, an' me left with
what's shinin' in th' palm of me hand! I'm not dhreamin',
mind you! Have yous nothin' to say to relieve me feelin's?
[*He moves towards the door to go.*] Jasus, it's a cruel thing to
do on anyone.[20]

Red Muffler's genuine need for the doctor is brought to
contrast with the trumpery ailments and frothy resentments
of the other patients. While attention is being paid to gimcrack
issues in the dispensary his daughter dies, and his wife comes
to fetch him home:

Come on Frank, till you see her. She's got all her old good
looks back again. [*Brokenly*] Oh, me little one'll be runnin'
round frightened, lookin' for her mammy, among the spirits of
the blest![21]

The naive fear of the mother may be compared to that of
Mrs Breydon in *Red Roses for Me*, where she begs the Rector to
leave the church lights on for the night so that her dead son
may not feel lonesome in the dark. Human sentiment, springing from an artless sincerity, brushes all reasoning aside and
makes the tragedy profoundly moving. O'Casey may not be a
master of logic, but of the human heart he surely is.

[20] *Hall of Healing*, pp. 267-8.   [21] *Op. cit.*, p. 272.

IX

Conclusion

I EARLIER suggested that before we pass any judgment of
our own as to whether O'Casey was right or wrong in exiling
himself, we must acquaint ourselves with all his plays. The
question of exile is a personal, if not a domestic, matter, and
the critic is only indirectly concerned with it: only in so far as
it affects the writer's creative output. In bulk this certainly has
been large. Since 1926 O'Casey has given us seventeen plays,
his life story in six volumes,[1] two books of criticism, and one
small anthology of poems written mostly when he was in
Dublin. His plays and autobiographies are read throughout
the English-speaking world, and have become a part of the
literature of Europe. Today he owes his fame as the greatest
living dramatist in English as much to *The Silver Tassie*, *Within
the Gates* and *Red Roses for Me* as he does to his early masterpieces. If he had remained in Dublin and written a dozen plays
in the tradition of his Abbey works, I am sure his place in
dramatic history would not have been higher than it stands
now. In the provincial atmosphere of Dublin his genius, then
limited to portraying the tenement world around him, might
not have flowered in variety, and his reputation could have
declined through uniformity and surfeit. To single out an
instance, *Within the Gates* might never have been written had
O'Casey not spent a considerable time in London. And we
know what a rare thing in dramatic literature this play is:
one in which the dramatist breaks away from the convention
of treating one facet of life, in favour of life itself. Though I
personally like *The Plough and the Stars* better, I can quite see
why Wilson Knight hails the former as O'Casey's greatest
achievement.

This is but one point of view, and justifiable only when we
take into consideration the best of O'Casey's exile plays. But

[1] See "A Note on O'Casey's Autobiographies," Appendix A, p. 250.

when we come across plays such as *The Star Turns Red* or *Oak Leaves and Lavender*—which are poor only when we compare them with his best—we feel that O'Casey, though a dramatist of undeniable genius, has lost his way. We then turn to agree with John O'Shaughnessy that after O'Casey left Ireland he "never again found an enemy so able to draw out of him all the passions and the furies of an Olympian as was afforded by the cause of Irish Freedom, bound up as it was with the cultural renaissance of nationalism, the religious struggle of Protestant against Catholic, the historical and political orientation against monarchical control, and the growing power and effectiveness of socialism."[2] But let us remember that there is no certainty that had O'Casey remained in Dublin all his plays would have been as powerful as *The Plough and the Stars*. Let us not forget that between the presentation of *The Shadow of a Gunman* and *Juno and the Paycock* there appeared *Cathleen Listens In*, the poorest of all his plays.

I cannot express my opinion on the problem of O'Casey's exile as firmly as some critics have done.[3] But if forced, I would say, taking into consideration the question of his personal happiness, that O'Casey did well in exiling himself. England in a large measure compensated for what he lost by breaking away from Ireland. In his new home he freed himself from the bitterness, the cynicism and the horrible impact of poverty that underline his Abbey plays. If not a new force, at least a new strain came into his writings: he began to sing of joy, love, healthy sex and the basic sorrows and pleasures of ordinary living. From England he could freely express himself on matters religious, political and social without any fear of interference or oppression. In Ireland his Communism and anti-clericalism would not have been tolerated for long, and exile would have eventually been thrust upon him.

There is one aspect of O'Casey's exile which is fundamentally more important than the controversy over it. The Irish expatriate writers, except for a few like Shaw and Ervine who cut themselves off completely from Ireland, still find their material in Irish life, but their treatment of it is often affected

[2] John O'Shaughnessy, *The Nation*, CLXXXIV, 16 Mar. 1957.
[3] See above Chapter III, pp. 100-1.

by alien considerations. O'Casey also finds his matter in Irish life but he differs from the other expatriates in not subjecting his treatment to outside considerations. The majority of his exile plays, in spite of their wider symbolic application, are essentially localised in Ireland. His plays are Irish before they are anything else, and Ireland unfortunately has decided to decry them.

Richard Findlater writes somewhere that "The story of Mr O'Casey's later evolution is the story of a dramatist in search of an audience."[4] Very true, but the reasons for it are not O'Casey's exile or his failure to transplant himself fully to England. Neither in England nor in America are people very keen on Irish plays; and even when the play has a universal significance, they are not anxious to view the world through Irish eyes. Moreover, the average playgoer wants plays with a "tidy parcelled message" and is frightened of experimental and symbolic drama. Then there arises the problem of the modern theatre's inability to contend with O'Casey's unique genius. John Gassner says on the subject:

> Our spiritually diminished theatre in a spiritually diminished world cannot quite assimilate his particular genius—cannot even adjust itself to it. His alleged and real faults of rhetoric, wordiness, and sentiment would be less formidable in a theatre like the Elizabethan that was vigorous enough to contain them and even make a virtue of them. His excellence—his wild humour of words and farcical action, his vast anger, and his vast love—threatens to burst the confines of a small-spirited theatre such as we mostly have in London and New York. The fermentation of the wine seems to be too strong for the pint-sized bottle.[5]

Besides these, there are other causes that have led to the neglect of O'Casey; the lack of first-class Irish actors outside Ireland, and O'Casey's espousal of Communism and his insistence on going his own way. Lastly, his constant criticism of other dramatists, and of producers and critics has turned the theatre entrepreneurs against him. But what does it matter? In his own lifetime he has heard some of the very eminent critics

---

[4] Quoted in *Evening Press* (Dublin), 29 Jan. 1955.
[5] John Gassner, *Theatre Arts*, xxxv, Jun. 1951.

refer to him as the greatest living playwright. That suffices for the present, and as for the future—

> AN IRISH CRITIC: The long view of posterity may turn out to be a poor one.
> O'CASEY: So it may, indeed, but I won't be there to hear it.[6]

But we need have no fear of that. Posterity will know its man if it has to choose from our generation.

[6] *The Green Crow*, p. 15.

Appendix A

A Note on O'Casey's Autobiographies

A sense of the world around him is the basic attitude of the work; not what is here but what it leads to; not what is now, but what can be, what will be, is important. Only this can explain the joyousness of the whole. Even in the caustic dissection of the pompous, the smug, the rich; in the setting down of criticisms, quarrels, bitter blasts against the stately, the powerful, the well-fed, the corrupt, there runs a constant and wildly exulting stream of joy. Life, "a wide branching flame good to see and to behold," has room for all things. There is meanness, ugliness, bitterness; there is poverty and oppression, stupidity and blind, bigoted ignorance: dark colours woven through the tapestry; but the red colour of blood and battle, the gold of sunshine and song, the green of all living things, purple of wine and fire, and blue of the sea and the sky dominate. O'Casey is an idealist, not a pessimist. [J. O'SHAUGHNESSY, *The Nation*, CLXXXIV, 16 Mar. 1957.]

O'Casey has written his life story in six volumes: *I Knock at the Door* (1939), *Pictures in the Hallway* (1942), *Drums Under the Window* (1946), *Inishfallen Fare Thee Well* (1949), *Rose and Crown* (1952) and *Sunset and Evening Star* (1954). It is almost impossible to get the first four volumes today, but the whole work is available in two volumes under the title *Mirror in My House* (1956).

The six volumes sum up an eventful life. O'Casey has set down his impresssions in an objective form: no doubt he follows the instinct of the dramatist in him. In the first three books he recalls vividly his childhood, boyhood and manhood days—"plodding, dodging and dancing through the rhetoric-laden atmosphere of Dublin in the years which bore bitter issue in the Easter Rebellion of 1916, . . . with all his swans still swans and all his geese geese."[1] In the fourth book, perhaps the most impressive of all, he relates with modesty and great clarity the memorable days of his early fame, and his meetings with Lady Gregory, Yeats, Lennox Robinson, A.E. and others. The last two volumes seem to be an anticlimax after such exciting and impressive records of his Dublin life. In them he writes too much of the world around him and too little about his own self. His wife remains shadowy and one hardly hears about his children. Still the six volumes are remarkable for the light they throw on O'Casey himself, and the man that emerges

---

[1] *The Times Literary Supplement*, 17 Nov. 1945.

from it remains as vivid in the consciousness of the reader as Boyle or Fluther. No wonder Frank O'Connor, reviewing them, wrote: "There he stands painted, as even Augustus John failed to paint, an international expert, insulted and oppressed by bowsies and gutties who wouldn't know a Giorgione from a hole in the wall."[2]

The autobiographies are also a "triumph of style." There are many passages in them which are great literature: such as the description of the Lord Lieutenant's procession in *I Knock at the Door* or his mother's death in *Inishfallen Fare Thee Well*. Not all of the writing is even; it varies greatly in style. When roused O'Casey can be Biblical, Shakespearian or Joycian by turns. He can also be rhapsodical, sentimental, rhetorical, or argumentative as the occasion demands. On the whole his prose is supple, bold, exciting and pictorial;[3] soaring into free verse without any conscious effort on the author's part. But at times he uses alliterations and perpetrates puns and jingles which, though neatly done and extremely amusing, are not everybody's dish. Yet the reader gladly puts up with it, for the force of the man comes through the good and the bad alike. "The styles are the men, the many men that O'Casey is, but always one feels the man behind the multiplicity."[4]

Splendid as these autobiographies are they have not escaped criticism. Some critics feel that the work is blemished by self-pity and proletarian snobbery. Others feel that O'Casey is unable to relinquish a grudge, an unfounded grievance. To point to an instance, he suffered greatly through Yeats's criticism of *The Silver Tassie*, and yet no writer of our time has spoken more movingly of Yeats than O'Casey. Then there are the Irish critics and reviewers who damn an author for speaking his mind freely on religious matters. When *Sunset and Evening Star* appeared in 1954, Padraic Colum described it as "cantankerous, intolerant, unfair and dogmatic—in a word, cornaptious."[5] The reviewer for the *Irish Independent* called it an occasion for O'Casey to sprawl in print his contempt for the world in general and the Catholic Church in particular.[6] How very different these two views are from those expressed by Harold Clurman and Gerald Weales. Harold Clurman says:

> He seems at moments to hate Ireland; yet he is Irish in his every breath. He strikes out wildly at institutional religion; yet he is

[2] Frank O'Connor, *Holiday*, XIX, Jan. 1956.
[3] J. C. Trewin, "Lord of Language," *Drama*, Winter 1954.
[4] G. Hicks, *The New Republic*, CXXXV, 22 Oct. 1956.
[5] P. Colum *The New Republic*, CXXXI, 27 Dec. 1954, p. 19.
[6] *Irish Independent*, 30 Oct. 1954.

deeply religious. . . . He who seems to be bursting with rebellious indignation is essentially all love. "And who can claim a share in God," O'Casey asks apropos of T. S. Eliot, "who does not take the part of man?"[7]

And Weales writes that to "O'Casey living has always meant a wealth of song and dance, loving and laughter, healthy sex and close-in fighting, it has also involved a recognition of sorrow, a respect for pain, and a continued determination that there shall be as little as possible of both in the world."[8]

A student who uses the autobiographies for a critical study of the man faces one serious difficulty. O'Casey rarely gives dates and seldom tells us his age or gives the time of a particular incident. Thus it becomes hard to relate events to their surroundings. However, one must remember that these books are not written to serve the purpose of a record, but to be read as a story showing the reactions of a sensitive poet to the world around him. Another problem, and a minor one, is that some of the accounts are not very factual. For instance, reading *Inishfallen Fare Thee Well* and *Rose and Crown* it would appear that O'Casey never visited Dublin after he left for England in March 1926. But this is not so, as O'Casey himself acknowledges in a letter to me:

> This is also a mistake. Came back to get books and papers. Stayed the night in a hotel opposite station for boat-train, and left first thing in the morning.[9]

He was in Ireland twice again: the first time in 1927 to spend his honeymoon in Howth; and later to stay as a guest of Lennox Robinson in Dalkey in 1935. But slips such as these are few (perhaps inevitable as O'Casey writes from memory) and on the whole the autobiographies remain remarkably accurate. They are indispensable for the study of the man and his works.

[7] H. Clurman, *The Nation*, CLXXIX, 27 Nov. 1954.
[8] G. Weales, *Commentary*, XIX, Feb. 1955.
[9] Letter to me from O'Casey dated 31 Mar. 1959.

Appendix B

O'Casey's letter on his affinities with George Bernard Shaw

Mr Ron Ayling, a very close friend of O'Casey, wrote to St John Ervine saying that the one fault in the latter's biography, *Bernard Shaw: His Life, Works and Friends* (1956), was his failure to record O'Casey's relations with Shaw. Ervine wrote back in a letter dated 12 Sep. 1957, saying that O'Casey was not one of Shaw's friends, and that he could not record something that "never existed as an important fact." Ayling forwarded this letter to O'Casey and got the following reply. The last sentence shows O'Casey's final generosity even towards those who attack him, and often unjustly:

I wonder how and where St. John Ervine got his dogmatism? He is more dogmatic on everything under the sun than a newly-fledged Irish Bishop. I have no doubt that G.B.S. was a friend of his and of W. Archer; but, I imagine, in a limited way. . . .

As a matter of fact, St. John wouldn't have understood, and can't now, the bond between me and G.B.S. Here are a few: He was a Dublinman, so was I; he was reared up a Protestant, so was I; he suffered the humiliation of living in the genteel poverty of the Irish lower middle-class, while I suffered the squalid, but more vigorous, poverty of the proletariat; Shaw was mainly a self-educated man, so was I; Shaw hated poverty in all its forms, so do I; Shaw fought against it most of his life, so do I, and still do; Shaw thought Stalin a great man, so did I, and so do still; Shaw was passionately devoted to the USSR and all the USSR did and was doing, so was I; Shaw hated all British Imperialism, so did I; Shaw rejected the Christian beliefs, so did I; Shaw saw through the Romantic idea of Irish nationalism, so did I; Shaw was a fighter, and he knew I was one, too (I've never heard that he ever said in a letter to St. J. "Bravo, Titan!"); in almost his last words to Mrs. O'Casey he said, "It is for Sean, now, to carry on the fight"; not St.J., but Sean; Shaw was a born Communist, so was I; Shaw called Jim Larkin "the greatest Irishman since Parnell," and Shaw knew how I had fought for the workers with Jim; Shaw was deeply interested in the Chinese Workers and Peasants Red Army and its long and terrible march from Kiangsi in the south to Shensi in the north, wondering if they could do it, and if they did it, what effect it would have on the whole of China, so was I; . . . Shaw had a deep affection for Lady Gregory, so had I (I hope St.J. won't next say somewhere I was never a friend of hers; but he would hardly do that, for he disliked her, I imagine, or, certainly, she did him); his initials are carved on the great tree in Coole, so are mine, but I have never seen St.J.'s there; while St.J. mentions a number of American Drama Critics, I noticed he never mentions Nathan, yet Nathan had a deep reverence for Shaw, and Shaw thought highly of him, and so did, do, I; . . . Shaw was always delighted to see John Dulanty, the then High Commissioner for Ireland—it was he who brought the Roll of Dublin's Freeman to G.B.S.; Shaw loved his humour and his stories, and so did I; Shaw was always ready to talk about Ireland, and so was I.

Well these are a few of the affinities that went to and fro between Shaw and me, cutting out, even, the tremendous interest we both took in the Theater; affinities that could hardly have existed between St.J. E. and the Dublin sage. . . .

St. Jay [*sic*] is, though not in the first class in fancy or imagination, I'm afraid, but forcible, though too dogmatic. His book on Shaw, in my opinion, is a fine biography, and a great tribute to Shaw.[1]

---

[1] Letter dated 3 Nov. 1957. In Mr Ron Ayling's possession.

Appendix C

"A Son of Granuaile"[1]
(Air: "Granuaile")

No more the blackbird blithely sings within the tangled brake,
No more the lark's high soaring notes the morning echoes wake,
No more the thrush her sweet song sends along each balmy gale,
For all are sad and silent now, since Larkin went to jail.

REFRAIN:
For the greatest man that ever trod the land of Inisfail,
Now lies in a dark prison cell, far, far from Granuaile.

I nourished great men at my breast that fought and died for me,
Or pined in exile far away that I might yet be free;
And great as greatest of the chiefs that marshalled Clan-na-Gael
Is dauntless Larkin—dearest son of poor oul' Granuaile.

REFRAIN:
The Irish workers join to smash the door of Larkin's jail,
And bring my great son back to me—ses poor oul' Granuaile.

With fearless, strong and lavish hands he scattered freedom's seed,
He made the Irish workers men and show'd them all their need;
His hand struck down the strong, to save the helpless, weak and frail,
Till hope's eternal song was sung by poor oul' Granuaile.

REFRAIN:
Then Irish workers join to smash the doors of Larkin's jail,
And bring my great son back to me—ses poor oul' Granuaile

And shall the workers leave to pine within the prison cell
The man who strove to raise them from their dismal hell?
No! while the sons of Labour live their efforts shall not fail
To break his prison bonds, and bring Jim back to Granuaile!

REFRAIN:
Then Irish workers join to smash the door of Larkin's jail,
And bring my great son back to me—ses poor oul' Granuaile.

---

[1] A print copy of the poem is in the possession of Mr Wedge, Dublin.

Bibliography

I. SEAN O'CASEY

1. Unpublished Material

Cathleen Listens In.
"A Stand on the Silver Tassie."
Letters to the Solicitors for the Abbey Theatre, Cyril Cusack, the author, and others.

2. Plays

Collected Plays. 4 vols., London (Macmillan) 1951-7.
   Vol. I (1957) *Juno and the Paycock; The Shadow of a Gunman; The Plough and the Stars; The End of the Beginning; A Pound on Demand.*
   Vol. II (1952) *The Silver Tassie; Within the Gates; The Star Turns Red.*
   Vol. III (1951) *Purple Dust; Red Roses For Me; Hall of Healing.*
   Vol. IV (1951) *Oak Leaves and Lavender; Cock-a-doodle Dandy; Bedtime Story; Time to Go.*
The Bishop's Bonfire. London (Macmillan) 1955.
Drums of Father Ned. London (Macmillan) 1960.
Behind the Green Curtain. London (Macmillan) 1961.

3. Autobiographies

I Knock at the Door. London (Macmillan) 1939.
Pictures in the Hallway. London (Macmillan) 1942.
Drums Under the Window. London (Macmillan) 1946.
Inishfallen Fare Thee Well. London (Macmillan) 1949.
Rose and Crown. London (Macmillan) 1952.
Sunset and Evening Star. London (Macmillan) 1954.

4. Miscellaneous

Songs of the Wren (series 1). Dublin (Fergus O'Connor) 1918.
Songs of the Wren (series 2). Dublin (Fergus O'Connor) 1918.
More Wren Songs. Dublin (Fergus O'Connor) 1918.
Thomas Ashe. Dublin (Fergus O'Connor) 1918.
A Son of Granuaile. Dublin 1918.
The Sacrifice of Thomas Ashe. Dublin (Fergus O'Connor) 1918.
The Story of the Irish Citizen Army. Dublin (Maunsel) 1919.
Windfalls. London (Macmillan) 1937.
The Flying Wasp. London (Macmillan) 1937.
There Go the Irish, in *They Go—The Irish,* ed. Leslie Daiken, London (Nicholson Watson) 1944.
The Green Crow. London (W. H. Allen) 1957.
Under A Colored Cap. London (Macmillan) 1963.

5. Material from Newspapers and Periodicals

"The Bonnie Bunch of Roses, O!" in *The Irish Worker*, 11 Jan. 1913.

"Gut Ar an nGaort," in *Irish Freedom*, Mar. 1913.

"The Gaelic Movement Today," in *Irish Opinion*, 23 Mar. 1918.

"Life and Literature," in *The Irish Statesman*, 22 Dec. 1923.

"Irish in the Schools," in *The Irish Statesman*, 20 Nov. 1924.

"The Innocent at Home," in *The Irish Statesman*, 10 Jan. 1925.

"Y.O. and The Silver Tassie," in *The Irish Statesman*, 4 Aug. 1928.

"The Plays of Sean O'Casey," in *The Nineteenth Century*, Sep. 1928.

"The Dream School," in *Yale Review*, XXVI, Summer 1937.

"No Flowers for Films," in *The Leader Magazine*, 19 Feb. 1949.

"Jeep be Jeepers!" in *The New Statesman and Nation*, 18 Jul. 1953.

"Sean O'Casey and his Critics," in *Enquiry*, Jun. 1958.

"O'Casey's Lively Credo," in *The New York Times* (international edn.),
10 Nov. 1958.

II. OTHERS

1. Unpublished sources

HOLLOWAY, JOSEPH: *Impressions of a Dublin Playgoer*. National Library,
Dublin.
MS. 1877, Apr.-Jun. 1923; MS. 1881, Sep-Dec. 1923; MS. 1884,
Jan.-Mar. 1924; MS. 1885, Apr.-Jun. 1924; MS. 1886, Apr.-Jun.
1924; MS. 1888, Jul.-Sep. 1924; MS. 1889, Oct.-Dec. 1924; MS. 1892,
Jan.-Mar. 1925; MS. 1898, Oct.-Dec. 1925; MS. 1899, Jan.-Mar.
1926; MS. 1900, Jan.-Mar. 1926.

HOWSE, HANS FREDERICK: *The Plays of Sean O'Casey*. (Thesis presented
for the degree of M.A. to the University of Liverpool, 1951.)

KNIGHT, GEORGE WILSON: Study of *Within the Gates*.

NORDELL, HANS RODERICK: *The Dramatic Practice and Theory of Sean O'Casey*.
(Thesis presented for the degree of B.Litt. to Trinity College Dublin.)

McGUIRE, JAMES BRADY: *Realism in Irish Drama*. (Thesis presented for
the degree of Ph.D. to the University of Dublin, 1954.)

2. Books

AGATE, JAMES: *The Contemporary Theatre*, 1926. London 1927.

——: *First Nights*. London 1934.

——: *Red Letter Nights*. London 1944.

BARKER, HARLEY GRANVILLE: *On Poetry in Drama* (The Romance Lecture).
London 1937.

BENTLEY, ERIC: *In Search of Theatre*. London 1954.

——: *The Dramatic Event*. London 1956.

——: *What is Theatre?* London 1957.

BLAGHD, DE EÁRNAN: *Trasna Na Bóinne* [Crossing the Boyne]. Dublin
1957.

BOUCICAULT, DION: *The Shaughraun*. London 1885.

BROWN, J. M.: *Two on the Aisle*. New York 1938.

S

BRYNE, DAWSON: *The Story of Ireland's National Theatre.* Dublin 1929.

CARTY, JAMES: *Ireland (1783-1850).* Dublin 1949.

CLARK, BARRETT H. and FREEDLEY, GEORGE: *A History of Modern Drama.* New York 1947.

CORKERY, DANIEL: *Synge and Anglo-Irish Literature.* London 1931.

CUNLIFFE, JOHN W.: *Modern English Playwrights.* London 1927.

D'ARCY, M. C.: *Communism and Christianity.* Harmondsworth (Penguin edn.) 1961.

DENT, ALAN: *Nocturne and Rhapsodies.* London 1950.

DEVOY, JOHN: *Devoy's Post Bag,* edd. O'Brien and Ryan. 2 vols., London 1953.

DUKES, ASHLEY: *The Scene is Changed.* London 1942.

ERVINE, ST JOHN: *Mixed Marriage.* Dublin 1911.

——: *Oscar Wilde.* London 1951.

FAY, GERARD: *The Abbey Theatre.* Dublin 1958.

FERMOR, UNA ELLIS: *The Frontiers of Drama.* London 1945.

FINDLATER, RICHARD: *The Unholy Trade.* London 1952.

FOX, R. M.: *Green Banners.* London 1938.

——: *History of the Irish Citizen Army.* Dublin 1943.

——: *Jim Larkin.* Dublin 1957.

GASSNER, JOHN: *Masters of the Drama.* New York 1954.

GREENE, DAVID H. and STEPHENS, EDWARD M.: *J. M. Synge (1871-1909).* New York 1959.

GREGORY, LADY: *Journals (1916-30),* edd. L. Robinson. London 1946.

GRIFFIN, GERALD: *The Wild Geese.* London 1938.

GWYNN, STEPHEN: *Irish Literature and Drama.* London 1936.

HODSON, JAMES LANSDALE: *No Phantoms Here.* London 1932.

HONE, JOSEPH: *W. B. Yeats (1865-1939).* London 1942.

JACKSON, T. A.: *Ireland Her Own.* London 1947.

JEFFARES, A. NORMAN: *W. B. Yeats: Man and Poet.* London 1949.

KAVANAGH, PETER: *The Story of the Abbey Theatre.* New York 1950.

KNIGHT, GEORGE WILSON: *Christ and Nietzsche.* London 1948.

KOSLOW, JULES: *The Green and the Red.* New York 1949.

KUNITZ, STANLEY J.: *Living Authors.* New York 1930.

——: with HOWARD HAYCRAFT: *Twentieth Century Authors.* New York 1942.

LUMLEY, FREDERICK: *Trends in Twentieth Century Drama.* London 1956.

LYNCH, DIARMUID: *The I.R.B. and the 1916 Rising.* Cork 1957.

MACARDLE, DOROTHY: *The Irish Republic.* Dublin 1951.

MacCARTHY, DESMOND: *Drama.* London 1940.

MacDONAGH, DONAGH and ROBINSON, LENNOX (Edd.): *The Oxford Book of Irish Verse.* Oxford 1958.

MacLIAMMÓIR, MICHEÁL: *All for Hecuba.* Dublin 1946.

——: *Theatre in Ireland.* Dublin 1950.

MACMURRAY, J.: *Creative Society.* London 1935.

MALONE, ANDREW E.: *The Irish Drama.* London 1929.

MARX, K. & ENGELS, F.: *On Religion.* Moscow 1957.

——: *Marx Engels Select Correspondence.* London 1956.

NATHAN, GEORGE JEAN: *The World in Falseface.* London 1923.

NATHAN, GEORGE JEAN: *Art of the Night*. New York 1928.
——: *The Intimate Notebooks*. New York 1932.
——: *Encyclopaedia of the Theatre*. New York 1940.
——: *The Entertainment of the Nation*. New York 1942.
NICHOLS, BEVERLEY: *Are They the Same at Home?* London 1927.
NICOLL, ALLARDYCE: *Masks, Mimes and Miracles*. London 1931.
——: *British Drama* (4th edn.). London 1949.
O'BRIEN, WILLIAM: *Irish Revolution*. Dublin 1923.
O'HEGARTY, P. S.: *The Victory of Sinn Fein*. Dublin 1924.
——: *A History of Ireland under the Union*. London 1952.
O'SULLIVAN, SEUMAS: *Dublin Poems*. New York 1946.
OWEN, WILFRED: *Poems*. London 1920.
PAKENHAM, FRANK: *Peace by Ordeal*. London 1935.
PEARCE, PADRAIC H.: *Political Writings and Speeches*. Dublin 1952.
PELLIZZI, CAMILLO: *English Drama*. London 1935.
REYNOLDS, ERNEST: *Modern English Drama*. London 1949.
ROBINSON, LENNOX: *The Irish Theatre*. Ed. London 1939.
——: *Curtain Up*. London 1942.
RYAN, DESMOND: *Remembering Sion*. London 1934.
SHAW, G. B.: *John Bull's other Island and Major Barbara*. London 1907.
SPRIGGE, ELIZABETH: *The Strange Life of August Strindberg*. London 1949.
STANFORD, DEREK: *Christopher Fry*. London 1954.
SWAFFER, HANNEN: *Who's Who*. London 1929.
SYNGE, J. M.: *Plays*. London 1932.
TINDALL, WILLIAM YORK: *Forces in Modern British Drama 1885-1946*. New York 1947.
TOLLER, ERNEST: *The Swallow Book* (tr. Ashley Dukes). London 1924.
——: *Seven Plays*. London 1935.
TREWIN, J. C.: *The Theatre Since 1900*. London 1951.
USSHER, ARLAND: *Three Great Irishmen*. London 1952.
VEITCH, NORMAN: *The People's*. Gateshead-upon-Tyne 1950.
WHITE, J. R.: *Misfit*. London 1930.
WILLIAMS, RAYMOND: *Drama from Ibsen to Eliot*. London 1954.
WILLIAMSON, AUDREY: *Theatre of Two Decades*. London 1951.
WILSON, A. E.: *Post-War Theatre*. London 1949.
WILSON, EDMUND: *Axel's Castle*. London 1931.
WRIGHT, ARNOLD: *Disturbed Dublin*. London 1914.
YEATS, W. B.: *Collected Works*, III. Stratford-on-Avon 1908.
——: *Pages from a Diary Written in Nineteen Hundred and Thirty*. Dublin 1944.
——: *Letters* (ed. Allan Wade). London 1954.

3. Articles

ADAMS, PHOEBE LOU: "Readers' Choice," in *Atlantic Monthly*, Oct. 1955.
A.E.: "Two Plays by Sean O'Casey." in *The Irish Statesman*, 7 Mar. 1925.
AICKMAN, ROBERT F.: "Mr O'Casey and the Strikers," in *The Nineteenth Century*, Apr. 1946.
ALLDRIDGE, JOHN: "What's Wrong with the Abbey?" in *The Irish Digest*, Feb. 1948.

BOOTH, ARTHUR: "Lies and Libels," in *Dublin Opinion*, Mar. 1926.

BROWN, IVOR: "Life by the Liffey," in *The Saturday Review*, 21 Nov. 1925.

——: "Cautionary Tales," in *The Saturday Review*, 18 Jun. 1927.

BUGGY, BERTHA: "All the World's a Stage," in *The Irish Statesman*, 18 Oct. 1924.

CLURMAN, HAROLD: "Theatre of Broadway," in *The New Republic*, 19 Sep. 1949.

——: "Bard in a Pub," in *The Nation*, 27 Nov. 1954.

——: "Red Roses," in *The Nation*, 14 Jan. 1956.

CODMAN, FLORENCE: "Sean O'Casey," in *The Nation*, 25 Apr. 1934.

COLUM, PADRAIC: "Wallops in Autobiography," in *The New Republic*, 27 Dec. 1954.

DUKES, ASHLEY: "Social Basis," in *Theatre Arts*, Jun. 1940.

E.S.A.: "Mr O'Casey Again," in *Spectator*, 29 May 1926.

FALLON, GABRIEL: "My Friend Sean O'Casey," in *The Irish Digest*, Nov. 1946.

——: "Pathway of a Dramatist," in *Theatre Arts*, Jan. 1950.

——: "Fragments from a Biography," in *Modern Drama*, IV, Dec. 1961.

FOX, R. M.: "Realism in Irish Drama," in *The Irish Statesman*, 23 Jun. 1928.

——: "The Theatre Goes on *In Ireland*," in *Theatre Arts*, Nov. 1940.

GASSNER, JOHN: "The Prodigality of Sean O'Casey," in *Theatre Arts*, Jun. 1951.

GREGORY, HORACE: "Playwright on a Soapbox," in *The Saturday Review*, 20 Nov. 1954.

HEWES, HENRY: "Broadway Postscript," in *The Saturday Review*, 19 Nov. 1955.

——: "Sean O'Casey's One-Shilling Opera," in *The Saturday Review*, 14 Jan. 1956.

HICKS, GRANVILLE: "The More You Shout . . . the Less I Hear," in *The New York Republic*, 22 Oct. 1956.

HOGAN, ROBERT: "O'Casey and the Archbishop," in *The New Republic*, 19 May 1958.

The Irish Statesman: "Correspondence: The Abbey Directors and Mr Sean O'Casey," 9 Jun. 1928.

JENNINGS, RICHARD: "The Silver Tassie," in *Spectator*, 19 Oct. 1929.

JOHNSTON, DENIS: "Joxer in Totnes," in *Irish Writing*, Dec. 1950.

KIRWAN, H. N.: "Sean O'Casey, the Man and the Dramatist," in *Crystal*, Feb.-Mar. 1926.

KRUTCH, JOSEPH W.: "Mr O'Casey's Charade," in *The Nation*, 7 Nov. 1934.

LENNON, MICHAEL: "Sean O'Casey and his Plays," in *The Catholic World*, Dec. 1929.

LEWIS, ALLAN: "Sean O'Casey's World," in *The Nation*, 24 Dec. 1955.

LEWIS, THEOPHILUS: "Criticism: *Red Roses for Me*," in *America*, 21 Jan. 1956.

Life: "The World of Sean O'Casey," in international edn., 23 Aug. 1954.

LITTLEWOOD, S. R.: "Isles of Drama," in *The Bookman*, May 1926.

MAC: "Too Much Laughter at the Abbey," in *The Irish Statesman*, 20 Sep. 1924.

MacCarthy, Desmond: "Juno and the Paycock," in *The New Statesman*, 28 Nov. 1925.

MacDonnel, A. G.: "Chronicles, The Drama," in *The London Mercury*, Dec. 1929.

Malone, Andrew E.: "The Shadow of Sean O'Casey," in *The Bookman*, May 1926.

Mercer, Vivian: "The Riddle of Sean O'Casey," in *Commonweal*, 13 Jul. 1956.

Nathan, George Jean: "The Best of the Irish," in *Newsweek*, 29 Jan. 1940.

O'Connor, A. C.: "Synge and National Drama," in *Unitas*, Jul.-Sep. 1954.

O'Connor, Frank: "O'Casey and the Ghosts," in *Holiday*, Jan. 1956.

O'Faolain, Sean: "The Case of Sean O'Casey," in *Commonweal*, 11 Oct. 1935.

O'Hegarty, P. S.: "A Dramatist of New Born Ireland," in *The North American Review*, Jun. 1927.

Ó Maoláin, Mícheál: "An Ruathar Ua a nDeachaigh Leis," in *Feasta*, May 1955.

O'Shaughnessy, John: "O'Casey: Forever Fare Thee Well," in *The Nation*, 16 Mar. 1957.

Phelan, Kappo: "A Note on O'Casey," in *Commonweal*, 7 Oct. 1949.

Punch: "*The Bishop's Bonfire*," 9 Mar. 1955.

Redfern, James: "Red Roses for Me," in *Spectator*, 8 Mar. 1946.

Reynolds, Horace: "Sean O'Casey," in *The Saturday Review of Literature*, 3 Mar. 1934.

Shipp, Horace: "Juno and the Paycock," in *The English Review*, Jan. 1926.

S.L.M.: "Dramatic Notes," in *The Irish Statesman*, 6 Oct. 1923.

Spender, Stephen: "A Morality Play with no Morals," in *The New Statesman*, 16 Mar. 1940.

Starkie, Walter: "The Plays of Sean O'Casey," in *The Nineteenth Century*, Aug. 1928.

Stokes, Sewell: "New Play At Last," in *Theatre Arts*, Jun. 1946.

Time: "*The Bishop's Bonfire*," 14 Mar. 1955.

The Times Literary Supplement: "English and Irish," 13 Apr. 1940.

——: "The Unfulfilled Nation," 17 Nov. 1945.

——: "Poetry in the Theatre," 11 May 1946.

——: "Riches Scorned," 21 Mar. 1958.

Trewin, J. C.: "Lord of Language," in *Drama*, Winter 1954.

Verschoyle, Derek: "Within the Gates," in *Spectator*, 16 Feb. 1934.

Waldman, Milton: "Chronicles, The Drama," in *The London Mercury*, Feb. & Jul. 1926.

Walsh, Louis J.: "The Defiance of the Abbey," in *The Irish Rosary*, Sep. 1935.

Weales, Gerald: "A Toast to Life," in *Commentary*, Feb. 1955.

White, Jack: "*The Bishop's Bonfire*," in *Spectator*, 4 Mar. 1955.

Wyatt, Euphemia V. R.: "Juno and the Paycock," in *The Catholic World*, Mar. 1940.

Y.O.: "*The Silver Tassie*," in *The Irish Statesman*, 21 Jul. 1928.

Young, Stark: "Theatre Gates," in *The New Republic*, 7 Nov. 1934.

Index

Works by O'Casey only are included here. Those marked with an asterisk are unpublished.

PRINTED IN GREAT BRITAIN BY
OLIVER AND BOYD LTD.
EDINBURGH